MW00474754

The Yoga of the
Bhagavad Gita

Sri Krishna Prem

MORNING LIGHT
PRESS

Published by Morning Light Press © 2008

Cover Image: Werner Forman / Art Resource, NY

ISBN: 978-1-59675-024-1

Previously published as *The Yoga of the Bhagavat Gita.* New York: Penguin Books, 1973.

MORNING
◯LIGHT
P R E S S

Morning Light Press
10881 North Boyer
Sandpoint, ID 83864
morninglightpress.com

Printed on acid-free recycled paper in Canada.

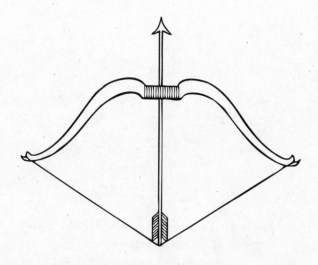

Having taken as a bow the great weapon of the Secret Teaching,
One should fix in it the arrow sharpened by constant Meditation.
Drawing it with a mind filled with That (*Brahman*)
Penetrate, O good-looking youth, that Imperishable as the Mark.

The *pranava* (*Aum*) is the bow; the arrow is the self;
Brahman is said to be the mark.
With heedfulness is It to be penetrated;
One should become one with It as the arrow in the mark.

—Mundaka Upanishad ii, 3, 4.

This book is dedicated to my guru, Sri Krishna Sevika,
Sri Sri Yashoda Mai, to whom alone is due
whatever truth its pages contain.

Table of Contents

Foreword

It is a matter of great happiness for all spiritual searchers that the classic commentary of Krishna Prem on the Bhagavad Gita is being republished. This important book has been out of print far too long, depriving the new generation of serious searchers of its great wisdom.

When I first encountered this book, I was struck by many things, but especially by its profundity, its sense of inner authority, and by its thoroughly non-sectarian character. Now, nearly half a century later, these characteristics still stand out.

Precisely because of the great importance of the Bhagavad Gita in the Hindu tradition, all the philosophic teachers (*acharyas*) are obliged to write commentaries on it. In these commentaries they feel called to read the Gita in a way that justifies their own philosophic position, or that of their school. The result is often a forced interpretation of many verses, giving these commentaries a sectarian flavor. This is well and good for winning intellectual arguments against those who have different intellectual points of view, but it does not help wayfarers along the path to find the Truth which by definition is beyond all sectarian considerations.

Krishna Prem is not interested in justifying one or another philosophical system. Nor does he have much patience for the historical or anthropological approach of many commentators, often from the West. His approach to the Bhagavad Gita, as is suggested by the title of the book, brings out the yoga expounded in the Gita. By yoga he understands not any specific set of practices, but the entire path which a searcher must tread in order to come to the Truth.

Krishna Prem quite rightly asserts that India does not have a monopoly of the path to the Truth. He gives many references to other mystical traditions, and especially to Plotinus and Hermes Trismegistus.

Here is an extraordinary exposition of the yoga of the Bhagavad Gita by someone who is equally at home in the East as well as in the West, and who speaks convincingly from his own inner experiences along the path of spiritual realization.

I do not know of any other commentary on the Bhagavad Gita, the paradigm text of perennial philosophy, which is more insightful than that of Krishna Prem.

—Ravi Ravindra
Author of *The Spiritual Roots of Yoga* and
The Wisdom of Patañjali's Yoga Sutras

Preface

This book originated in a series of articles which were written for *The Aryan Path* of Bombay on the significance of the chapter titles of the Gita. The editors altered the title to *The Song of the Higher Life*, and before I knew where I was, I found myself engaged on a running commentary on the Gita as a whole. Partly owing to the nature of the Gita itself, and partly because of the exigencies of publication in monthly installments, a certain amount of repetition was involved. I have tried to eliminate as much as possible, but for any that remains I can only beg the indulgence of the reader.

—Sri Krishna Prem
Mirtola, India 1937

Introduction

The Bhagavad Gita needs little introduction nowadays. Many have come to value it as one of the world's great spiritual classics and not a few take it as their guide to the inner life. Of its popularity in India there is no need to speak. Though its author is unknown (for we can scarcely adopt the orthodox view that it was, as we have it, spoken by the historical Krishna on the battlefield of *Kurukshetra*) it is revered by Hindus of all schools of thought, and is one foot of the triple base on which the *Vedanta* is founded, the other two feet being the Upanishads and the Brahma Sutras. Every teacher who wished to claim Vedantic authority for his teachings was obliged to write a commentary on it showing that it supported his views.

In consequence of this we have commentaries written from many points of view, monist and dualist, pantheist and theist. Enthusiasts for action, for knowledge (*jñana* or gnosis), or for devotion to a personal God, all find their special tenets in the Gita, and, though this universal appeal is proof of its catholicity, the various commentators have often devoted more energy to special pleading and refutation of opponents than to straightforward inquiry into the real meaning of the text.

Into the views equally diverse of the Western scholars with their incurably external method of approach, it is not proposed to enter. Garbe considered it a *Sankhya-Yoga* textbook overwritten by Krishna worshippers and then again by a Vedantist, while Hopkins held that it was a

Vishnuite poem worked up in the interests of the Krishna cult. Nearly all of them object to what they term its philosophical inconsistencies and loose use of terms.

Let me say at once that I care nothing at all for these learned pronouncements. To anyone who has eyes to see, the Gita is based on direct knowledge of Reality, and of the Path that leads to that Reality, and it is of little moment who wrote it or to what school he was outwardly affiliated. Those who know Reality belong to a tribe apart, the tribe that never dies, as Hermes Trismegistus puts it, and neither they nor those who seek to be born into that tribe concern themselves with the flummeries of sects and schools.

It is by such a seeker and for such seekers that this book has been written. Some may feel that the interpretation is a somewhat modernized one, but in answer to that I would only say that the words of an Enlightened One refer to eternal realities. Those realities are the same now as they were thousands of years ago, and the texts of the Gita should be interpreted in words that refer to those realities here and now, and not merely in words which did refer to them in medieval India or, for that matter, at the time when the book was originally written. As the Buddha teaches in the Lankavatara Sutra: "Meaning is entered into by words as things are revealed by a lamp. . . . So, I, making use of various forms and images of things, instruct my sons; but the summit of Reality can only be realized within oneself."

The point of view from which this book has been written is that the Gita is a textbook of Yoga, a guide to the treading of the Path. By Yoga here is meant not any special system called by that name, not jñana yoga, nor *karma* yoga, nor *bhakti* yoga, nor the eightfold yoga of Patañjali, but just the Path by which human beings can unite their finite selves with

Infinite Being. It is the inner Path of which all these separate yogas are so many aspects. It is not so much a synthesis of these separate teachings as that prior and undivided whole of which they represent partial formulations.

As such, it deals with the whole Path from the beginning to the end, from what Buddhists term "entry in the stream" to the goal of Nirvana. It follows that the sequence of the chapters is of great importance, and that it is a mistake to do as some expositors have done and expound the teachings with no reference to the place at which they occur in the general scheme.

The Path is not the special property of Hinduism, nor indeed of any religion. It is something which is to be found, more or less deeply buried, in all religions, and which can exist apart from any formal religion at all. That is why the Gita, though a definitely Hindu book, the very crown jewel of Hindu teachings, is capable of being a guide to seekers all over the world.

The psychologist C. G. Jung, in the course of some sympathetic and interesting comments on a Chinese Taoist book, found occasion to criticize those Westerners who practice Eastern Yogas. It is quite true that much of the so-called yoga practice indulged in by Westerners is foolish and misguided. That is, however, not because it is "eastern" in origin, but because it is not pursued for the right reason. Yoga is to be undertaken for the sake of Truth itself, for the sake of what the Buddha termed "unshakable deliverance of heart." To practice it, as many do, out of curiosity, in search of new sensations, or in order to gain psychic powers is a mistake which is punished with futility, neurosis, or worse. None should seek initiation into the mysteries from unworthy motives, or disaster will surely result.

In fact, though the particular dress in which it is presented in the

Gita is an Indian one, the Path itself is neither "eastern" nor "western." It belongs to no race and to no religion, being that on which all true religions were originally based. It is to make this clear that I have quoted so freely from other mystical literature, in particular from Plotinus and Hermes Trismegistus. For the former I have used the translation of Stephen McKenna,[1] and for the latter that of G. R. S. Mead.

The Path is not a purely Eastern one having, as Jung would say, no roots in a Western psyche, but is universal, found in all traditions, and open to anyone who has the will to seek it. If a person has a healthy mind, a worthy aspiration, sincerity (including what is less common, intellectual sincerity), courage, and tenacity of purpose there is no need to fear any serious danger on the Path. If it is approached from the scientific or philosophic side that is all that need be said. But if the approach is through some particular religion seekers will have to be careful to discard any idea that their own religion is a unique one and any clinging to authority in the shape of inspired scriptures. Failure to do this will result in delusions and blocking of further advance. Each one must, as the Buddha said, be their own Light and their own refuge. The only authority is within the Soul itself, and the would-be disciples must be ready to test everything and abandon their cherished conceptions if they prove inadequate.

Superstition is a deadly foe and must be conquered at all costs. As it says in *The Precepts of the Gurus*:[2] "Reason being in every action the best friend is not to be avoided."[3] While on the subject a few other aphorisms from the same source are so relevant that they may as well be set down:

"One should acquire practical knowledge of the Path by treading it and not be as are the multitude.

"Weakness of faith combined with strength of intellect are apt to lead to the error of talkativeness.

"Strength of faith combined with weakness of intellect are apt to lead to the error of narrow-minded dogmatism.

"Desire may be mistaken for faith.

"Attachment may be mistaken for benevolence and compassion.

"Sense perceptions may be mistaken for glimpses of Reality.

"A mere glimpse of Reality may be mistaken for complete realization.

"Charlatans may be mistaken for sages.

"A philosophy comprehensive enough to embrace the whole of knowledge is indispensable.

"A system of meditation which will produce the power of concentrating the mind on anything whatsoever is indispensable.

"An art of living which will enable one to utilize each activity (of body, speech and mind) as an aid on the Path is indispensable."

Those who seek after novel experiences, psychic powers, or the sweet-sounding consolations of religion had far better leave the whole thing alone or they will wreck their lives, and perhaps those of others as well. The path of Truth is a hard one, and the Inner Ruler will exact the last farthing of *karmic* payment for dallying with error.

The reader is recommended to have a copy of the Gita, and in order to facilitate references to the original the verses referred to have been noted in the margin. Where the interpretation seems to differ from generally accepted translations I can only say that the differences are not based on ignorance of the standard versions, but are the results of careful thought. A useful translation for the general reader is that of Mrs. Annie Besant, and for those who know even a little Sanskrit, the edition by Mrs. Besant and Bhagavan Das (T. P. H.), which gives the text and a word-by-word translation as well as the general one, will be found very helpful indeed. Another good translation is that by W. D. P. Hill (Oxford

University Press), which also gives the text.[4]

It is recommended that the Appendices should at least be rapidly glanced through before commencing serious reading of the actual book. Much explanatory matter that would have interrupted the general flow has been given there. A glossary of Sanskrit terms will also be found at the end of the book.

To any who read with a view to treading the Path, however inadequately here set forth, I would only add:

"Thine own consciousness, shining, void and inseparable from the Great Body of Radiance, hath no birth, nor death, and is the Immutable Light."

Notes

1   Published by the Medici Society.

2   *Tibetan Yoga and Secret Doctrines*, translated from the Tibetan by Lama Kazi Dawa-Samdup, and edited by Dr. Evans-Wentz. Oxford University Press, 1934.

3   But it is also necessary to avoid cheap "rationalism." It will not do to regard as superstition anything that is not understood by contemporary "reason." It is by no means always easy in practice to decide whether something is superstition or not.

4   Further references for the Gita:

The Bhagavad Gita. trans. Sri Aurobindo, Twin Lakes, WI: Lotus Press, 1995.

The Bhagavad Gita. trans. Annie Besant and Bhagavan Das. Adyar, India: Theosophical Publishing House, 1905.

The Bhagavad Gita: The Lord's Song. trans. Annie Besant. Adyar, India: Theosophical Publishing House. 1965, 1974

The Bhagavad Gita. trans. Eknath Easwaran. Tomales, CA. Nilgiri Press, 1985, 2001.

The Bhagavad Gita. trans. Barbara Miller. New York: Bantam, 1986.

Prolegomena

The General Setting

Before starting to discuss the Gita itself it will be desirable to say a few words about its setting—namely, the events recorded in the Mahabharata which serve as the framework of the Gita. For the sake of Western readers I will very briefly recount those events.

The Divinely born Arjuna,[1] with his four brothers, was brought up with his cousins, the Kauravas, at the Court of the latter's father, Dhritarashtra, the king who though legally disqualified by his blindness, had seized and held the throne. Not content with the seizing of the throne, the old king did not even hold the balance evenly between his sons and their cousins, the Pandavas, but constantly favored the former. Hostility soon developed between the two parties and, after a brief attempt to divide the realm between them, the Pandavas were defeated at dice by trickery and made to wander for twelve long years in exile, followed by a thirteenth year in which their very whereabouts had to remain unknown. At the conclusion of this period the well-meaning but weak king found it impossible to persuade his headstrong and evil-minded son, Duryodhana, to restore to the Pandavas their share of the kingdom and, in spite of fruitless attempts to bring about a reconciliation by Sañjaya, Dhritarashtra's charioteer, by Bhishma, his wise counselor, and even by the Lord Krishna Himself, war could not be averted, and the rival hosts faced each other on the field of Kurukshetra. It is at this point that the Gita commences.

Without going into the question as to whether all incidents of the Mahabharata have a symbolic significance and whether it is possible to trace a consistent symbolism all through the vast epic, it must be clear to all those who have eyes that there is an inner significance behind the events thus inadequately summarized. There is no need to ask the question whether the author of the Mahabharata had such a symbolism consciously in his mind. Many, perhaps most, great works of art are filled with symbolism that is often quite unplanned by the conscious minds of their creators, and sometimes this symbolism is truer and more profound from the fact of its having descended from a region beyond the realm of conscious thinking. It embodies not the head-knowledge but the soul-knowledge of the artist. Far more is this true of the Mahabharata, a poem in which all the culture, all the aspirations, and all the traditions of an entire race finds expression. Symbolism is, in fact, like beauty itself: either you see it or you do not. And if it is seen, then it is as irrelevant to inquire whether it was consciously intended by the author as it is to ask whether the beauty was consciously intended. It exists.

The skeleton interpretation that I shall indicate does not base itself upon the authority of scriptural texts, nor does it depend for its validity on anyone's ability to fit every event in the poem into the framework of this scheme. That may or may not be possible, and in any case is outside the scope of this work. Whatever value it may have for any reader will depend entirely on the light that it may succeed in throwing on the teachings of the Gita.[2]

In the first place we must notice that, though not the eldest, the chief of the Pandava brothers is Arjuna. It was he that won Draupadi at the *svayamvara*,[3] and it was he alone that she really loved, and he who

was the hero of the greatest exploits. Yudhisthira may excel in dharma
and Bhima in feats of strength, but it is on Arjuna's heroic prowess that
the Pandavas depend, and it was Arjuna who went to Kailash to get the
magic weapons from Mahadeva Himself. It is Arjuna, again, who is the
special friend of Krishna, and the latter confirms this view when, in the
tenth chapter of the Gita, he proclaims Arjuna and not Yudhisthira as
the chief of the Pandavas.[4] In the *Srimad Bhagavada*, it is Arjuna who
goes with Krishna to the abode of the *Purushottama* and is addressed by
the latter as a second Krishna,[5] and, returning to the Mahabharata, it is
Arjuna who is seen in heaven with Krishna, "those two foremost of all
beings," by Yudhisthira on the latter's arrival there.

Arjuna and Krishna, the inseparable friends, are well known to represent *Nara* and *Narayana*, the human soul and the Divine Soul, the
jiva and *Atman*.[6] They are the two birds that are described in the Upanishad,[7] the two birds, eternal friends, seated upon the same tree, the
body, of whom one, the human soul, eats the fruit, while the other, the
Atman, is a silent witness. It is true that the terms, *Nara* and *Narayana*,
are explained by a reference to the story of a dual incarnation of God
in the form of two Rishis, Nara and Narayana, who performed *tapasya*
and are believed to be still so doing, in the Himalayas. But this story is
itself symbolic. The word *Rishi* means a seer, and in truth the only seer
is the Atman. "That which sees through the eye but whom the eye sees
not; that is the Atman." So says the Upanishad, and this story of the two
Rishis is a symbol of the dual soul, human and Divine, incarnated in
one body. It is significant that the very name of the place in which the
two Rishis perform their austerities is *Badri*, the name of a tree bearing
sweet fruits, thus bringing us back again to the Upanishadic birds who
are seated on a tree which likewise bears sweet fruits (*svadu pippalam*).

The significance of Arjuna and Krishna having thus been indicated, we must next inquire into that of his brothers and cousins. We shall see that, in the sixteenth chapter of the Gita, Sri Krishna makes a division between two great tendencies or movements in creation which He terms the *Daivic*, or bright, and the *Asuric*, or dark. It is these two tendencies that are symbolized by Arjuna's brothers and by the hostile Kauravas respectively. Detailed treatment of these forces will come in its proper place;[8] it will be sufficient here to observe that the Asuric and Daivic creations, popularly identified with vices and virtues respectively, in reality signify the "outgoing" and the "ingoing" forces elsewhere called *pravritti* and *nivritti*, the forces which tend to enmesh the soul deeper and deeper in "matter" and those which help and accompany it on its return journey to Spirit.[9] It is evident that the popular identification of them with the vices and virtues is but a rough approximation to their true meaning and one on a much lower plane of thought than that of the Gita.

It should be further noted that the Kauravas and the Pandavas are cousins. There is none of the ultimate dualism that has marred so much of Christian thought, no God and Devil standing as ultimate irreconcilables. The Daivic and Asuric forces both spring from the same Supreme Source and in the end both return to It.

It is not necessary to go into the question of the significance of the individual Pandavas (except of course Arjuna, who has already been dealt with) or Kauravas. The only other figures we shall discuss are Dhritarashtra, the blind old king, and Sañjaya, his charioteer. These two are of some importance, as they figure directly in the Gita.

The teachings of the Gita are spoken by Krishna, who is acting as the charioteer of Arjuna; they are overheard by Sañjaya as the result of the blessing of Vyasa, the author of the Scriptures, and who signifies the power of inspiration, and they are repeated to Dhritarashtra. This is the framework in which the teachings of the Gita are set. Who are these persons, and what is the significance of the two charioteers?

Krishna, we have seen, is the Divine Soul who imparts the life-giving Wisdom to the individual soul. The symbol of the charioteer is one that occurs in the Upanishads and also in the *Dialogues* of Plato. In the Upanishads the individual soul is described as the Rider in the chariot of the body, while *buddhi*, a spiritual faculty that we shall discuss later, is the charioteer. In the Gita, however, the use to which the symbol is put is slightly different. True, the individual soul in the form of Arjuna is still the rider in the chariot, but the charioteer is, as we have seen, the Divine Self in the person of Krishna.

Dhritarashtra, on the other hand, represents the empirical ego, the lower and transient personality which, blinded by egoism and foolish infatuation, wields a nominal sway over the kingdom of the body which it has unjustly seized, the word Dhritarashtra meaning one who has seized the kingdom. Although he arrogates to himself the title of King, his rule over the kingdom is merely nominal, for the real power lies with his Asuric sons, just as the human personality which so proudly says "I" is the sport of a continual succession of involuntary desires and passions which are the real rulers of the body it calls its own.

Sañjaya, the charioteer and adviser of the blind king, is the link between the higher and lower minds. The mind has a dual status in Hindu philosophy. "The mind is said to be twofold, the pure and the impure: impure by union with desire, and pure, completely free from desire."[10] The impure mind is Dhritarashtra, the empirical ego controlled by desire (Duryodhana), while the pure mind is Arjuna, the individual soul. Sañjaya is thus the link between the two.

It is not easy to give a clear account of the relation between these two minds, or better, perhaps, these two aspects of the mind. The higher mind, though individualized, is pure and detached, and sees in its own clear light, while the lower mind is stained by its union with the principle of desire. Failure to understand this is at the root of those modern views which plausibly urge that the mind is but the slave of the hidden tides, quiet or tempestuous, of the so-called "unconscious." Of the lower mind (which is what most know as their minds) this is only too true, but the higher stands firm in its own being and is a rock of refuge in the surging waves of desire. It is of this that Plotinus has written:

"Even our human soul has not sunk entire; something of it is continuously in the Intellectual Realm, though if that part (i.e. the lower manas) which is the sphere of sense be mastered here and troubled it keeps us blind to what the upper phase holds in contemplation. . . . But there is always the other (the higher manas), that which finds no savor in passing pleasure, but holds its own even way."[11]

It is here that Sañjaya comes in as the link between the two. Plotinus speaks of the lower being loosed from its shackles and able to soar only when "it makes its memories[12] the starting-point for the vision of essential Being." The link should not be conceived as material, but as the purely mental connection between the two aspects of what is in essence one. When the lower thinks of the higher, the latter's knowledge shines upon the former and is manifest in the form of what Plotinus, following Plato, termed "memories," but what is perhaps more clearly described as perception of value—truth, beauty, or goodness. This is the root of what is usually termed conscience, though it must be carefully distinguished from the voices of social, family, and racial prejudices which are often dignified by the name. In some teachings it is termed *antah-karana*, "inward turning," though usually in Hindu philosophy that term is used, as meaning inner organ, for the various mental faculties taken as a whole. It is the drawbridge of the inner fortress, the gateway leading to immortality, the mediator through which the Voice of the Higher is heard by the lower.

Thus Sañjaya, though anchored in service to Dhritarashtra, reaches out to a faith in Krishna, and constantly counsels his master to abandon his weak egoism and submit himself to the latter. It is thus Sañjaya who, when aided by the inspiration derived from Vyasa, is able to "overhear" the dialogue between Krishna and Arjuna and so to form a link between the inner knowledge of the soul and the dark ignorance of the self-centered personality.

It may also be said that there is a correspondence between these four characters and the four states of consciousness taught by Hindu philosophy, the *jagrat*, *svapna*, *sushupti* and *turiya*, usually translated, more by way of analogy than of identity, as the waking, dreaming, deep sleep, and ecstatic states.[13] This correspondence, however, involves a different reading of the symbols and would only confuse the issue here.

We are now in a position to return to the outline sketch of the events that have led up to the delivery of the Gita. The Soul, leaving behind its Divine ancestry, became attached to a personality and lives amidst the conflicting forces that make up this world. The conflict, at first latent, as the Daivic and Asuric forces are not clearly differentiated, gradually increases in strength. Attempts at partition of their respective spheres of influence having failed, as indeed they must fail since all is one unity, and action and reaction must necessarily take place, the Soul and its associates are deceived by the illusions of the Asuric, or downward-tending forces, and are condemned to long wanderings in the wilderness. During this period, a period which in reality extends through long ages, the Soul wanders about from birth to birth performing actions and reaping their fruits. Reduced to powerlessness as it is, it yet slowly gathers wisdom as a result of its manifold experiences, and though exposed to countless hardships and perils, it is yet saved from utter disaster by the unseen power of its Lord, the Divine Soul. Experience, wisdom, and also powers are gained, for it is during this period that Arjuna gains his magical weapons that are later to be of such immense value to him. The Asuric forces rule the world unchecked and at length the thirteenth year arrives, the year of *ajñata vasa*, in which the very existence of the Soul and its brothers has to remain unknown.

It is the darkest hour, the hour before the dawn, and the Soul, reduced to performing the tasks of a servant, is lost to sight altogether. The forces of materialism seem triumphant and the very existence of the Soul becomes a matter of doubt, or even denial.

But not forever can the Soul be thus buried in darkness. The allotted period draws to its close, and the Soul emerges from its obscurity with all its flashing powers. Significantly enough, the first event is a battle in defense of the right, the battle fought of behalf of King Virata, in which the Soul, though still disguised, displays its prowess and puts to flight the powers of the Dark. So decisive, indeed, is the Soul's intervention that none can stand against it. All are aware of the rising star, and all foresee the terrible conflict that must now occur.

But the Soul seeks no autocratic power for itself. It is for its brothers, the dispossessed Bright Powers (*Daivic Sarga*), that it is prepared to fight, and even for them it claims no undivided sway. Knowing, as it does, that the Asuric forces are as much a part of the cosmic play as are the Daivic ones, it proposes only a just division of the kingdom, but this the Powers of the Dark will not grant.

Bhishma and Drona, the aged warrior counselors, symbols of blind faith of established Law and Order and ancient Tradition, foreseeing the disastrous conflict, plead for peace and reconciliation, as does Sañjaya, the conscience. Sri Krishna himself sets forth in persuasive words the advantages of harmonious peace, but all is of no avail. Duryodhana refuses to listen, and the old king professes himself powerless to control his headstrong sons. War is inevitable. The conflict of the Daivic and the Asuric can no longer be averted, and the rival hosts face each other on the field of Kurukshetra. It is at this fateful moment that the Gita commences. The opposing hosts are drawn up in battle array, and the long-expected conflict is about to commence.

Dhritarashtra said: "In the Holy Field of Kurukshetra what did they do, O Sañjaya, my sons and the Pandavas, gathered together eager for battle?"

Notes

1   Arjuna's putative father, Pandu, was disqualified from having children by a curse, and so his wife, Kunti, bore the five Pandavas by five Gods, of whom Indra, the chief, fathered Arjuna.

2   I may also add that no claim is made that these thoughts are original. Anyone who considers that they belong to him is welcome to take possession of them.

3   A *svayamvara* was a sort of tournament at which a maiden of the warrior caste used to choose her husband. In this case the princess became the wife of all five brothers.

4   Gita, x, 37.

5   *Ityadishtau bhagawata tau krishnau parameshthina.*

6   See Appendix B.

7   Mundaka Upanishad, iii, I, 1-3.

8   Chapter 16.

9   See Appendix B.

10   Maitri Upanishad, vi, 34.

11   Plotinus, *Enneads*, iv, 8, 7.

12   Memories in the Platonic sense of course: memories of what the soul (*manas*) knew and knows on its own level, not mere memories of life experience down here. *Cf.* Gita, xviii, 76, 77.

13   See Appendix C. Transcendent perhaps renders the meaning better than ecstatic. Literally the term *turiya* simply means "the Fourth."

Chapter One

The Yoga of the Dejection of Arjuna

Too many readers pass by the first chapter of the Gita hurriedly considering it a mere introduction to which no special significance need be attached. This, however, is a mistake. It is an introductory chapter, but introductory to what? Not to a historical situation or to a body of philosophic teachings, but to the Yoga itself, and, if properly understood, it has a great significance for all of us.[1] Like all the other chapters, it is termed a yoga, and is entitled "*Arjuna Vishada Yoga*"—the Yoga of the Dejection of Arjuna.

We have seen that the Gita commences at the point where the Soul, like one awakening from sleep, has emerged from the obscurity in which it lay buried. Arjuna, as the individual Soul, finds himself on the battlefield of Kurukshetra faced by the necessity of a terrible conflict in which all his friends, relatives, and former teachers are ranged against him, "eager for battle." On this field, significantly enough termed *dharmakshetra*, the field of dharma or duty, the opposing forces of pravritti and nivritti stand face-to-face and Arjuna as the Soul, from a position to which he has been guided by the Divine Krishna, is stationed between the rival armies, surveying the situation.

Verses 24–28

We are shown that as long as the Soul remains hidden in the inner worlds, the conflict does not come to a head. The individual passes from one experience to another in an apparently unordered fashion, as described in the introductory section. But this cannot last forever, and after the intoxication of the awakening, symbolized by the triumphant battle fought on behalf of King Virata, has passed off, the Soul finds itself in a situation which may well inspire dejection.

Verse 14   It was easy to sound the war conches in defiance and to feel the thrill of anticipated battle with the Asuric forces of pravritti. But, suddenly, in a flash of insight which comes while the Soul is poised inactive between the two opposing tendencies, Arjuna realizes for the first time all that is involved in the struggle. Relations, friends of his childhood, and revered teachers are entangled amongst his enemies, and he realizes that it is his own heart's blood, as it were, arrayed against him. During the long ages of slumber the Soul has contracted all sorts of relationships and has submitted to the guidance of various ideals and traditions, and only now does it realize that all these relationships must be destroyed and all these ideals, ideals that have often seemed the very goal of life, must be ruthlessly sacrificed on the battlefield. Now they are seen to be in league with the outgoing forces of pravritti and opposed to the destined triumph of the Soul.

Up till now the individual has been content to live within the narrow circle of race and family. Bounded by the ties of kinship he has felt that it was enough if he fulfilled the duties that he owed to his society and nation and attempted to live according to the ideals of his *gurus*, the religious and ethical systems in which, by birth, he found himself. But societies and races are all temporary, while the Soul is eternal and, in the end, can rest on no support but Itself. The simple creed of "my country, right or wrong" lies in ruins, destroyed by conflicting loyalties, and the ideals which had uplifted him in earlier days are powerless to guide him any longer, as they are seen to be mental constructions, inadequate to the needs of the Soul.

Nor is the conflict to which the Soul is called merely one with outer ties, established institutions and recognized standards of conduct and belief. In the inner world, too, Arjuna is faced with the same situation. Arrayed against him he finds the army of his desires. Not merely those desires that are conventionally considered "evil" but many others too, the desire for "harmless" enjoyment, the desire to shine in society surrounded by friends, and the desire to lead a secure and comfortable life. All these and many more have taken the field against the Soul under the leadership of the various ideals that have been harnessed to their service. The glittering ideals of patriotism, of family affection and of devotion to his religion have also "eaten the food of the Kauravas,"[2] and, though they served as guides and teachers in the past, are, like Bhishma and Drona, in arms against the soul and must be slain.

This is the situation with which every aspirant is faced and through which, sooner or later, all have to pass. Small wonder is it that Arjuna is overcome with utter dejection and that his bow slips from his nerveless hand as he sinks down overcome by an intolerable sadness, a sadness that is the inevitable experience of those who seek the Path. What will be the worth of victory if "those for whose sake we desire kingdom, enjoyments, and pleasures" must first lie dead on the field? If all desire is renounced, will not the whole of life become an empty waste, a vast desert in the midst of which the victorious Soul will sit enthroned in desolation, exercising a vain and empty rule? For what purpose are we called to such a sacrifice and, in the end, how shall we benefit by it? "Better to eat beggars' crusts in the world than to partake of such

Verses 29-30

Verses 32-35

blood-besprinkled feasts."[3] Better that is, to enjoy what simple enjoyments can be had than to set out on this perilous path, a path to an as yet quite inconceivable Goal, and of which the only certain thing is that it requires the destruction of all that we hold dear in life.

A further doubt arises in the heart. "In the ruin of the family the immemorial traditions perish and in the perishing of traditions lawlessness overcomes the whole community." Will not the destruction of all these desires—and, above all, of these ideals—cause great confusion in the world? Can it be right to disturb in the name of the Soul's progress to an unknown Goal an equilibrium which has at least stood the test of time? Will not the aspirant, by the renunciation of desire, become unfit to participate in the everyday life of the world, to share in the joys and sorrows of fellow-beings, and by shattering the ideals enshrined in ancient traditions will chaos not be brought into the world?

> *Wilt thou dare*
> *Put by our sacred books, dethrone our Gods,*
> *Unpeople all the temples, shaking down*
> *That law which feeds the priests and props*
>   *the realms?*[4]

Such, at least, are the doubts which present themselves in the heart, some of them well-founded, others ill, but all alike having their source in the gloom which invades the heart at the prospect of a life in which all desire for self will have to be renounced and utterly slain.

Nor, at this stage, is the darkness lit by any ray of light, and although the Divine Teacher is standing beside the Soul, His Voice has not yet been heard. Brought by its past evolution to the field of conflict, poised, as it were, upon the very edge of battle, the Soul loses heart and sinks back terrified at the desolate outlook, an outlook in which victory seems as cheerless as defeat.

The real source of this desolation is the prospect of a life in which all desire and ambition will be dead. We are so used to a life in which all action has its roots in desire that we can conceive no other. Not yet has the Soul learnt that, having Krishna, it has all; that it is not for their own sakes that parents, wives, and children are dear, "but for the sake of the Atman."[5]

Nevertheless, this experience of the *vishada*, or sorrow, is a very necessary one, as we may see from the fact that the Buddha, too, set forth in eloquent words the essential sorrow of life as the first of his Four Noble Truths.

The Voice of Krishna can be heard only in silence, and as long as the heart is filled with the clamor of desire the silver tones of the Voice cannot be heard. It is only when the outer world becomes utterly dark that the Ray of the Divine Star can be seen by us, for, although It shines eternally, it is only when the glaring sunlight of so-called life is eclipsed that we can at first perceive It.

Later, that Star will shine with such a Light that "if the splendor of a thousand suns were to blaze out together in the sky, that might resemble the glory of that Mahatma,"[6] and not all earth's tumult will be able to deafen us to the majestic rhythm of that Voice, that Voice that reverberates throughout the Eternities as the tides of Being thunder upon the beaches of the worlds.

But the time for those glories is not yet. At first the Light is but a dim Star twinkling faintly within and the Voice is but the sound of a nightingale "chanting a song of parting to its mate."[7] Before the bright Path of the Sun can be trodden, aspirants must enter the valley of gloom, must close their eyes and ears to the light and laughter of life, and must realize in sorrow that all that they are and all that they have is nothing.

Verse 47   "Casting away his bow and arrows, Arjuna sank down on the chariot, his mind overborne by grief," and thus, in dejection and sorrow, closes the first chapter of the Gita and the first stage of the Path.

Notes

1   It is by no means intended to suggest that all the kings and warriors mentioned in this chapter have symbolic significance as individuals. Attempts to interpret them have been made, but such as I have seen bear an artificial stamp.

2   Bhishma explained his blind acquiescence in the injustice done to Draupadi in the Kaurava Court to his having for long eaten the Kaurava food. In other words, the power of faith had long been harnessed to ancient traditions now degenerated into superstition and forces of Darkness.

3   Gita, ii, 5.

4   *The Light of Asia*, iv.

5   Brihadaranyaka Upanishad, ii, 4.

6   Gita, xi, 12.

7   *The Voice of the Silence*.

Chapter Two

The Yoga of Discriminative Wisdom

"If emancipation means dissociation from all objects of pleasurable enjoyment, for what reason would men cherish a desire for action? What do we gain by knowledge and what lose by ignorance?"

These words of King Janaka to the Sankhyan teacher Panchashikha well describe the mood of Arjuna as the discourse opens. Surrounded by desolation on all sides, the Soul has no alternative but to turn within Itself and seek the Divine Teacher there. Wherever else it looks it sees nothing but bitter emptiness, and even the appeal to fortitude fails, for when all one's world is in ruins, such an appeal seems a mere posturing in the void.[1] In despair the Soul turns within to the Divine Krishna and, weighed down by wretchedness (*karpanyadosha*), a wretchedness in which self-pity plays a prominent part, cries out: "I am Thy disciple; teach me, I am Thy suppliant." *Verse 7*

Verses 2, 3

But the Soul is not yet ready to abandon itself, for we see that there, at the very feet of the Teacher to whom he has just proclaimed his submission, Arjuna refuses to abandon his dejection, and cries out bitterly, "*na yotsya*" ("I will not fight").

These words express the very fault we are always committing. The disciple appeals for teaching to the Guru, either to the divine Lord within or to His embodiment in human form, and professes his willingness to serve Him utterly. But, spoken or unspoken, there always remains a reservation: "Lord, I am Thine and will do Thy bidding, but—ask not of me one thing, for that I cannot do. I will not fight!" This is why the appeal to the Teacher seems so often to bring no result and why many lose faith in His presence, feeling that, were He really there, they would assuredly hear His Voice.

But the impossible is not demanded and, slowly, if only there is patient perseverance, a new and Divine knowledge is felt obscurely stealing into the Soul and lighting up the darkness within. For true Knowledge is to be found within the Self; that which is merely derived from books or hearsay is no real knowledge. Outer teachings may help to give expression to what is at first only dimly intuited, but it can form no substitute for the latter. The work of any real Teacher is to bring to birth that which already exists within, as has been well expressed by Browning in his poem, *Paracelsus*:

> *"Truth lies within ourselves; it takes no rise*
> *From outward things, whate'er you may believe.*
> *There is an inmost center in us all*
> *Where Truth abides in fullness; and to KNOW*
> *Rather consists in opening out a way*
> *Whence the imprisoned splendor may escape,*
> *Than I effecting entry for a light*
> *Supposed to be without."*

The first stage in the manifestation of this inner knowledge comes in the form of a perception that within the self is That which is immortal. This perception is of fundamental importance, because without it the spiritual life can find no lasting basis, and even at this

early stage a dim perception of the Immortal rises up within the
heart. At first this perception is likely to be clothed in the somewhat crude theory of an unchanging soul-entity dwelling within the   *Verse 13*
body. Time, however, will bring clarification. We must not expect at
this stage the clear vision that will come, but, even now, the disciple
should be able to realize that the Dweller within is something separate from the matter in which he dwells.   *Verse 14*

"Things themselves touch not the soul, not in the least degree.
. . . Let the part of thy soul which leads and governs be undisturbed
by the movements in the flesh whether of pleasure or of pain; and let
it not unite with them, but let it circumscribe itself and limit those
effects to those parts."[2]

Only those thus resolutely attempt to withdraw themselves from   *Verse 15*
the life of the senses are worthy to realize immortality, and to those, as
they struggle, will come a perception that "this too too solid" world of
names and forms is but a passing phantom show which veils from sight
the true and unchanging Eternal Reality which is forever unmanifest.   *Verse 16*
"The Unreal hath no being; the Real never ceaseth to be." An echo of
the same truth is found in Shelley's beautiful lines:

> *"The One remains, the Many change and pass;*
> *Heaven's light for ever shines, Earth's shadows fly.*
> *Life like a dome of many-colored glass*
> *Stains the white radiance of Eternity."*

With this perception comes a realization that this Unchanging
One, the Unmanifest in which all beings have their true selves is   *Verses*
indestructible. "Weapons cannot cleave It nor fire burn It, nor can   *17-25*

any compass the destruction of that Imperishable One." Just as the all-pervading light of day is not destroyed with the perishing of the material forms in which it is reflected, so the Unchanging One passes from one form to another, as a person changes a worn-out garment, and, though invisible, remains forever even though the whole world perish.

This is no piece of theological dogma to be taken as an article of blind belief. The Gita is not concerned with beliefs but with knowledge, and the above is a truth that becomes clear to the disciple even at this stage, and a calm descends upon the Soul as it realizes that neither can one slay nor is any slain. Forms and personalities come and go inevitably, but That which lies behind them all can neither come nor go. It forever IS.

Verses 27, 28

Moreover, since all forms are the same in kind, whether they be forms of flesh and blood or forms of conduct and belief, the Soul learns not to grieve over the passing away of familiar social forms and cherished religious creeds, for it sees that the Reality behind them all, the Reality which gave birth to them, is the same forever, and neither comes into being at birth of a new religion nor perishes with its decay. From the Unmanifest they take their rise, on the Unmanifest they float and into that Unmanifest they sink again. What room then for lamentation, since all form is transient and must pass away, while all that is Real is eternal and perishes not throughout the ages.

Verses 29-36

Therefore, having perceived, if only dimly, that the Marvelous One is also the Dweller in the bodies of all, the Soul is exhorted to cease from vain lamentations over the disappearance of what is transitory by nature and to stand up and fight, fulfilling the duties that lie before it.

Even if the disciple loses the battle, the fruits of heroic endeavor will be enjoyed in the shape of better opportunities in the future.[3] *Verse 37* And if victorious, the earth will be won, for one who is the master of all manifested being. No longer a "procession of fate," as Hermes graphically puts it, but a king, throned in the Sunlight, ruling all that is.

This knowledge is what is referred to in the Gita as the wisdom of the *Sankhya*, but it should not be confused with the brilliant but purely scholastic version that is to be found in the much later *Sankhya Karika*. Partial accounts of the older Sankhya are to be found in the *Shanti Parva* of the Mahabharata, and suffice to make it clear that, while the later system was a frank dualism, the original teaching was monistic. The latter set out to explain the world as an evolution in a graded series of manifestations proceeding from one eternal Reality, referred to as "That," or the *Avyakta*, the Unmanifested. The duality between *prakriti* and *purusha* that forms the center of the later system is here transcended, since both are but aspects of the *avyakta* and are ultimately absorbed in It.[4]

Thus we see that essentially the Sankhya was a body of teaching designed to give a coherent intellectual expression to the intuition of the Unchanging One that arises at the proper time in the soul of the disciple when stimulated into activity by the words of the Teacher.

It is, as Shankara rightly maintains, a system of jñana yoga, of yoga by knowledge, and, like all such partial systems, it suffers from a certain one-sidedness that Krishna makes it his business to correct. At the time when the Gita was spoken (as indeed now) there were several such yogas in existence, and we shall find that the first six chapters of the Gita (or rather chapters 2 to 6) contain expositions of the Path according to their various teachings, and also corrections of their deficiencies.

In this chapter we are taken along the path of the Sankhyan knowledge, because the first cry of the Soul when it awakens to a dim perception of the Eternal is for a coherent scheme of principles by which it may explain to itself its new knowledge. But there is a danger in the demand for detailed explanation, a danger that the original intuitive perception may be swamped by the clear-cut intellectual expression, a danger that knowledge, divorced from the love and activity that are the other aspects of the Path, may be considered as the whole.

Many must have had the experience of seeing the flashing intuitions of the one Atman, which come from a reading of the Upanishads, fade and grow pale as the reader seeks to fix them by the help of even such a writer as Shankara, who made those intuitions the very cornerstones of his philosophy. The Soul flees just at the very moment when we seem to hold its gleaming splendor in our hands.

Therefore the disciple has ever to keep in mind the fact that the clear intellectual grasp that is craved and may to some extent be gained by the study of the "Sankhyan wisdom," is but a substitute, a symbol of the true knowledge which alone can bear the Soul upward on swift and flashing wings.

It is here that the one-sidedness of the pure Sankhya comes in. In proportion as the inner vision fades, the disciple endeavors to recapture its fleeing spirit and to galvanize it into life once more by a violent effort. Separating more and more from the world of action and emotion, disciples withdraw into the realm of the abstractions and, bending upon them the whole power of their psychic energy, they often succeed in imparting a kind of life to them at the cost of an ever sterner and more forcible warping of their nature. This "life," however, shows by its very lack of balance that it is not the authentic life of the Soul. Only in perfect poise and harmony can the Soul blossom and be developed, and not by any such forced and unnatural straining will the disciple reach the true Goal. Origen's act of self-castration did not enable him to attain that state that Hindu tradition terms *brahmacharya*, and rigid isolation in a mountain cave will not bring about that inner detachment from the passing show of things which is the soil in which alone the flower of true Wisdom can grow.

The battle of life must be won and not run away from, and so, after a repetition of the injunction to prepare for the fray, the disciple is instructed in the all-important buddhi yoga which is necessary to supplement the static analytic technique of pure Sankhya. The latter attempts to gain its goal of emancipation (*Kaivalya*) by a forced isolation from the whole of the manifested universe which, even if at all practicable, can only result in a strained and unnatural attainment. The true Path aims at a detachment from the lower manifestations by a progressive union with the higher, and is as different from the former method as is the natural blooming of a flower from the forced opening of the bud.

Verses 38, 39

What is therefore emphasized is the buddhi yoga, the union with the buddhi as a preliminary step to the utterly transcendent state of the goal. The manas, or mind, must cease to be united to the senses, but must become *buddhiyukta*, or united to that which is higher than itself, if the Path is to be really trodden and not merely talked about. For by climbing the ladder there is none of that loss of effort which is in store for him who attempts to leap in one bound to the roof of the world. Nor is there any transgression of the law that all that lives is one.[5] And at this point it is necessary to say a few words about the nature of buddhi.

Nowhere does the purely intellectual nature of the *later* Sankhya come out more clearly than in its account of the nature of buddhi, which it treats as simply one of the intellectual faculties, the faculty by which the mind comes to a decision after a period of doubt and hesitation. True it is that the buddhi is the faculty that gives determined knowledge (*nischayatmika buddhi*), but the knowledge that it gives is no mere collection of intellectual propositions, but a living knowledge that is closer to intuition, save that it has none of the sporadic flashing that we associate with that term, but on its own level, burns with a steady radiance. In the Katha Upanishad, buddhi is termed the jñana atman, and it is at once the knowledge of the Atman and the faculty by which that knowledge is attained. Symbolically it is the yellow cloth that is worn by Krishna, and its particular significance for the disciple lies in the fact that it is beyond the limitations of individuality.

On the level of the manas, the Light of the One Atman is split up into a number of separate individualities, each standing on its own uniqueness. The buddhi, however, is non-individual, being the same for all.

This certainty-giving buddhi (*Vyavasay atmika buddhi*), which is one in all, is contrasted with the wavering and uncertain thoughts[6] of the ordinary person. It is the source of all real knowledge and, for one who can attain to it, it supersedes all the scriptures of the orthodox. Not that the latter have no value at all. Veiling in rites

Verses 42–46

and ceremonies the eternal Truths behind, they serve as guides to the great mass of human beings and furnish checks upon the grosser forms of desire; but they can do little for the serious aspirant for knowledge. "The Vedas deal with the three gunas,"[7] says the Gita, while the disciple, steadfast in *sattva* alone, must reach out to what is beyond. The reason for their failure is that they depend on hope and fear (manifestations of *rajas* and *tamas* respectively), whereas only the sattvic devotion to Truth for its own sake can serve for him who seeks to tread this Path. The orthodox may thunder forth their dogmatic assurances, but all their books are, literally, as useful to the enlightened disciple (*vijanata*=possessed of *vijñana* or buddhi) as "a tank in a place overflowing with water on all sides." Hence the extreme importance of the buddhi yoga, for this union, when achieved, brings about a liberation from "the knots of the heart," the fetters which had bound the Soul within the prison of separate individuality. Only when this union with the super-individual buddhi has been achieved will it be possible for the Soul to "escape from the tangle of delusions" and to "stand immovable," unshaken alike by the pleasures and pains of life and by the conflicting and partial views of reality that are all that can be achieved by the unaided manas.

Verse 45

Verses 52, 53

Only one who is thus established in the *prajña* (a synonym for buddhi) will be able to make the final leap to the *anamayam padam*, the Sorrowless State, with any hope of success, and in order to attain this union with the buddhi, the method recommended is skill in acting (*karmasu kaushalam*), the maintenance of a balanced attitude that remains the same in failure as in success. Disciples are to keep their minds indifferent to the results of their actions while, in a spirit of utter detachment, performing such acts as are their

Verse 51

Verses 47-51

duty. Acting in this way the disciples' actions will be guided by the impersonal knowledge of the buddhi and they will then transcend the limits of selfish good and evil.

This is the method of the karma yoga, whose theoretical basis will be gone into in the next chapter, of which it forms the specific subject. In this context it is enough to point out that its purpose is to gain control of the desire-prompted impulses of the senses and to harmonize the mind so as to render it possible for the latter to unite with the buddhi and enable the Divine knowledge to blossom forth. It is only through the buddhi that this knowledge can shine freely in; below that level it is obstructed and broken up by the play of the separated individualities, and it is only when they are united with what is beyond them that the unifying Divine Wisdom can become manifest and the fetters of duality begin to fall away.

It is easy to say "unite the mind with the buddhi," but usually such words have but little meaning for the disciple, since he has as yet had no experience of the buddhi and does not know what it really is. Moreover, the mind remains obstinately separate and will not suffer itself to be united with anything. Hence the supreme importance of supplementing the theoretic technique of the Sankhya by a practice designed to harmonize and control the mind in action. In reply to Arjuna's question about the characteristics of the man who has united with the buddhi, Sri Krishna describes how the disciple must detach the self from the desire-life of the senses as a tortoise withdraws its limbs from contact with the outer world. Mere withdrawal is, however, not enough, for though the sense objects lose their power over one who habitually practices restraint, the desire for them remains in the heart and dies only when something higher

Verses
56-58

Verse 59

than the sense life is actually seen.

In the last resort, nothing but the vision of the Atman itself can cause the utter dying-out of desire, and therefore the disciples are instructed not to remain content with negative restraint but to center their gaze upon the Atman within, unseen though yet it be. "Silence thy thoughts and fix thy whole attention on thy Master, whom yet thou dost not see, but whom thou feelest."[8] The slightest wavering, the slightest turning back in thought to that sense world on which the disciples have turned their backs, will energize anew the desires that they are striving to abandon, and as the tension increases in their desire-nature (what some psychologists term the unconscious) those desires will burst out in a great flash of anger utterly devastating to spiritual progress, shattering inner perception and causing a loss of those "memories"[9] by which they hoped to mount.

Verses 62-63

It is not that the sense life is to be negated or outwardly discontinued, as impracticably taught by some Sankhyas. It is an inner withdrawal that is to be practiced, a withdrawal to higher levels that will in itself bring that outer harmonization which is essential if the buddhi is to be attained. In the old symbol of the chariot, the horse of the senses are to be held back (*nigrihita*) by the reins of the mind, but it is not intended that they should be unyoked from the chariot, or that their movement should be stopped altogether. The aim of this practice is that the mind should, to some extent at least, be purified by the practice of selfless action and at least partially liberated from the thralldom of attachments, so that it may cease to assert its unique viewpoint at every moment. Then, as the wind of desire subsides, the disciple will feel a luminous peace and wisdom reflected in the heart, like the images of the eternal stars reflected in the depths

Verses 65,71

of a lake, and will have gained a preliminary perception of the actual nature of buddhi that will be a thousand times more useful than all the descriptions of the books.

For the first time the command to unite the manas with the buddhi will begin to have a meaning, and only now will the disciple be able to address the task with any hope of success. Far overhead, Its blazing Light as yet a mere pinpoint to his vision, burns the Star of the Supreme Atman, the Goal of all his efforts. Dimly It shines in the darkness and seems to flicker as Its rays pierce the unsteady middle air, but once seen It can never be forgotten. Offering the self to It, in utter devotion and worship, the disciple must press on, straining vision to the utmost, to pierce through what appear to be the abysses of non-being, through to the fully awakened eye of the Seer, to a radiant pleroma of Light, the "Light that shines beyond the broken lamps," the glorious sunshine of the Eternal Day.[10]

Verse 61

Verse 69

Verse 72

"This is the *Brahmic* State, O Arjuna, which having attained, one is deceived no more," and though, the disciple has but a distant glimpse of that Farther Shore its memory will remain forever, with one who has "reached the stream" and for whom the promise of final Salvation has been uttered: "Whoever, even at the final hour, is established therein attains the Supreme Nirvana."

Notes

1   Compare Bertrand Russell's *A Free Man's Worship*. His appeal for a Promethean defiance of the universe "based on the firm rock of unyielding despair," however thrilling it may be to the armchair agnostic, will scarcely nerve anyone who is actually in the abyss, and for all Russell's sincerity his glowing rhetoric rings false.

2   Marcus Aurelius, *Meditations*, v, 19, 26.

3   Compare *The Voice of the Silence*: "For either he shall win or shall fall . . . and if he falls, e'en then he does not fall in vain; the enemies he slew in the last battle will not return to life in the next birth that will be his."

4   See the teaching of Panchashikha, a pupil of Kapila and a traditional teacher of the early Sankhya, given in *Shanti Parva*, chapter 219. The soul (Kshet-rajña) is said to "rest upon the mind" (cf, what was said in the introduction as to the Mind's (*manas*) being the higher ego) and to obtain emancipation or absorption into the Unmanifest Reality by complete renunciation of all that is manifest. For other early accounts see *Shanti Parva*, chapter 311 and 312; also Caraka's account quoted in Das Gupta's *History of Indian Philosophy*, p. 213.

5   The all-renouncing flight of the soul to the Unmanifest is in some sense a transgression of this law and it is for this reason that the *Mahayana* stigmatizes the *Pratyeka Buddhas* (treaders of that Path) as spiritually selfish.

6   The word *buddhi* in addition to being used of the super-mental level is also, as it were by courtesy and common usage, applied to ordinary mental knowledge. Hence the plural in the second half of the verse.

7   Sattva, rajas, and tamas, the three gunas, or characteristics of *Mula-prakriti*, and so of all forms derived therefrom. Though not very easily translated, they may be rendered as harmonious purity, passionate activity, and dark inertia respectively. See Chapter 14.

8   *The Voice of the Silence.*

9   See Prolegomena, p. 24, second note.

10   Compare Plotinus: "The sphere of sense is of the Soul in its slumber, for all of Soul that is in body is asleep and the true getting-up is not bodily but from the body" (*On the Impassivity of the Incorporeal*, vi).

Chapter Three

The Yoga of Action

The third chapter opens with the disciple in doubt. "If it be thought by Thee that knowledge is superior to action, why dost Thou, O Krishna, urge me to this terrible deed?". The Teacher has praised the wisdom of the Sankhyas, but then urges the necessity of action, the one thing, which, above all, was shunned by the followers of the Sankhya. Lastly, the disciple has heard him praise knowledge and describe a state in which action would, at best, appear an irrelevance. Small wonder that the disciple is confused and begs to be taught clearly the one way to the Goal.

Nevertheless, it is not the teaching that is confused; it is only that the disciple, in demanding a clear-cut intellectual presentation is looking for something which cannot be given. The method of a true Teacher is not to demand assent to an intellectual scheme. Such an assent, even if given, is entirely useless, as it does not lift the disciple above the levels of the manas, the thinking mind. Rather, He aims, by setting forth apparently conflicting but actually complementary aspects of Truth, to force the disciple to transcend higher intuitive knowledge of the buddhi and thus bring to birth in the soul a new and harmonious knowledge which shall be built into the disciple's very being.

The reader is apt to make the mistake of concluding that the thought of the Gita is actually confused, or of picking out that aspect that most appeals to him and ignoring the rest. But the Gita is neither a confused eclecticism nor a one-sided sectarianism. It aims at setting forth the Yoga or Path to the Goal as a coherent whole, but in so doing, it is inevitable that the mind, which loves to pursue one train of thought to its logical conclusion regardless of others, should be brought up sharply from time to time and made to grasp the other sides as well.

In answer to the disciple's query, the Teacher states that from *Verse 3* the beginning of time there have been two main types of aspirant, corresponding to the duality that pervades the manifested world. Modern psychology speaks of introverts and extroverts. Corresponding to these we have the yoga of knowledge practiced by the Sankhyas and the yoga of action of the karma yogis. Urged on by the lack of balance in their own natures, one-sided exponents always attempt to show that one of these is the chief teaching and the other only subsidiary. But the duality in the universe is not ultimate. In the end all is resolved into the unitary Brahman, and therefore no one-sided view can be the whole truth.

The doctrine of the karma yogis starts from the plain fact that a cessation from all action is simply impossible. Even a forcible abstention from outer actions will leave the mental actions quite unchecked, and in fact more riotous because of the enforced outer inactivity. Psychologically it is certain that excessive and long-continued introversion will have disastrous results upon the psychic health and—as Jung, I think, puts it—the attempt to escape from all entangling outer relationships will result in an eventual domination of the ego by relationships of a neurotic and inferior type. "Not by *Verse 4* mere cessation of activity shall the soul rise to the state of actionlessness." Therefore, since action is a necessity, we must make an effort to come to grips with it and prevent it from exerting its fatal binding power on us.

The great objection to action as ordinarily performed lies in its connection with results. We are bound by the results of our actions and must experience the consequences whether pleasant or painful. This so-called law of karma is apt to strike the Western mind as unverified dogma or, at best, as philosophical speculation. In fact, however, it is nothing of the kind, but a fact of nature which may be experienced by anyone. Even on the ordinary levels it is obvious that our destinies are largely shaped by the sum-total of our past thoughts, and particularly those which have crystallized into actions. Those who think cruel thoughts usually proceed to cruel deeds, and thus, becoming an object of fear and hatred to others, are at least extremely liable to meet with cruelty in their turn. Ordinary everyday experience can perhaps not take us much farther than this probability; but ordinary experience is not the final arbiter in these matters, and one who advances on the inner path, the Path of Knowledge, becomes immediately aware that it is no mere probability with which we are connected but a perfect and unerring law—

> "By which the slayer's knife did stab himself,
> The unjust judge hath lost his own defender."

The world of life is no less a unity than the world of matter, all lives being interlocked in one vast whole. It follows that any act— even any thought—sets up a tension in the whole which, however delayed the response, inevitability brings about an "equal and opposite" reaction. I repeat that this is a profound truth of experience, which may, like other natural laws, be disregarded only at one's peril. The same perception is expressed in Christ's flashing words: "They that live by the sword shall perish by the sword."

. Thus, if action is inevitable, it is none the less a source of bondage, and, by tying the soul to its own position, whether good or bad, prevents that self-transcendence in union with the All that constitutes the Goal.

The method proposed by the karma yogis was that of scrupulous performance of the prescribed code of ritual actions which, according to Hindu custom, filled a Brahman's life and regulated conduct down to the minutest detail. At the same time the yogi was to perform these actions without any desire for the fruit, in the shape of worldly prosperity and heavenly bliss, that the scriptures promised as the result of such actions. In this way they hoped to avoid the impasse created by the inevitability of action and its no less certain binding power. They rightly perceived that the binding power came not from the action in itself but from the desire with which it was performed, and therefore taught that if the latter could be eliminated the poison fangs of the acts would have been removed.

"The righteous who eat the remains of the sacrificial offerings are freed from all sin, but those who merely prepare food for their own sakes verily eat sin."

This doctrine, literally understood, like the detachment of the Sankhyas, is not enough in itself. Taken literally and by itself it fails, because it reduces the vigorous creative life of action to a dead round of sterile ceremonies and smothers the spirit under a tedious formalism quite inapplicable to the ordinary actions of life. For them, as to the typical follower of the pure Sankhya, this rich and wondrous life was no better than a ghastly mistake.

This ignoble view of action is by no means that of Sri Krishna. For Him, as for the karma yogis, action is a sacrifice, but one far different from the formal ceremonies of the Brahmans. The lower or sense mind is to be sacrificed to the higher and that higher to be united with the buddhi, as we have seen in the last chapter.

It is time now to say a few words about the actual process by which this is to be accomplished. We have seen (in the Prolegomena) how between Arjuna, the higher mind, and Dhritarashtra, the lower, stand Sañjaya, the second charioteer, the voice of conscience speaking in the heart of the eternal values. Just as the buddhi, the Divine Knowledge, serves as a link between the individual ego and the One Life (*Mahat Atman*), so does Sañjaya on a lower plane serve as a link between the empirical personality and the true individual Self. By uniting with the buddhi the mind is raised into transcendence, and similarly, by making the empirical personality or lower mind the servant of the voice of Sañjaya, the personality is raised to union with its own true Self.

Verse 8

This is the reason for so much emphasis upon performing action as a duty. The lower self is not to be destroyed by self-mortification, but to be united with the higher by being trained to obey the voice of the higher under all circumstances. "Right action" is to be performed, the test of rightness being its accord with the commands of that voice and not with any outer scriptural injunctions. The disciple must always listen for that voice, and having heard it must always act in accordance with it. By this means the lower self will be purified of its attachment to desire and will in time become united with the higher. This must be achieved before the next stage, that of union with the buddhi, the *dhyana paramita* of the *Mahayana* Buddhist, becomes possible.[1]

Having dealt with the practical importance of action, Sri Krishna next goes on to show its moral and cosmic significance. In a few rapid words He sketches the *yajña chakra*, the great Cycle of Sacrifice[2] that forms the manifested Cosmos, and shows how action is rooted in the Imperishable. Into all quarters of space streams forth in sacrifice the life-blood of the Supreme Purusha. But for that sustaining life the worlds would "fall into ruin," and ceaselessly does the Supreme pour Itself forth in action for the welfare of all. Round and round circles the One Life through all beings in the worlds as It weaves the pattern of the universe, and none can claim a proud independence of his brothers. The knowledge of the world that comes to us so easily today we owe to countless thinkers and discoverers of the past, and we cannot walk down the street of a town without treading on the bowed backs of the nameless toilers of bygone ages. Our intellects owe their every possibility of thought to those who strove to grasp new conceptions long ago, and even our eyes are what they are only as a result of long and painful struggles of which no record now remains. No record, that is, but the debt inscribed in the imperishable characters of the book of *Karma,* a debt that claims our actions in return and from which not the proudest yogi in a Himalayan cave is free, though he may choose to ignore it. "He who on earth doth not follow the Wheel thus revolving, sinful of life and rejoicing in the sense, he, O Arjuna, liveth in vain."

Verses 10-16

Thus action is seen to be not only a physical necessity for those who are embodied. It is also a moral necessity, since out of sacrificial action spring the worlds and by sacrifices are they maintained in their ceaseless whirling around and in the Central Sun. Consciousness (the Gods) nourishes the forms, and forms in their turn sustain that Consciousness in manifestation. Thus is the whole universe linked in one stupendous Sacrifice, each separate element being related to all else that is.

It is important to realize, however—and that is why the instruction in the Sankhyan wisdom preceded the teaching about action—that without knowledge of the Atman the sacrificial action is not possible in the true sense. Until the One Self, or at least Its shining Light, is known, the abandonment of all desire for the fruits of action remains but a matter of grand words. The Light of the Atman must be known to some extent at least, and just in proportion as It is known, not as a matter of theoretic philosophy but as a vivid reality present in every moment of experience, will the disciple be able to discard any wish for the fruits of his actions. The *Verses 17, 18* desire for fruits is an utter irrelevance which will fall away of itself, though *only for as long as the disciple is thus centered in the Light.* When at last, after long and persistent struggles, this centering of life in the Atman is permanently established, when the disciple rejoices in the Atman and is content with the Atman, there will remain nothing further to be accomplished and "no object of his will depend on any being."

Nevertheless, in thus escaping from "private" action, disciples *Verses 22-24* have but united themselves with the Divine and Cosmic action, and of them it will be said, as of Krishna Himself, that, though there is nothing in the three worlds that is unattained by them, they mingle in action unweariedly for the sake of the welfare of all. Note the word "unwearied." The Sacrificial Action is no tiresome carrying out of dull and spiritless acts such as are too often called up in our minds by the words sacrifice and duty. We saw how, at the beginning of the Path, the disciples were filled with despair at the thought of the joyless life which awaited them when all the desires which made life seem worth living should be slain. But this is an illusion which has to be dispelled. "As the ignorant act of out attachment to action, so should the wise act without attachment, desiring the welfare of the world." The glow which accompanies the desire-prompted actions of the worldly, the enthusiasm and zest of youth and the tireless energy of the ambitious, must all be preserved and transmuted into something higher and not allowed to drain away into desert sands. The true *vairagi* is not a dull, dried-up, "holy" person, but a tireless fountain of joyful and inspired life based on the eternal *ananda* of the Brahman which overflows into creation out of Its own inherent fullness. *Verse 25*

This, then, is the charter of action, the fact that the whole Cosmos is established on sacrifice; not on mere formal acts of ceremonial offering but on that of which these were but the outward symbol, the Great Sacrifice of which we read in the Vedas,[3] in which the One Purusha was offered in the fires of the worlds and His Limbs scattered like those of Osiris to all the quarters of space. This is the Sacrifice which the disciple is called to cooperate in. But, though he acts ceaselessly, he is not bound by karma, for his grounding in the Sankhyan wisdom has taught him that actions are performed by the modifications of prakriti alone. His bodies, gross and subtle, act, and the unwise are entangled in the acts, but he who has mastered the lesson of the previous chapter has learnt to see that the Atman, the True Self, is forever but the detached Witness, serene and impartial. *Verses 27-30*

Actions can no more bind Him than weapons can pierce Him, and, clinging firmly to this knowledge in his heart, offering his actions to Krishna as the symbol of the Great Sacrifice, free from the fetters of selfish hope and fear, he engages with zest in the great battle against evil and sorrow, the evil of his own lower nature and the sorrow of his brothers.

For let none think that the battle is won at the first triumphant blare of the trumpets. The knowledge that has been given must be practiced and built into the heart by constant struggle. Again and again must the battle be fought, and those who, shutting with subtle sophisms their eyes to the imperfections still existing in their lower nature, and their ears to the cry for help that sounds pitifully from suffering humanity, are unworthy of the Wisdom they have received and are doomed to fall, however proudly they may carry things off for the time.

Doubts will assuredly come tormenting the heart with the suggestion that the struggle is useless:

> *"All things are vain and vain the knowledge of their*
> *vanity;*
> *Rise and go hence, there is no better way*
> *Than patient scorn, nor any help for man,*
> *Nor any staying of his whirling wheel."*[4]

Verse 33   All beings follow their own natures. The Atman is the impartial Witness of all; good and evil are but empty words and the fight against the latter is in vain. What shall restraint avail since actions flow inevitably from the workings of Nature and the Soul is but the passive witness of the phantom show?

But these deceiving half-truths must be conquered. It is true that the play of Nature follows fixed laws and that effect follows cause with unerring accuracy. Deeply embedded in the Cosmos is the power of attraction and repulsion by which all things move and change. From the chemical elements with their "affinities," to humans with their loves and hates, all are bound by this power within the iron circle of Necessity—all, that is, save one who has conquered desire and acts from a sense of duty (*svadharma*) alone. As long as the disciples do certain acts because they like them and abstain from certain others because they dislike them, so long must they whirl helplessly upon the Wheel; for, though they may be of "virtuous" disposition, and so perform but "virtuous" acts, they are nonetheless victims of their own nature.

Verses 34, 35

But the Atman, the One Self, is forever free in Its own being; Its apparent bondage comes only from the self-identification with Its lower vehicles, the mirrors in which Its Light is reflected. The higher the disciple climbs up the Ladder of the Soul, the more the inherent freedom of the Atman will shine forth and dominate the play of Nature instead of blindly suffering it.

Those who act from the dictates of manas are freer than those who act from the dictates of the senses, and freer still are those whose manas is united with the buddhi and suffused by its Light, the Light of the glorious Flame Beyond. Therefore, instead of allowing themselves to be guided by the likes and dislikes of the senses, disciples must constantly strive, by acting from a sense of duty alone, to rise to higher and even-higher levels of their being. Bound as they are by their nature at any given level, yet are they free with the inherent freedom of the Atman to choose whether they will act from their

Verse 42

lower nature or from the higher. True the "higher" will ever recede as they climb, and what is "higher" now will become "lower" in time; but at each stage freedom will increase until the Unreachable is reached and all desire is dead in that blazing Unity.

Verse 43

"Thus understanding Him (the Atman) as higher than the buddhi, restraining the lower self by the Atman, slay thou, O Mighty-armed, the enemy in the form of desire, difficult to be overcome." Let the disciple dwell on this concluding verse, for in its few words is contained the secret that has baffled so many ascetics and philosophers, the secret of the conquest of desire. True, it is a secret that cannot be imparted in words, one which must be experienced in the heart; but those who have even partially understood the meaning of the words "restraining the lower self by the Atman" may know for certain that their foot is on the ladder, and that if they will resolutely put their knowledge into practice their further progress is assured, and neither gods nor human beings can hinder their ultimate attainment of the Goal.

Notes

1   See Chapter 6, which deals with this stage.

2   "Food" signifies the gross material world of which forms are built and "rain" the forces of desire which brings those forms into being. The sacrifice is the sacrificial self-limitation by which the many issue from the One and "karma," action, is the Mula-prakriti from which all action issues (*cf.* Gita, viii, 3, and xiii, 29). While "karma" is the Mula-prakriti considered as the source of all action, "Brahma" (verse 15) is the same considered as the source of being, the great matrix (*cf.* Gita, xiv, 3), while the Imperishable is of course the supreme *Parabrahman*.

3   Rig Veda, x, 90.

4   *The Light of Asia.*

Chapter Four

The Yoga of Partial Knowledge[1]

"The same imperishable yoga that I taught to Vivaswan[2] long ages ago I am again setting for thee today." Thus opens the fourth chapter, and in so saying Sri Krishna reveals the source and credentials of the teaching He has to impart. It is no "new" doctrine, the private property of a particular teacher, that is being set forth; nothing, either, that is intended to form a new sect, shut off by the fortress walls of dogma from the life all around, walls which will have to be broken with infinite pain before the imprisoned souls. *Verse 1*

It has to be clearly understood that there is no ownership in the realm of ideas. Rather is it the fact, as Plato rightly taught, that when we entertain a "new" idea we do but participate in something that is eternal, and that when two people "think" of the same idea they are united with each other by this very fact since both are participating in a particular facet of the Eternal Wisdom. Ideas are greater than any of the finite minds that think them and the Wisdom is greater than any particular teacher. Therefore it was that the Buddha made no claim to originality, being content to say that what He taught was but the echo of the teaching of all the former Buddhas, and therefore it is that Sri Krishna is careful to explain that the Yoga He is teaching to Arjuna is but a restatement of the Eternal Wisdom taught under the same Divine sanction to Vivaswan long ages before.

Let none suppose, however, that by the phrase "Eternal Wisdom" is here meant some body of teachings set down in intellectual form in any books however old. It is the Norm by which all teachings must be judged, the Fount from which all great religions and philosophies have sprung, and being beyond the level of individuality it is utterly impersonal. It is *the Truth*. Fortunate are those through whose minds even a ray of that Wisdom Light can manifest, for, though they still may make frequent mistakes, they have in their hands an Ariadne thread with which, if they will but follow it up, they can make their way safely through the labyrinth of theories and avoid the quicksands of doubt. It is this Wisdom which inspired the ancient Sages and the

Verse 2   Divine Kings of whom the records of all the archaic people tell, and it is this Wisdom, or rather Its manifestation, that has "decayed here on earth through great efflux of time" as the warring schools sought each to imprison in its own system the gleaming splendor that shone in the words of its Founder.

Verse 3   Jñana yoga, karma yoga, bhakti yoga, dhyana yoga, all are but one-sided glimpses, fragments of that mighty whole, the "imperishable Yoga," the imparting of which in its all-sided beauty is the aim of Sri Krishna.

Sri Krishna, in fact, *is* that Wisdom, incarnate here on earth not once but many times in order to reveal in every act and gesture that which is hidden in all mere "teaching," the ultimate Mystery of His own Divine Being, beyond the reach of mind.

Verses 6-8   It is the birth of this Wisdom in the human soul that is celebrated each year at the *Janmashtmi* festival,[3] the Wisdom that destroys the demons of ignorance and selfishness, the Wisdom whose other names are Love and Sacrifice. Though Unborn and

Undying, this Wisdom-Love manifests in human souls from time to time,[4] and especially at times of great spiritual stress when materialism and the cosmic forces of disharmony are straining at the personalities of individuals and forcing them away from their contact with the Inner Watcher. At such times a terrific tension is set up in the inner worlds, a tension which manifests itself in a psychic unrest in the heart of each one, and also among the peoples of the earth, tossing them hither and thither in wars and revolutions like corks upon a sea of sorrow.

Then, like the lightning flash cleaving the night, comes at the dark *Verse 9* midnight hour the great Mystery, the birth of the Birthless, the action of the Actionless, and once again the Light of the World is revealed to them that walk in darkness. Therefore does Sri Krishna say that they who know the *essential nature* of His Divine birth and actions wander no more in the cycles of suffering but attain to His exalted Being.[5]

But not only at certain seasons in the outer world must that Birth take place. It is not enough to look with longing backward-turned eyes at the Light which once blazed with such splendor in Muttra, at Buddha-Gaya, or in Nazareth. In the dark soul of every disciple the Divine Krishna must be born, and throughout the ages many are those who, filled with the newborn Wisdom, the Slayer of the demons of passion, fear and anger, have passed along by the ancient narrow Path (the *anuh pantha puranah* of the Upanishads) and, piercing through the Darkness, have entered His Being.

"In all ways[6] men follow My Path," says Krishna, and indeed, *Verse 11* there is no other Path, *nanyah pantha vidyate' yanaya.*[7] The only bridge that spans the sea of sorrow is the Bridge of Light, the many-colored rainbow bridge, and, though one may give what names one pleases to the various stages, and may use primarily intellect, emotion, or unselfish action as the stick by the help of which one essays the crossing, yet is it the same Path for all, the Ladder of Souls figured on many an Egyptian papyrus[8] and known to all the ancient teachers of the world, "the ladder whose foot rests in the deep mire of the disciple's sins and failings but whose summit is lost in the glorious Light of Nirvana."[9]

But no mere theoretical knowledge of the Path will enable the disciple to tread it. It can be trodden only by *becoming* oneself its various stages. "In this Path, to whatever place one goes, that place one's own self becomes."[10] The consciousness must be raised step by step, and it is useless to think as did certain Sankhyas, that if only action could be abandoned the soul would fly up at once, like a bird released from a cage. Useless, because even if the more obvious outer actions be forcibly abandoned, the subtle actions of the mind will remain to bind the soul as firmly as ever.[11]

Verse 14

The only way to tread the Path in reality is by the knowledge of Krishna, of the Atman which is present as the unseen background of every action, of the smallest as of the greatest, of the action that sends the pen across this page as of the action that hurls a million men into battle. Just as nothing can move except within the framework of space, so nothing can take place except within the Light of the Atman, which yet is no more entangled in the actions than space is entangled in the movements of objects. Therefore Krishna says that those who know Him are freed from the bonds of action.

Verse 18

Such people are wise, for they see inaction in action and action in inaction. They see, that is, that while in the midst of all movements broods the motionless Atman, yet do all actions spring from Atman, or, rather, take place *within* that calm and passionless Light. This is the knowledge whose fire burns up all actions, slaying desire for selfish fruits and making those Sages who, though body and mind are forever engaged in action, do nothing since they cling to nothing.

"Of one with attachment dead, liberated from bondage, with his thoughts established in knowledge, his works sacrifices, all action melts away."

The instinct which leads so many to reject the idea of an action-less life is a sound one. To reject action is to create a dualism between the Brahman and the universe, which leaves the latter on our hands as a vast cosmic folly. But it is not so. There is no ultimate dualism in the Reality. It is not action that binds. What binds us is a wrong attitude to action, the "knots of the heart" which, springing from ignorance, make us fancy that we are so many separate individuals, isolated from each other and "free" to perform actions for our selfish ends. This, and not action in itself, is what binds us, and therefore Krishna returns again and again to the theme of unattachment to the fruits of action, for there is no freedom for the selfish actor any more than for a bird that is in the meshes of a net.

Once it becomes clear that the manifestation is also an aspect of the Supreme Brahman, it will be evident that there must be a way of action which does not bind the Soul. And this is the realization that now begins to dawn in the hearts of the disciples. They see, though as yet but with the mind, for there is still a long and weary road to be traversed before the vision will permeate their whole being, that the action, the actor, and the act are all so many manifestations of the stainless Eternal, and that if all action be offered as a sacrifice in the consuming fire of that Brahman there can be no bondage; for the root-cause of the bondage, the ignorance which makes a dualism, and a multiplicity where there is in truth but One, is now removed and, if not yet eradicated entirely, is at least seen for what it is, an unreal phantom, like a rope mistaken for a snake.

Verses
25-30

This knowledge has now to be applied if it is to be made effective, and so the Teacher proceeds to enumerate various types of practice by which the knowledge may be made to pervade the whole life of the disciple. Some will practice restraint of the senses as a prelude to that more advanced stage in which the now controlled senses can be used for the service of the Atman which is in all. Others endeavor to serve with their wealth or learning, or with that concentrated force of character which is the result of self-discipline (*tapasya*). Others again devote themselves to yogic practices with a view to gaining that inner poise which will enable them to keep their balance in the whirlpool of activity and to hold out helping hands to others.

Verse 33

All these strive to sacrifice themselves in various ways to the Atman who is in all, and all these sacrifices culminate in the wisdom[12] sacrifice, the effort to gain the life-giving wisdom, not, again, in order that oneself may be wise, but because in wisdom lies salvation for all.

Verse 34

All action and all efforts find their completion in gaining of that Wisdom, but just as life springs only from other lives, so the flame of wisdom can be lit only by contact with those in whose heart it already shines. The disciple must find a wise teacher, one who is an embodiment of that Teacher Who is already in his heart, the Eternal Wisdom referred to before. Some will wonder why, if the Teacher is already present in the heart, there should be need for an external guru at all. True, the Teacher is there, but we are so used to listening only to the trumpet tones of desire that the voice in the heart passes unheeded. Too often does the disciple mistake the promptings of desire and of unpurified emotion for the intuition which is the Voice of the Teacher, and therefore needs the guidance of one who, because their whole being has become one with the Wisdom, can speak with the same voice as that Teacher in the heart and do so in tones which can be heard with the outer ear.

Such gurus are always to be found at the right time, for the earth is never without those who know the Truth, who, however scattered and unlinked with each other they may appear, constitute a tribe apart, a tribe whose Light shineth in darkness though the darkness comprehendeth it not, a tribe which never dies, for it is constantly renewed throughout the ages as the torch of Wisdom passes from hand to hand.

But it is not by wandering restlessly here and there, by searching out the remoter corners of the earth, that the guru can be found. The Path which leads to the feet of the guru, outer as well as inner, is an interior path, and only by treading the preliminary steps by oneself can one reach the outer guide. It is only when this stage has been reached, the stage at which the disciple is ready to offer up this self in sacrifice to the Self in all, that the guru can and does manifest himself: "When the disciple is ready the guru appears."[13] For him whose aims are selfish, however "refined" the selfishness may be, no teacher will be forthcoming, for he could be of little use, since his work is but to make more manifest the Voice in the heart. Until the disciple has learnt to listen always for that inner Voice a blind obedience to an external authority can do more harm than good, destroying self-reliance and so rendering fainter that which is too faint already.

Verse 34

When, however, the right stage of development has been reached and the disciples have found their Guru, they must, by the obedience of self-effacement, and the service which consists in putting their will at the disposal of the Teacher, so unite their being with that of the latter that the Wisdom which shines in him may light up in the disciples too.

Verse 35

Then will the disciples begin to *see* that all beings are within the Light of the One Self, just as all things exist within the matrix of space, and, by the raft of this Wisdom Light, they will commence to cross over to the Farther Shore. For, just as fire reduces fuel to ashes, so does the Wisdom Light destroy all sense of difference and multiplicity.[14] The actions which fatally bound the self are powerless to affect the Self, for action binds through ignorance and the Self is free through Wisdom.

But though the Wisdom will save those who lay hold of it from bondage to their past sins, none can serve God and Mammon, and those who are guilty of that egoistic self-assertion which is the essence of all are by that very fact far removed from the Wisdom whose heart is sacrifice of self.

Verses 36–39

True, the Wisdom is hidden in the hearts of all, "even of the most sinful," but it is only he who is "perfected in yoga," in sacrificial action, that finds It there in due season. For this disciples need faith (*shraddha*),[15] the firm aspiration of the soul which seeks to give itself, an aspiration which is itself a reflection of the Wisdom that it preludes. Not only must they have this faith. They must also have gained the mastery over their senses, else will they carry them away "as the wind hurries away a ship upon the waters,"[16] and the sails of aspiration that were set for the voyage to the Deathless will but bear the Soul more swiftly to the black rocks of death.

Above all must disciples beware of doubt[17] that creeps in like a dark fog over the sea, blotting out the guiding stars and filling the soul with despair. From time to time as they try to advance this fog of doubt will enwrap their hearts. The Light by which they have hitherto been guided will be eclipsed, and all that has been accomplished will seem vain and a delusion. If they waver and lose heart they are lost indeed. Clinging to the compass of the Wisdom, an intellectual memory of which is all that remains in this condition, they must press on in confidence that the fog will lift in time and the familiar stars shine forth once more. For, in the end, it is only the Wisdom which can silence doubt. As long as there is any clinging to a separate self, so long is there fear for that self, since all that is separate must one day cease to be. Only the Wisdom which knows the Self as One in all can silence the whisperings of fear and cleave the fog of doubt. Only those shall live who feareth not to die, and such fearlessness can be theirs alone who, by the buddhi yoga, have united themselves to the Light and, by the karma yoga, have offered up the self in sacrifice to Self. These ones alone will stand rock-like in the Self when selves are scattered like leaves by the burning winds of sorrow.

Verse 40

Verse 42

"Therefore with the sword of the knowledge of the One Self cleaving asunder the ignorance-born doubt dwelling in thy heart, be established in Yoga and stand up, O Arjuna."

Notes

1   This chapter, a literal translation of the title of which would be "the yoga of the section of knowledge" as distinguished from the full knowledge of chapter 7, deals with the knowledge as applied to the Sacrificial Action. Just as the

theories of the Sankhyas and karma yogis formed the backgrounds of the two previous chapters, so the sacrificial theories of the *Mimansakas* form the background of this one.

2   Vivasvan, Manu, and Ikshvaku may be taken as standing for the Divine Kings of the prehistoric period. Even as late as the time of the Upanishads we find Brahmans going to Kshatriyas for instruction in the secret wisdom. In Egypt the same is true: above all the priests stood the Pharaoh. Rama, Krishna, Buddha were all Kshatriyas, rulers of the world—and of human hearts. Tilak has pointed out that these same names occur in the *Guruparampara* of the very old Vaishnava School termed *Bhagavadas of Pancharatrikas*. See Mahabharata, *Shanti Parva.*

3   The Hindu Christmas, the birthday of Sri Krishna, occurs in August-September.

4   This does not imply that it is *only* in the soul that the Descent or *avatarana* takes place. Stress has here been laid on the inner (*adhyatmik*) significance, but it is in no way intended to suggest that Sri Krishna was not "born" in the outer world as well.

5   See "Avataras," appendix D.

6   "From all sides" is another translation, but both Shankara and Sridhara paraphrase *sarvashah* as *sarvaprakaraih.*

7   Shvetashvatara Upanishad, vi, 15.

8   E.g. *Book of the Dead,* xcvii (Theban Recension).

9   *The Voice of the Silence.*

10   *Jñaneshvari,* vi, 160.

11   For discussion of the "four castes" (verse 13) see chapter 18.

12   See chapter 18, verse 70, for explanation of the *Jñana Yajña.*

13   Popular superstition has it that no Guru can give *diksha* (initiation) unless he is given *dakshina* (a fee). Corrupt as all such practices are, this is a symbol of a profound truth. Of all who seek a Guru the question is asked: "What do you offer and what will you give in return for the Wisdom that you seek?"

14   Christians may see here the meaning of the salvation of sinners by faith in the crucifixion of Christ. The blood of Christ is the Wisdom Light which is shed through the sacrifice of self for the sake of all. That Light, if clung to, has power by its very nature to save "even the most sinful of sinners."

15   The nature of "faith" will be further discussed in connection with chapter 17.

16   Gita, ii, 67.

17   The doubt referred to here is not mere intellectual doubt, which is the usual precursor of any advance in knowledge; still less is it doubt of orthodox dogmas, for all clinging to dogmas must be destroyed, root and branch. It is the doubt of the reality of what has once been perceived, and springs from the inevitable pendulum swing of reaction after an advance has been made. If it is conquered further advance will come, but if given way to all progress is stopped.

Chapter Five

The Yoga of Renunciation

Verse 1   "Renunciation of actions Thou praisest, O Krishna, and then also (karma) yoga. Tell me decisively which of the two is better."

The Wisdom which is not filtering into the consciousness of the disciple is a unifying wisdom which fuses the broken lights of the mind into a living unity which the unaided intellect cannot reach. None who have reached this stage can view the seated majesty of the Buddha without *knowing* in their soul that renunciation alone gives peace. But neither, when they contemplate the many-faceted figure of Krishna, warrior, statesman, lover, friend, can they refuse their souls' assent to that marvelous revelation of the Divine action, free and unfettered in the very midst of the cosmic whirl.

Verses 4,5   The interpreting mind asserts that these are incompatible ideals and with facile logic seeks to lead the disciples to one side or the other; but they must cling, instead, to the inner wisdom of their soul, which will teach them how these seeming irreconcilables are in reality two aspects of the same truth. They truly see who see that the true meaning of the renunciation of actions taught by the Sankhya is the same as that of the action taught by the karma yogis.

Verse 6   True renunciation cannot be attained by any sudden wrench of the will, even though, when it does come, it may seem to appear with all the swift glory of lightning. "Without yoga, renunciation is hard to attain to." As long as there is the feeling of a separate self, true renunciation is impossible, for it is the personal self which is the seat of attachment, being but the illusory center of the bundle of attachments, likes and dislikes, that make up the so-called self.

Psychologists can tell us how this "self" is gradually built up in the originally "selfless" infant, how it expands and becomes more complex with experience, how strains in the imperfectly integrated experience may sometimes distort and split it into two or more separate "personalities," and how these may be welded into one again by harmonizing the conflicting stresses. They teach, as the Buddha taught long before, that in all this there is nothing permanent, no hard changeless center in the ever-changing flux of experience which could in truth be called a self. This self that we prize so dearly and to which we subordinate all is the empty heart of a whirlpool, a mathematical point which changes its position, not only from year to year, but even from hour to hour, as we shift from home to workplace to social gathering.

Therefore does Sri Krishna teach that the disciples must utterly destroy the false sense of self, realizing in all that they do, "speaking, giving, grasping," no self is involved; only "the senses moving among the objects of the senses." *Verses 7-9*

But a whirlpool is real even though its center be empty,[1] and Life is real though lives are devoid of permanent selves. There is a Life that is the Light of men, "a Light that shineth in darkness though the darkness comprehendeth it not." That Life, the Atman, is the Self of all beings, the very Breath of the Eternal, of which the Rig Veda says: "The Only One, the breathless, breathed by Its own nature; apart from It was nothing whatsoever."

Verse 10

It is that One Life which is the life of all beings, that One Self, if it may be called a Self, which is the inmost heart of all. In that Life alone can immortality be achieved, and only when it is realized that it is in the bosom of that Ocean of Light that all these whirlpools of activity have their being can the disciple "place his actions in the Eternal" and, in renouncing the illusory finite center, achieve that renunciation of attachment which leaves the actions free and divine.

Verse 11

Disciples must, then, learn to divest themselves of egocentricity. They must no longer act for the separate self but for that Self which is in all, which means in practice that, seeking neither gain nor fame, they must work for the welfare of their fellow-beings. Body, mind and senses will act as before, but their actions must no longer find their meaning solely in the point within them, but in that mystic Circle whose center is everywhere and circumference nowhere.

When some success in this yoga of disinterested action has been achieved the disciples will notice a change taking place within themselves. Instead of the elusive personal center, the empty and featureless point of reference, they will perceive a Light shining where before all was darkness, will hear a Voice where previously all was silence.

Verse 13

"Having renounced all (desire-prompted) action with the mind, the Inner Ruler sits blissfully in the nine-gated city of the body, neither acting nor causing to act.".

For the center within is illusory only when considered as an independent self, a monad separate from all others. In reality the "point" within is a window, a point of view *through* which the Eternal One as subject looks out upon Itself as object. Just as a window, empty in itself, is yet a focus through which the all-pervading sunlight can illumine the world of objects, so is the self a focus through which can shine the Light of the One Consciousness illumining the objective world which is the other aspect of the Great Atman or Universal Mind (*Mahat Atman*).

This Light, differing in no way from that which shines through the innumerable other foci which constitute the world of beings, is the real Self, and, as stated in the text, it dwells blissfully in the body, *Verses* neither acting nor causing to act. Serene in Itself, It is untouched by *14, 15* the good and evil deeds of the personality and constitutes a fortress in which the disciples can take refuge, unharmed by the tides of battle, and yet not in selfish isolation, for they will be one with all that is.

This inner Self, however, as is shown by the use of the word *vibhu*, the all-pervading one, is not to be regarded as an eternally *Verse 15* existing monad, separate for each disciple. In all the worlds there is nothing eternal but the one Brahman, and to consider the "inner point" as a permanent separate self, even if a "higher" one, is to attempt to repeat on a higher level the unwisdom which sets oneself over against others.[2]

As long as this delusion of separateness exists, so long is "wisdom enveloped by unwisdom." When, however, this clinging *Verses* to separate existence is abandoned, the disciples are able to pass *15-17* through the inner door of the heart and to enter a realm in which they are one with all, and in which the wisdom light of the one Atman shines forth unobstructedly, revealing the Supreme, the nameless Eternal. All names are based on the discriminating analysis of the mind, and how should names be given to that which is one and indivisible in all? Therefore have the sages referred to It merely as "That," that Reality "from which the mind turns back together with the senses, unable to comprehend."[3]

This is not the first knowledge which the disciples have had of "That." Long before, in chapter two, they had their first intuitive glimpse of It, though, at that time, It presented Itself to them merely as the Unmanifest, the unchanging background of all that is. Again, at the stage represented by chapter four, they perceived It a little more clearly as the mysterious source of all the action in the world.

Verses 18, 19

Thus, circling round in spiral progress, they get ever nearer to clear vision, and now, peering through the open "inner door" they see that the Eternal is the same in all, in learned Brahmin and in despised outcast, in animals as in human beings. Stainless and equal in all is the Supreme Eternal Brahman, and the disciple who has seen that Light *sees* that it is folly to suppose that It can be affected by good or evil deeds. As the pure sunlight is not affected by the foulness of objects that it falls upon, so the Brahma Light is not touched by the differences in the bodies which It illumines. This is a plain fact and those who have seen it will of necessity look with a very different eye upon their fellow-beings. Behind all the masks, beautiful or repulsive, is the one Clear Light, and no longer can others be thought of as beings to be praised, criticized, or condemned. With a gaze centered on the Light, the one thought will be how to help It to shine more clearly through the obstructing bodies, and, acting with that in view, they will gradually achieve in practice that abandonment of self-prompted action which constitutes the true renunciation.

On this Path action and vision go hand in hand, and that is why the teachings of the Gita alternate between knowledge and action in a way so baffling to the purely intellectual person. Purified and disciplined action opens the inner eye and grants the vision of the highest that the disciple is yet capable of seeing. But that vision must not remain a mere private ecstasy. It must be translated into action, and incorporated into the personality before any other range of vision can present itself to the inner eye and the way be opened for yet another cyclic advance.

A causal reading of this section (for example, verses 17 or 24) might suggest that the full attainment is being described or, at least, that it is now possible for the disciple to go "straight through," as it were, by the longed-for shortcut. But it is not so. The disciple at this stage is as one who has got one's head through the inner door but whose body is too big to follow. Once again the vision must be translated into practice. The body, the personality, must be so refined by vision-lit action that it will cease to be an obstacle to passing right through, and, though these verses may describe the condition of attainment, they are meant only to encourage the disciple and to help keep in mind the Goal to which tend all these weary strivings and disciplinings of the self.

And so, firmly attached to the Light that has been seen behind the phantoms of the senses, the disciple must strive to live in the Eternal, to realize in practice the stainless balance of the Reality and cease to be whirled away by the pleasant or painful "contacts of the senses." *Verses 21, 22*

Sensations will still come and go as before, but the inner vision which has been achieved will give a new power of withdrawing from them even while experiencing their pleasure and pain. What characterizes pleasure and pain is not any quality in the sensations themselves so much as the psychic attraction or revulsion *Verse 23* that takes place within. When, through a grasp of the Light of the Eternal, the disciples are able to master this inner revulsion, they find that the pain sensations, though unchanged in themselves, have, in some quite undescribable way, become "different," have lost their power to storm their being or to lead to blind reaction; though rational and controlled response is more possible than ever before. No longer are they masters, smashing their way brutally into the consciousness, demanding instinctive reaction as a right, but mere phenomena to be observed, studied, and deliberately attended to at will.

The teaching about the control of desire that was given at the end of the third chapter now begins to bear fruit. Previously disciples had no means of dealing with unwelcome sensations except stoic endurance of them, and no method of resisting the surging waves of desire. Now, however, the position is different. They have only to use their will to establish themselves in the inner fortress and, for the time being at least, desires will drop before their eyes like butterflies killed by frost as they emerge from a warm house. True, they will rise again from the dead, and again have to be faced, but a great gain has been achieved in that, instead of the grim setting of the teeth of the personal will that was necessary, only relatively small effort of will is needed to enable the disciple to take up a position in the fortress, and, once that is done, victory is assured.

But any surging up of personal pride at this stage will ruin all. Great as is the achievement that has been attained, the power of slaying desire at will, much has yet to be accomplished before the Brahma-Nirvana, the utter "blowing out" of personal desire in the calm Light of the Eternal, is reached, before the disciple will become a Rishi and be able to echo the triumphant words of the Buddha:

> *"Now art thou seen, O Builder. Never again shalt*
> *thou build a house for me. Broken are all the beams*
> *and sundered lies the ridge-pole. My mind is set on the*
> *Eternal; extinguished is all desire."[4]*

Pride implies duality, and all duality must be rooted out for-   *Verse 25*
ever. Therefore the disciples are reminded that it is not as a personal
refuge from the sorrows and pains of life that they must enter the
fortress. The Brahman is One and the same in all, and only those
who have developed the all-embracing compassion of a *Bodhisattva*
can attain Supreme Enlightenment of a *Buddha*.

Nevertheless, great is the achievement of one who has got even
so far as this. If only personal pride can be suppressed the disciple's
further progress is assured, for "the Brahma-Nirvana lies near to   *Verse 26*
those who know the Atman," and who are able in consequence, by
the method outlined, to "disjoin themselves" from desire and anger.
The next chapter will indicate a method which will enable the disciple to leap the consciousness across the gap that still separates the
conscious mind from the Ocean of Light beyond. Here it should be
noted, however, that it is only to one who has reached this point, to
one who has seen through the inner door to the Light on the Other
Side, who has mastered the lower self and who is "intent on the welfare of all beings," that the Brahma-Nirvana lies near at hand.[5]

For one who has not trodden faithfully the Path so far, it is quite
useless to attempt to flash the consciousness into Enlightenment by
any meditative yoga for, if anything at all results from a premature

practice, it will only be in the nature of dangerous, neurotic dissociations of the personality, perhaps even insanity itself.

Verse 28   But for the fit disciple—for one who has mastered the senses, mind and buddhi,[6] who is free from all selfish aims, who has cast away desire, fear and anger, desire for any enjoyments, fear of any consequences, and anger against those who obstruct progress, who has seen though as yet only through the "door," that eternal Krishna

Verse 29   who is the One Self of all, the One for whom the Cosmic Sacrifice was undertaken, the Great Lord of all the worlds, the *Lover of all beings*—for such a one all doors stand open, further progress is assured, and speedily the Peace will be attained, the Peace that only Enlightenment can give.

Notes
_____

1   Empty of any *thing*, that is. See appendix B.

2   This is the great heresy of *satkayadrishti* against which the Buddha directed so much of his teaching, the theory that there are permanent soul monads, eternally separate. What has here been described as the higher Self, the true Ego, constitutes no doubt a relatively permanent individual center, but it is in reality only a focus of the One Self and not a separate unity. Its separateness lies only in its content, not in itself. Strictly speaking, even the One Universal Self (the Mahat Atman) is not permanent, since it is part of the manifested Universe and is withdrawn at the universal dissolution (*pralaya*) into the Parabrahman, which is alone eternal in the strict sense of the word.

3   Taittiriya Upanishad, II, vi, 1.

4   Dhammapada, 154.

5   Verse 27 does not refer to sitting in trance with the eyes turned upwards (as practiced by some *hatha yogis*) but to the habitual attitude of the disciple at this stage. Externalizing the outer (sense) contacts—that is to say, considering them as something external to the self—the disciple transfers the eye, the center of vision, to the symbolic spot between the eyebrows. Seeing with the ordinary

eyes stands for the ordinary sense vision, seeing with or in the heart for the eye of the individual Self, the manas, while seeing from the spot between the eyebrows symbolizes seeing with the third eye, the eye of spiritual knowledge, the calm, all-illumining knowledge of the buddhi. Compare the symbolic description in the Mahayana scripture, the *Saddharma Pundarika* (introduction): "And at that moment there issued a ray from within the circle of hair between the eyebrows of the Buddha. It extended over eighteen hundred thousand Buddha fields . . . and the beings in any of the six states became visible without exception." See also *The Voice of the Silence*: "Then from the heart that Power shall rise into the sixth, the middle region, the place between thine eyes, when it becomes the breath of the One Soul, the voice which filleth all, thy Master's voice." Buddhi is, as it were, the breath of Mahat, the One Soul.

6   The reference to the mastery of the buddhi should be understood as anticipatory in the context. It will occur before liberation (*mukti*) is attained.

Chapter Six

The Yoga of Meditation

The Path has been divided into three stages, called respectively the Way of Purification, the Way of Illumination, and the Way of Unity. The first six chapters of the Gita correspond to some extent with the Way of Purification. This sixth chapter marks the transition to the Way of Illumination, for, as was mentioned in the last, it sets forth the technique of a mental discipline which is meant to transfer the consciousness from its ordinary waking state to those higher levels which, up to this point, have been working, as it were, behind the scenes, glimpsed perhaps in occasional flashes of inspiration, but always as something beyond, something outside the dominion of the will, coming and going with the apparent caprice that veils an unknown law.

This technique is called *dhyana yoga*, the yoga by meditation, and it corresponds, more or less, with the method systematized by Patañjali in his *Yoga Sutras*. But, at the very outset, it should be clearly understood for whom this practice will give results and for whom it will not. This is vitally important, since there are many who consider the practice of meditation as the yoga *par excellence* and eagerly seek to practice it without having passed through the all-important earlier stages. As stated before, nothing but dangerous neurotic dissociations of personality can result from the practice of meditation without the qualifications mentioned at the end of the last chapter.[1]

It is not one who gives up rites that symbolize social duties in order to plunge into meditation in some Himalayan cave who is the true *yogi* or *sannyasi*, but one who performs such actions as are enjoined by duty without any selfish desire for fruit.

Verse 1

It is not work which has to be renounced by the *sankalpa*, the formative will which seeks its own aims, an attitude that is found in too many would-be yogis who seek in yoga, not the Atman, but an enhanced power of molding the environment to a pattern more pleasing to the personal self.

Verse 2

For it is in action, disinterested selfless action, that the way to yoga lies. Forcible opening of a bud will not produce a blossom, and it is only when the disciple is *yoga-ruriha*, firmly established in the Path, that the serenity of meditation can be a means of further advance.

Verse 3

It is easy and common to fancy oneself already at this point, but the stage is a very high one. Only those may be said to be established in the Path who feel no more attachment to the objects of the senses nor to self-seeking activity, and who have thoroughly renounced the above-mentioned desire to impose their own formative will upon the course of events.

Verse 4

Before the practice of meditation can be available to flash the consciousness now centered in the lower or personal self across the gulf which separates it from the Atman, or higher Self, it is essential that there shall be a harmony between the two. If the self is in harmony with the Self, if it ceases to exert its personal will, if its impulses are under control and it is able to offer itself as an instrument through which the Self can work, then the Atman is its friend, a source of inspiration and guidance, the Inner Teacher of

Verse 5

Verse 6

whom mention has previously been made. But if the self is allowed to sink down in inert depression, if it pursues its own aims and stands proudly upon its own individual uniqueness, then, indeed, the Atman is felt as something hostile. No more a source of inspiration, It makes itself known as the mysterious source of misfortunes and sicknesses, of those "blows of Fate," which are the teachers of the Law that all life is one.[2]

Verse 7

In order that disciples may know whether they have truly arrived at this stage or not, certain signs are given in the text and, impartially scrutinizing their own mind, they must see whether they are present or not before they venture farther. If the self is really controlled and harmonious, then the Higher Self will be felt always as a calm background to all the activities of the mind. The "pairs of opposites" that torment others will have no power to disturb that inner serenity. The gratifications of honor and the death-like sting of dishonor, those infallible testers of claimants to the yogi's title, can have no effect on one whose only honor is the approval of his Teacher, whose only dishonor is the shame of having subordinated Self to self. Wealth is nothing to one who feels within the living waters of the sacred wisdom, and the distinctions that mean so much to others are absurd in the eyes that have caught a glimpse of the One Life which is in all.

Verses 8, 9

Now comes the time for the practice of meditative yoga and, accordingly, the Gita proceeds to give some teachings about the technique to be pursued. Essentially the method consists of gaining control over the mind-processes so that they can be stilled at will, enabling the consciousness to perceive the Truth like a calm lake reflecting the eternal stars above.

Only brief indications are given in the text because the full process cannot be set forth in writing. It varies for each disciple and must be learnt from the guru, who, as explained before, is always available at this stage. It is true that there are books which apparently give full instructions about the practice, but their apparent fullness is misleading. It is easier to become an artist by the study of a manual of oil-painting than to become a yogi by the study of books on meditation, whether those books were written yesterday or whether they were written five thousand years ago.

The few notes which are here given are intended merely to help the reader to follow the text and by no means are a sufficient guide to practice.

The first necessity is a quiet place to practice meditation, undisturbed by friends or visitors whose presence would be apt to agitate the disciples' mind with thoughts of what so-and-so is thinking of them. This too is the meaning of the phrase that the place should be "pure," that is to say, it should be free from any features likely to give rise to aesthetic irritation or to distraction. Certain natural surroundings, such as the banks of rivers, the tops of mountains, or the open sky, are particularly helpful, as such surroundings exert a calming influence on the mind and have, moreover, a symbolic reference which works powerfully even if not consciously attended to.

Verses 10-11

The directions about the seat (*asana*) are of an entirely practical nature. The seat should not be so high that there is risk of falling if trance (or more likely sleep!) supervenes, nor so low that there is danger from poisonous insects such as scorpions. The other specifications are that it should be soft enough to give ease of body and of such a nature that it will keep the yogi off the damp ground, hence the use of a leather skin in days when waterproof materials were unknown. More important than these technicalities are the instructions that the disciple should make the mind calm and free from hope and greed, that is to say, from that attitude of wishing to grasp things to and for oneself which is characteristic of the lower mind.[3]

The next point is posture (also called *asana*). The postures used in this yoga have nothing to do with bringing pressure to bear on centers in the body, whether nervous or "occult." The essential is, as·Patañjali said, that it should be steady and pleasant. By pleasant, however, it is not meant that it should be an arm-chair sort of attitude but one which can be maintained for a long stretch without sensations of cramp or fatigue, and at the same time it should be one which is conducive to mental alertness, hence the traditional instruction to keep the spine straight.

Verse 13

The direction of the gaze is another point on which there is often confusion. A wandering gaze means a wandering mind, and therefore the eyes are to be kept fixed in one direction. In practice it has been found that the best way to do this is to direct the eyes along the line of the nose and then to half-close the eyelids. This should not be confused with the fixing of the gaze between the eyebrows which is often referred to, and which means that the center of consciousness should be transferred to the buddhi which is often symbolized by that spot (see note 5 on page 76 of the previous chapter). "When one fixes the *thought* on the mid-point between the two eyes, the Light streams in of its own accord."[4]

The breathing is also to be kept regular and smooth, as there is a vital connection between the flow of thoughts and the rhythm of the breath. To quote the same Chinese book: "Because breath comes out of the heart, unrhythmical breathing comes from the heart's unrest. Therefore one must breathe in and out quite softly so that it remains inaudible to the ear." That is all: elaborate processes of holding the breath and breathing through alternate nostrils (*pranayama*) find no place in this yoga.

All these are the preliminaries and can be understood by anyone. The heart of the yoga is more difficult and is what cannot be taught in words. It is the "checking of all the modifications of the mind," the "holding of the heart to the center of the midst of conditions," the "making of the mind one-pointed," and its direction towards Him, the Atman, the Light that "streams in of itself between the eyebrows." This is the essential thing, and produces the detachment from the desire nature and the union with the buddhi (*buddhi yoga*) that gives Enlightenment. The center of consciousness withdraws its attention from the world of outer phenomena, whether of sense or of thought, passes through the central point, which is itself, and emerges in the spiritual world of the buddhi, which is in deepest truth the same world seen in a different manner. It is the same world because all "worlds" are but illusions. All that exists, exists within the One, and what we see as a world depends upon the point of view from which we see; that which we see is One. As the Maitri Upanishad puts it: "Thought is verily the world and therefore should be purified with care. As one's thought is, so one becomes; this is the eternal mystery."[5]

The process will be clear to one who is ready for it. "This is the pathway to Brahman here in this world. This is the opening of the door here in this world. By it one will go to the other shore of the darkness. When the five sense knowledges cease together with the (lower) mind, and the buddhi (here the higher mind) also stands motionless, that they say is the highest Path."[6]

Verse 14   Two absolute essentials are brahmacharya, or control of the sex-impulse, and utter purity of aspiration. Brahmacharya must not be confused with mere celibacy. It is the *control* of the sex-impulses that is meant and not their inhibition alone, a control that will take varying forms under differing circumstances. There is no merit in the sexlessness of the eunuch, whether his castration be a physical or a mental one, and Hindu tradition is right in affirming that the householder whose sex-life is controlled is as truly a Brahmachari as the ascetic who observes the vow of total sex-abstinence. In any case it must be borne in mind that the inner world of sex-fantasy is as important as the outer one of procreation. Without control of sex, in both its inner and its outer manifestations, it is safer to play with dynamite than to practice the yoga of meditation.

Turning now to the other essential, the aspiration must be purely directed towards the One Self, as, under any other circum-
Verse 14   stances, the practice of meditation will give rise to visions that may even delude the disciples into fancying themselves *Avatara*, or other great personages.[7]

Purity of aspiration and the proximity of a *wise* guru are the only safeguards against such delusions. It must never be forgotten that visions and other psychic experiences prove absolutely nothing whatever. True knowledge is possessed by the Atman alone, and no dualistic knowing can be relied on, whether the senses which mediate it be the outer or the inner ones. It is the knowledge of the Atman
Verse 30   alone that is the true knowledge. Therefore is it said that he alone is safe "who sees Me, the Atman, in all beings and all beings in Me."

Hence all the emphasis on the Self, the Atman. The yogi must be united with the Atman, with thought fixed on the Atman, absorbed in the yoga of the Atman, seeing the Atman by the Atman. It cannot be too emphatically stated that no true yoga is possible by the unaided personal will. Thought may be stilled to the point of trance, but unless the self is surrendered to the Atman there can be no yoga in the true sense of the word. The preliminary effort at concentration may be made from the lower level but the complete stilling of the mind by sheer will is like balancing a pyramid upon its apex, a feat of balance which, even if accomplished, is so precarious that no useful result can be achieved.

The true concentration comes when the disciple is able to surrender to, and identify with, the Atman, that Self which is present as the unchanging Witness of every thought and of every sensation. It is only when this is achieved that the mind of the yogi becomes *Verse 19* steady "like a lamp in a windless place,"[8] a state which, to anyone who has seriously tried to concentrate from the lower level alone, will always seem an almost fantastically difficult feat.

It is because of this impossibility of achieving success in meditation without some perception of the Higher Self that it is only in this sixth chapter that instructions for its practice are given. Up to this point "action is called the means," that is to say, the means of *Verse 3* getting a preliminary perception of the higher level of consciousness, the buddhi, by which the yoga is to be achieved.[9]

"Little by little let him gain tranquility by means of the *Verse 25* buddhi, firmly adhered to," and thus, securely seated in the Atman, to which the buddhi is a bridge, it will be possible to bring all thoughts to a standstill and yet remain in a stable state of serenely

Verse 22

blissful consciousness, "which having attained, he thinketh that there is no greater gain," and which all the assaults of pain and sorrow can never shake.

Verse 23

"That should be known as yoga, this disconnection from the union with pain." Profound words, which gain an added profundity when we remember the teaching of the Buddha that *all* experience is (*in itself*) *dukkha*, painful by reason of its finite and transitory nature. This "disconnection" from union with all finite experience is the

Verse 25

secret of successful yoga, or rather, it is half the secret, the other half being the *atma sanstha*, the abiding in the Atman. The two processes, negative and positive, go on side by side, as someone climbing a ladder loosens the hold on one rung while simultaneously attaching to the next.

These two processes are the "detachment and practice" referred to in verse 35. Without their aid there is no possibility of stilling the restless and fickle mind and of climbing up the ladder. For countless ages the mind has been turned outwards and has been given a free rein to attach itself to objects of desire, and it is not to be expected that it will be possible to wrench it away from them at once. A bamboo that has long borne a weight will not be straightened merely by its removal. So with the mind; long bent by the forces of desire, it must first be detached from them and then, by constant practice, united with that which is higher than itself.

This practice is not a matter of an hour, or even of several hours, of daily meditation. Throughout the day (and even, in a sense, throughout the hours of sleep as well) constant effort must be made to retain in the consciousness as much as possible the detachment and insight that were achieved during the meditation period.

Throughout the day the disciple must hold on firmly to whatever degree of realization was able to be gained in those calm hours, for a short period of uncontrolled thought, an hour of despondency, or even five minutes of anger, will undo all that has been accomplished, and, like the web of Penelope, what was woven in the morning will be unraveled by next day.

It is a long and uphill struggle, and one which, to the disciple, will often seem hopeless. Progress is slow and attainment looms far away. The night of Death may come before the haven is reached, but the disciples must not despair, for the Path is one that must be trodden through many lives, and they may repose serenely in the arms of the Cosmic Law, knowing that not the slightest effort is ever wasted, and that, like one completing on the morrow the unfinished task of today, they will be able to begin in the next life at the point where they left off in this. *Verse 37* *Verse 45* *Verse 43*

If only the effort is steady ultimate triumph is secure, and at last, like a tree long bound by winter frost, bursting suddenly into glorious bloom, the arduous struggles of many lives will bear fruit and will burst into the Light and attain the *Brahma-sansparsha*, the contact with the Eternal, no longer sensed as a vague background, no longer even glimpsed fitfully through the inner door, but felt in actual contact, contact that will drench the soul in bliss. *Verse 44* *Verse 28*

Gone is the sense of a separate finite self, with its individual gains and losses, its personal hopes and fears, and in its place comes the experience of the One Atman abiding in all beings, of all beings as eddies in that all-pervading ocean of bliss. *Verse 29*

This stage may be reckoned as the third great landmark on the Path. The first was the Entry on the Path; the second, the consciousness of the Divine Birth in the heart; and now, with the over-whelming perception of the unity of all life in the One Self, the third, termed in some traditions the Mystic Marriage, may be said to have been accomplished. It is the fifth (in some traditions sixth) or Dhyana Paramita of the Buddhists, after which the shining path of Prajña lies open before the disciple's feet. Thrice great is the one who has traveled thus far. The bridge which separated self from Self has been crossed, and now no obstacle remains to prevent the Divine Light from irradiating the personality with Its wondrous rays.

Verse 31
Wherever they may be, and whatever they may be doing, yogis are now established in the ever-living Divine Unity. The touch of the Eternal Krishna has awakened the flame of love in their hearts—love the great liberator, the breaker-down of all barriers. Borne out of the self on its rushing wave, they see no more themselves or others, but everywhere and in all things the blue form of Krishna flashes forth. Beneath the frowning brows of their foes no less than within the smiling glances of their friends, they perceive the gleaming eyes of the Divine Lover, and they pour themselves forth in utter worship of the Unchanging One seated within the hearts of all.

Worship is a word which conjures up before us ideas of hymns and formal offerings but the worship which the disciple now offers is something quite different. It is the worship which gives itself because it can do no less, the worship of self-forgetful service compelled by the sovereign power of love.

What need have they of temples when every form enshrines their Lord, and how shall they withhold their service when they see the Divine beauty distorted by the gloomy ugliness of the world, the Divine bliss masked by the myriad sorrows of humanity?

Great is the *tapasvi*, the ascetic who disciplines the self; great   *Verse 46*
the *Jñani* standing firm in the calm knowledge of Reality; great, too,
is the person of action, for that one is the instrument, albeit unconscious, of the unresting cosmic tides. But greater than all is the yogi
for such a one is a combination of all three. United with the Divine
Lover in the heart, the yogi sees Him as the One Self in all and,
offering a disciplined personality on the altar of self-sacrifice, such a
one serves unrestingly the Wisdom-Love that ever plans the welfare
of the worlds. "*Sa me yuktatamo matah*—He in my opinion is the
greatest yogi of all."

Notes

1   This warning against the premature practice of meditation refers only to the
     deliberate attempt to scale the Ladder of the Soul by a meditative technique.
     Meditation on the symbol of the Supreme or on the figure of the teacher, reflec-
     tion on the eternal truths about the Soul and the world, and the calm analysis
     of one's character are practices which are useful and desirable at all stages of the
     Path.

2   It was perhaps some realization of this truth (though from a different angle of
     vision) that prompted the words of Jung: "Only when in disharmony . . . do we
     discover the Psyche; we come upon something that thwarts our will, which is
     strange and even hostile to us."

3   Compare the Buddhist practice of removing the five "Hindrances" (sensual
     passion, ill-will, sloth and torpor, worry, and perplexity) from the mind before
     beginning the meditation (*jhana*) proper. Note also the Buddhistic emphasis
     on the "Middle Path" in verses 16 and 17. It is needless to say that the purpose
     in adducing these and other parallels is not to suggest "borrowing" but to point
     out that the true yoga is the same wherever it is found.

4   *The Secret of the Golden Flower*, a Chinese Taoist book of yoga, translated by
     Wilhelm. Compare also the following quotation from the same book: "There-
     fore the Master makes especially clear the method by which one enters in the
     cultivation of life, and bids people look with both eyes at the end of the nose, to

lower the lids, to look within, sit quietly with upright body and fix the heart on the center in the midst of conditions [the "point of view" or central reference-point, the higher ego]. Keeping the thoughts on the space between the two eyes allows the Light to penetrate. There upon the spirit [buddhi] crystallizes and enters the center in the midst of conditions. The center of the midst of conditions is the lower Elixir-field [the lower immortal or higher ego], the place of power [that is, the seat of will]." The words in brackets have been added.

5   Maitri Upanishad, vi, 34.

6   Maitri, vi, 30. Compare also the words of Hermes: "Whenever I see within myself the Simple [*i.e.* unitary as opposed to multiple] Vision brought to birth . . . I have passed through myself into a Body that can never die. And now I am not what I was before but I am born in Mind. The way to do this is not taught" (from the *Secret Sermon on the Mountain.* The part in brackets is added).

7   Such delusions are common in India and elsewhere, and are by no means always due to deliberate imposture. Often the Avatara is his own first victim.

8   The point of this simile—evidently much older than the Gita—is often missed. It is useless to try to make the flame steady in a windy place. The mind must withdraw to a region where the winds of desire no longer play before it can become more than momentarily steady.

9   See chapter 2.

✿

Chapter Seven

The Yoga of Knowledge

With this chapter the Way of Illumination, the Prajña Path of the Buddhists, commences, and the glorious Knowledge dawns on the disciple's inner eye, the Knowledge "which, having known, there is nothing more here that needeth to be known." It would be a mistake, however, to suppose that the actual Knowledge is or can be described in the verses that follow. As a two-dimensional photo is to its three-dimensional original, or as a map is to the actual countryside, so is this or any other description to that wondrous Knowledge, and none should imagine that a grasp of the statements set forth is the same thing as the illumination itself. *Verse 2*

At the very outset it is desirable to dwell for a moment on the extreme rarity of this Knowledge. The vast majority know nothing of its existence, and though a few by strenuous effort have succeeded in establishing themselves upon the Path that leads to it, at any given time, only one or two gain it in its fullness. This is not said in order to depress the disciples, but in order to keep them humble now that they are on the Path of Illumination. Let them not suppose themselves Gods because they have attained a measure of Light, nor think that they have scaled the eternal Snows because they stand upon a foothill peak. *Verse 3*

What is this wondrous Knowledge that is now to be described?

It is the knowledge of Krishna, the Undying Atman, the Eternal Being that lies behind all change. This should be borne in mind in all that follows, for though there are many who worship Krishna, few of them, though they may be on the Path, know His Essential Being. Who or what Krishna in essence is, is what is attempted to be set forth in this and the four succeeding chapters. Here, more than ever, must the disciple beware of words, for, as the Upanishad says: "It is not known by him who knows It though known by him who knows It not."[1] The knowledge that can be expressed in words is not the true Knowledge. The description that is given is useless if interpreted by the intellect alone, and its words are but a shining curtain through which the disciple must pass to "that from which all words, together with the mind, turn back unable to attain."

Verses 4, 5

Before the disciple can apprehend that Supreme Unity, the two-fold nature of the Manifested Universe must be understood. In all that is manifested, whether gross or subtle, whether living beings or what we call "dead" matter, there are two aspects which must be understood. These are the ever-changing forms, and the unchanging "consciousness" that supports them. Whether the forms of matter, the "five elements,"[2] or whether the more subtle forms of thought, all form is but a transient play that is upheld in the light of consciousness, the higher or living (*jiva-bhuta*) nature. Apart from this witnessing consciousness no forms could exist at all.

But, it may be asked, what about "brute matter," as it is sometimes called, the sheer "stuff" of which the world is made? The answer, an answer more acceptable now that even physical scientists have reduced matter to "waves of probability," is that there is no stuff in that sense at all. Analyze matter to its furthest limit and it evaporates, as it were, or is resolved into something incomprehensible but non-material. It is in fact true, as Plotinus said, that matter in itself is sheer negation; it is the unmanifest substratum of the ever-changing forms in "consciousness."

This is a subject that will have to be further dealt with later, but here it is sufficient to know that these two, consciousness and form,[3] are the womb in which all beings are born. But beyond this duality is That with which Krishna here identifies Himself, the Marvelous, Incomprehensible One, not the blank absolute unity of intellectual philosophy, but the rich and unspeakable Infinite Wonder which is the ground of all, of consciousness and form alike, on Whom all this is threaded like pearls upon a string. *Verses 6, 7*

This is the essential being of Krishna, to which He says so few attain. Words fall away, useless and empty labels, and the mind, dizzied in ceaseless whirlings, sinks and is dumb before that viewless Wonder, the Void which is the Full, the Full which is the Void. Let us bow down in awe before that Sacred Mystery and keep our words for realms where words can live.

But since it is just this fathomless Mystery that must be known, some ladder must be found, some means of knowing That which the mind cannot reach. And so Sri Krishna goes on to teach that, though the manifested cosmos is illusion, yet is it a divine illusion, and at its throbbing heart stands He Himself.

The disciple must in all things—in earth and fire and water, in sun and moon and in all splendid things, and in all living beings— seek for the Essence, for that which makes them what they are. Undistracted by the accidents of outer form, the passing phantom shapes which are the great illusion, the disciple must hold firm to *Verses 8-12* that essential nature of which the forms are crude embodiments. For those essential natures are the Divine Ideas, ideas which live forever, shaping all things from within, "molding blind mass to form."[4]

Verses
13, 14

The eye of flesh sees but the changing forms, and, holding fast to them, is utterly deluded by the false shows of things. Like Plato's dwellers in the cave, humans see only the shifting shadows on the wall. They cannot see the Light, nor yet those truer forms from which the shadows come. This Divine illusion is indeed hard to cross, because long ages spent in grappling with material things have taught our minds to dwell exclusively on what is without. A doctor, trained to view all bodies in terms of health and disease, cannot with ease see with the artist's vision, and we, who owe our mastery over nature to this fidelity to outward fact, cannot at once pass to the higher vision and reverse our customary modes of thought.

This reversal is the jñana-yoga, and, as the Katha Upanishad says, "some few wise men, seeking the Immortal, with eyes turned in, saw the Undying Atman." Disciples must avert their gaze from the manifold illusion. In its place they must see "Me," the Divine idea of Fire in all things fiery; "Me," the divine Strength in all things strong; "Me," the Divine Life in all that lives and breathes.

Verse 15

Only by turning thus to the Eternal Atman can the illusion be crossed. Those who look outward, who embrace the illusions, the treaders of the Asuric path,[5] can find no foothold in the cosmic flux and are tossed here and there on its unresting tides.

Verse 16

In contrast to these are those who tread the inner Path, they who serve[6] Krishna. They are divided into four classes, graded according to the degree of perception they have attained. First come the *arta*, those who have seen that all life is but sorrow.

Ache of the birth, ache of the helpless days,
Ache of hot youth and ache of manhood's prime;
Ache of the chill grey years and choking death
These fill our piteous time.[7]

Seeing that life is transient, that all things pass and die, they turn from them in sorrow and seek consolation from That which is beyond all suffering, the Undying Krishna, beyond the reach of change.

This is the first stage, the first of the Buddha's four noble Truths, but it is the first only because it is based on mere recoil from suffering. Insight has shown disciples that life is shot through and through with sorrow, its so-called joys mere cheats, and so they sadly turn away their eyes. Were life to be more joyful they would not thus have turned their face to Krishna.

The next class is the *jijñasu*, the inquirer, the seeker after knowledge. Knowledge gives mastery and power, and, the one who sees that life is sorrow seeks the understanding that shall master it, the knowledge of the causes of woe.

Next comes the *artharthi*, who seeks the Real.[8] Knowing that it is the outgoing forces of desire that are the sources of all sorrow, knowing, too, that all manifested life is transient by its very nature, this disciple turns away from all desire for anything that is manifest and seeks the anamayam padam, the Sorrowless State of Liberation, lifted on high above the bitter waters of life.

But beyond this stage there lies another, the stage of the jñani, the Wise One, who treads the Path of perfect self-surrender. For the seeker after Liberation there is a dualism between the world and Nirvana and this disciple rejects the one to cleave unto the

*Verses
17-19*

Other. But jñanis are those who see that all duality is false. "Here," as "There," their opened eyes see nothing but the One. They seek no liberation for themselves "beyond the flaming ramparts of the world," for they have seen that "all is *Vasudeva*"[9] and, in the words of the Upanishad, they know that "what is There is here; what is not here is nowhere at all."

This glorious realization, as rare as it is wonderful, comes as the fruit of countless lives of effort. Noble are all who tread the Path, but noblest of all are the jñanis, for their realization leads them to unite themselves with the One Self in all, and, seeking no selfish gain, they reject not the bitter waters of sorrow but rather seeks to sweeten them in service of his Lord. Not their own self but the One Self is dear to them, therefore they are supremely dear to Krishna. Because they know that nothing but Krishna is, they seek no gain or Goal but to serve Him. Like Krishna Himself, they pour themselves forth in sacrifice and love. They are made one with Krishna's very Atman, and, knowing themselves to be the One in all, they are established in the highest Path.

Verse 20

Few reach these lofty heights. To give oneself utterly, caring for no reward, is not for those whose hearts are clouded by desire. The worship of the majority is not the true worship of Krishna even when they use His name in their prayers. Seeking to gain some good for their own selves they worship various Gods "according to their natures."

What are these Gods and what the nature of their worship? In all manifested nature there is, as we have seen, duality of life and form. Nowhere is there life without some form and nowhere, also, form without the Life. The powers of Nature, which to modern eyes are but so many dead "forces," are in truth embodiments of that one Living Power which wields the universe in Its unceasing play. They are not "persons," but in ancient times they were given personal form to symbolize their living nature.[10] *Indra*, *Agni*, and other Vedic Gods are the personified symbols of the Living Power ensouling Nature's "forces," a Power no more to be identified with the physical embodiments than is the Life ensouling us to be identified with our physical frames.[11]

Modern people seek to gain benefit from these Powers of Nature by an understanding of their outward being's laws, but ancient people sought the same ends by different means. By various rituals they attuned their consciousness to the Life that ensouls all nature and sought to control her powers from within by lending their human imagination and will to their living but will-less being.

Acting in this way, it is possible to obtain from the "Gods" the benefits desired, but that is so because beneath the varied powers is the One Power, the Cosmic Harmony known in the Vedic age as *rita*. Krishna it is who, from behind the scenes, makes steady the faith of such worshippers and by His Eternal Laws secures to each the fruits of all his deeds. *Verses 21, 22*

All things are possible if the right means are known, yet their price must be paid, for in all things the law of karma rules and action and reaction are inseparable. Therefore it is said that the fruits of all such worship are but finite and "to the Gods will go their worshippers; My devotees come unto Me." *Verse 23*

Let it not be thought, however, that this "Me" is but one God among the Gods. Krishna is the Unmanifest Eternal, imperishable, supreme. The Eternal One is never one among the many: always He is the One without a second, hidden, unborn, beyond the changing *Verse 24*

Verse 25

flux. He cannot be found in the manifested world. Deluded by the great illusion of plurality, human beings seek Him fruitlessly, saying "Lo here! Lo there!"—but all they find is some one thing among the many, searching in this way they can never find the One.[12]

Seeing only the "pairs of opposites," whirled about by the forces of attraction and repulsion, seeing only the many, they go "from death to death." They cannot know the Deathless Being of Krishna, for none save the One can ever know the One.

Only by the yoga that seeks the One at once within[13] and beyond the many, can He be found, and, as the Upanishad says, "having known Him, one crosses beyond all death, there is no other Path for going there."[14] Fire of the fires, Life of the lives, Light of the lights, He stands beyond all forms; past, present, future—all are one to Him.

Verse 28

This knowledge, however, can only come to those whose sins are at an end. Sin does not mean the infringement of any arbitrary code of morals worked out by human reason or set forth in "holy" books. Sin is the assertion of the separate self, the making of difference where, in truth, none exists. Sin is the central ignorance which sees the separate, personal self as real and seeks its own gain though the whole world perish.[15] To this assertion of the personal self all sins are due, and only those can win the Truth who have renounced such sin and whose pure selfless deeds are all directed to the service of the One who dwells in all.

Verses 28–30

They, the selfless ones, refuged in the One Self, strive for the liberation of that Self from the illusion of birth and death. They are the true *mumukshus*, or seekers after liberation, for they scorn to seek a liberation for their own selves alone, knowing that all that lives is One. They also are the true jñanis, for they know the primordial Unmanifested Trinity, the one Eternal Brahman and Its aspects, *Adhyatma*, the Unmanifested Self (the Shanta Atman of the Katha Upanishad) and the Unmanifested *Mula-prakriti*, here referred to as the totality of (potential) action.[16]

But this knowledge is not enough in itself. The Three are eternally the same. They dwell beyond the "Abyss" which separates the manifest from the Unmanifest, and he who tread the "selfish" Path seeks but to lose himself forever in their unchanging timeless bliss. Not so the follower of Krishna, who treads the Path of Sacrifice and seeks to gather up in the Treasure-House (*cf.* chapter ix, v. 18) the pearls of which have been buried in the Cosmic Ocean, to reunite the scattered limbs of the dismembered Osiris.

For this disciple the knowledge of the transcendent Eternal is not enough. There are not two realities, Nirvana and the world, for all is Vasudeva and what is "There" is likewise "here" as well. One who would tread the Path and knows the Self, not in its own eternity alone but here amid the changing play of life and form, sacrificed here upon the cross of matter, becomes one of the "fishers of men" spoken of by Christ. Others may scorn the world *Verse 30* as mere illusion, and, at the death hour, wing their way across the blackness, alone to the Alone. However, the fully harmonized one, seeing the One here in the midst of the many, knows no black gulf of death, but in full Light of Consciousness garners the fruits of the Divine Adventure, and, in the words of the Isha Upanishad: "*Avidyaya mrityum tirtva, vidyaya'mritamashnute*—Having crossed over death by knowledge of the many, by knowledge of the One he gains the Deathless State."

Notes

1   Kena Upanishad, ii, 3.

2   On "consciousness" see appendix A; on "matter" appendix B; and on the "five elements" appendix H.

3   United on the level of the Mahat Atman.

4   *The Light of Asia.*

5   The Asuric path is the outgoing pravritti path, of which more will be said later. See chapter 16.

6   *Bhajate*, usually rendered worship, comes from the root *bhaj*, to serve.

7   *The Light of Asia.*

8   This term *artharthi* is often misunderstood and applied to one who seeks for wealth or worldly objects. The order of the words in the verse is sufficient to show that this is not the true meaning. The artharthi is not one who seeks for the *artha* (wealth) which is *anartha* ("illth"), but one who seeks the true Wealth, the *Paramartha*, which is *mukti* or liberation.

9   A patronymic of Krishna, but here signifying "the Light which dwells in all."

10 Moreover, it is a characteristic of psychic Powers that, when they manifest, at least to human beings, it is as personal or quasi-personal beings that they do so. "Personification" is a characteristic of the Psychic realms.

11 The modern notion that because the winds and waves move according to law they are therefore "dead" is wrong. Do not our own bodies move by law as well? The fact is that nowhere in all the universe is there any form that is not subject to Law, and nowhere, either, is there anything that is "dead"; for all forms move and have their being in the one all-pervading Life.

The Vedic Gods have also another aspect, in which they are the symbols of the various levels of the Consciousness, but that is not the aspect with which we are here concerned.

12 Compare the saying of Eckhart: "Some people expect to see God as they would see a cow."

13 Note the contrast between *among* the many and *within* the many. Even the word "within" is not strictly correct, for, as we shall see in chapter 9, He is not within the many but the many within Him. Nevertheless, at this stage, it is as within them that He will be perceived.

14   Shvetashvatara Upanishad, vi, 15.

15   This is the meaning of the Buddha's teaching that as long as there is belief in *atma* (here meaning separate self) there can be no Nirvana. Christians also teach that salvation from sin is found only in Christ, the meaning of which is clear to those who know that Christ is the One Self in all, and therefore is it said that "No man cometh unto the Father but by Me."

16   For explanations of the technical terms used in these last two verses see the next chapter.

Chapter Eight

The Yoga of The Imperishable Eternal

The farther the disciples proceed upon the Path the clearer the Light that comes flooding into their hearts. The last chapter ended with the mention of terms that are now seen to refer to the Ladder of Being, the Rainbow Bridge, down which the Soul has come and up which it must return. This Ladder has been described in all the ancient traditions, for instance as the Sephirothal Tree of the Kabala, and the disciple who has reached this stage can read the symbols the Teachers have employed for the reality behind them all is one.

Verse 3   Beyond all and alone stands the Supreme Eternal, the Imperishable Brahman, dark in utter mystery, the Root of all that is, was, or shall ever be. Neither subject nor object, neither knower, knowing, or known can exist in the unspeakable Being of That which is beyond all names.

All manifestation springs from the self-limitation of that Brahman. Brahman as subject sees Itself as object and thus emerges the first, though still unmanifest, duality. The essential nature (*svab-hava*) of the One as transcendent Subject, here called *adhyatma*, separates out, as it were, leaving the other aspect of the Brahman to stand as the eternal Object, Mula-prakriti.[1] This Mula-prakriti, the unmanifest basis of all objectivity, is, from its very nature, the source of all the manifested Many. Reflecting as it does the Light of the

One Atman, It is the root of all plurality. In Its dark being lie all the seeds of action, seeds that, under the Sun's bright rays, will shoot and grow into the great World Tree.[2]

Because it is thus the root of all action, the Gita terms it *Karma*, but it should be borne in mind that it is not any sort of primordial "brute matter" existing in its own right but merely the objective aspect of the Brahman, the unmanifest Substratum in which forms live and move and have their being. It cannot stand alone apart from the Brahman of which it is an aspect. It was a failure to perceive this that led the later Sankhyas into dualism. Remove the dualistic knowing[3] and the Mula-prakriti collapses into the Brahman of which it is but the appearance. If the Brahman is to appear as an object at all it is only as the Mula-prakriti that It can so appear.

Passing now to the manifested Cosmos, we find that the inter- *Verse 4* action of these two, the Unmanifested Subject and the Unmanifested Object, gives rise, on the one hand, to the changing world of forms, the "perishable nature" (*adhibhuta*), and, on the other hand, to the witnessing Consciousness, the One Life, the *adhidaiva*, termed in the Katha Upanishad the Great or Mahat Atman.[4]

Then comes the *adhiyajña*, the Mystic Sacrifice by which Krishna, the One Life, unites Himself with the passing forms. Just as the Unmanifested Two find their unity in the Supreme Unmanifested Brahman, so do the manifested Life and Form find union in the sacrificial act of Krishna. This is that Mystic Sacrifice mentioned in the Rig Veda in which the Purusha was dismembered to create the world of beings, and this the crucifixion of the Christ, pouring out His life-blood on the Cross of matter, redeeming thus the duality of the world.

The One Self, seeing Itself reflected in the myriad forms, willed by Its mystic yoga to identify Itself with them and share their limitations. Thus were the individuals formed, the central being of human beings, sometimes termed (higher) manas, sometimes *ahankara*,[5] the scattered limbs of the Divine Osiris. These are the Immortal Sparks, the Shining Threads, dying in myriad forms and yet, unseen, passing from life to life in age-long immortality.

This "Sacrifice" has also been described in the *Poemandres* of Hermes Trismegistus:

"He (the Cosmic Man), beholding the form like to Himself existing in Her water, loved it and willed to live in it; and with the will came act, and so He vivified the form devoid of reason. And Nature took the object of her love and wound Herself completely round Him, and they were intermingled; for they were lovers. And this is why beyond all creatures on the earth man is twofold; mortal because of body, but, because of the essential Man, immortal."

Verses 5-7   On account of this twofold nature of the human being it is of great importance that the disciples should at all times, and especially at the critical hour of death, identify with what is immortal within, should cleave to the Undying Krishna in their hearts and not to the mortal form which constitutes the body. Imagination is the power which wields the universe. From imagination sprang the dualism of the Cosmos and through imaginative union came about the Mystic Sacrifice. As one thinks, so one becomes. Therefore is it of such supreme importance how the disciples use their imagination. Identifying themselves in thought with the perishable body they share the latter's death, while if they can unite themselves with what is Deathless they will partake of immortality.

There is no appeal here to the authority of ancient texts. It is plain fact of which, as the Gita says, "there is no doubt at all." To one who doubts it only needs to say: "Make yourself ready, try it and reap the fruits." Try it and *see*; you are the immortal Spirit: "Thou wast not born for death, immortal bird! No hungry generations tread thee down."

But, as in the ancient myth, the elixir of immortality must be churned from out of the Cosmic Ocean. How will the Soul's immortality benefit those who think they are the body? It is useless to rely on any mere death-bed thoughts. Only those who in life "strive with continual practice" to know themselves as that which is immortal can meet the illusions of the death hour with unruffled mind and place their being in the Deathless Spirit, treading the Bridge of Souls to the Eternal.

Verse 8

Five are the stages on the Rainbow Bridge, five gates of consciousness through which the soul must pass. First comes the Ancient Seer,[6] the world creator, Brahma the Demiurge, red-colored with desire. It is the Light we know as the desire-consciousness, the Light that shines through the senses, inner as well as outer, for this it is that makes the world of beings, and from this point must the ascent commence.

Verse 9

Next comes the Inner Ruler, smaller than the small. This is the inner "Point" mentioned in chapter five, the Higher Self, shining in the pure Mind. He sows the field and He reaps the harvest; happy the man ruled by that Inner Lord!

Above this comes the Buddhi, All-Supporter, the luminous Sea in which the separate Sparks are all united in one Living Flame. It is the Light that shines above the Mind, uniting individual points of view in one all-seeing Wisdom. It is the vestibule that leads beyond to the Great Being of unimagined form, the Cosmic Ideation which is Krishna,[7] the farthest edge of manifested being. This is the Plane of the Creative Word, and whoever has attained this lofty height can hear the thunders of the mystic Sea that ebbs and flows throughout the Universe, "and hear its might waters, rolling evermore."

Beyond it lies the dark unfathomed mystery of Unmanifested Nature, and beyond again burns the White Light, the Sun beyond the Darkness, the calm and peaceful Light of the Unmanifested Atman.

Beyond once more is the Supreme Eternal, the Nameless Mystery symbolized by the one-syllabled *Om*.[8] One who can tread the Path of Consciousness, sinking the senses in the mind, the mind in buddhi, buddhi in the "Great Self," and then go on Beyond, enters the bliss of that Supreme Eternal and comes no more to birth.

Verses 12, 13 ⸱ This description of the Path has been taken from the Katha Upanishad, but the same thing has been stated here in more symbolic terms. The gates of the senses are to be closed by withdrawal of the consciousness from them and the lower personality (the mind) to be merged in the higher Self, here called the heart. Then, as Shankara puts it, "ascending through the subtle path to the head," the yogi is to establish the self in the buddhi, here termed the "breath of the Atman." From here, contemplating the symbol of the Eternal, one performs the Great Passing-On (*samparaya*).

Verses 16-21 Between the Unmanifested and the manifest lies an Abyss which thought can never cross. Up to the farthest edge of manifested being, the great Self or Cosmic Ideation, here referred to as the world of Brahma, all things are transient, even though they last a thousand ages. From out of the dark Unmanifested Nature they issue forth at every Cosmic Dawn. They last for untold ages, but the eternal rhythm of Day and Night is on them and, at length, there comes a time when, like plants that have flowered, they sink back in the Unmanifested Root of all. In that dark matrix of the Universal Mother the seeds of all that has been lie in latency through the long Night till the next Cosmic Dawn. This mighty rhythm of Cosmic Day and Night, towards an idea of which modern astronomers are perhaps dimly groping, was clearly known to the great ancient Seers. They knew that nothing Cosmic lasts forever and that even the Unmanifested Mother, Mula-prakriti, sends forth her shoots again each Cosmic Dawn. Therefore they sought to live in the Eternal, in that Supreme Unmanifested Brahman, the Indestructible, the Highest Goal. Beyond the Cosmic Tides, That stands forever, the Great Nirvana, the Supreme Abode. Those who attain It know Day nor Night. Like seed destroyed by fire, no Cosmic Dawn can bring them forth again to worlds of sorrow. Of them nothing can be said save the great mantra of the *Prajna Paramita*: "*Gate gate paragate parasangate bodhi svaha!*—O Wisdom gone, gone to the Other Shore, landed on the Other Shore, *Svaha!*"[9]

This is the Goal reached by the Rainbow Bridge; what of the means by which to tread that Path? It is one thing to know of the different levels of Consciousness but quite another to be able to raise oneself at will to higher levels. The best means to accomplish this is "unswerving love and devotion to Him in Whom all beings abide, by Whom all this Cosmos is pervaded." Let there be no misunderstanding here. This is not said in the spirit that has marred some of the bhakti schools of India, the spirit of rivalry with those who

Verse 22

teach the Path of Knowledge. Knowledge is indeed the very Path itself. The Path is made of various levels of Knowledge and we have seen the Jñani described as Krishna's very Self. But this Knowledge is not the knowledge found in books. It must be gained by making the ascent to higher levels; and how in fact may that same rising be accomplished? Who is there that has tried to tread the Path and does not know what is referred to here? Above our heads, like the full moon, shines forth that higher level of our being. We see it there, drawing our hearts with beauty, and yet, for all our efforts, inaccessible, beyond our reach.

The best and easiest means to make the ascent is for the disciples to give themselves in love and devotion to that which is above their present level. Loving devotion is the easiest way by which human beings can transcend their limitations. This is the great force which will carry the disciples out of themselves.[10] One's self is dear to all, but one who loves or worships with unswerving heart loses the self to find a higher Self in the Beloved or the Worshipped one. Thus do they find themselves upon the level which, up till then, had gleamed beyond their reach. Thus do they tread the Path and "sink the senses in the Mind," and so on till they reach the One Self, the Shining Atman within which all live.

This Atman may be symbolized for them as their own Teacher or as some great Avatara. But, through the symbols, they should ever bear in mind it is the One Great Self on all they worship, for as it says in Brihadaranyaka Upanishad, not for the son or husband are son and husband dear but for the Atman which is dear to all. For though one cannot scale at once the heights of being, one can reach them step by step through love, giving oneself to that which stands above one, climbing in this way till the Goal is reached.

It is true that there are other ways of making the ascent. Plotinus said that only he attains the One who has the nature of a lover or philosopher. The disinterested passion for Knowledge, which was what he meant by philosophy, is also capable of lifting human beings out of their personality, of making them forget all self in contemplation of the universal Truths. But few are they whose feet can tread this latter Path. Many, no doubt, desire Knowledge intensely, but of them, most seek it for the power it confers and not for its own sake. It is in that rare case alone where knowledge is desired for Truth's own sake that man can lose all self in its pursuit.

Love is, in any case, the power by which we rise, whether that love be of the True or of the Beautiful or, best of all, of the One Atman, Krishna, Who shines through everything we love or worship. Truth of all truths, Beauty of all things beautiful, Soul of all things beloved, to Him at last all come, losing themselves to find their Self in Him.

There are two Paths, two everlasting Paths; by one or other *Verse 23* must all souls go forth. "By the one he goeth who returneth not, by the other he who again returneth." These are the "Way above" and the "Way of Death" of Hermes Trismegistus; probably also the Two Paths, one through the sky and one beneath the earth, mentioned by Plato in his *Vision of Er*. These Paths, the Path of Light and the Path of Darkness, have been veiled in symbolism throughout the ages. This particular symbolism is far older than the Gita, and these so-called "times" are no times at all. It does not matter when we may die; if we have Knowledge we will tread the Upward Path, if not, the Path of Gloom to birth and death.

Verse 24   These "times" are stages on the Paths that Souls must tread; the one, the Bright Path of the Consciousness, the Path Beyond, trodden by one who knows the Self in all; the other, the Dark Path of Matter, trodden by the ignorant. One who goes by the first climbs the steep inner Path from flickering firelight to the Sunshine of Eternal Day. Rising from Light to Light in ever-widening splendor, one treads the trackless Swan's Path till the blazing Goal is reached.[11]

Verse 25   The other is the Path of gloom and sorrow. Here the only Light is that reflected in the Moon of matter, and the traveler in that pale radiance, taking foes for friends, losing the self in forms which are illusions, knowing not the Immortal, goes from death to death.

Verse 27   Those who know these Paths have, as it were, a compass with which to guide their steps at every instant, in death as in life. For these teachings are not for this life and world alone. There, in those worlds beyond the grave, the mind, freed from the dragging fetters of a gross material body, treads its own path, the path prepared for it by its own thoughts and actions, done while yet "alive." Either it shines serene in its own Light or else it burns in self-enkindled flames of hatred, greed, and lust, the "threefold gate of hell" (chapter xvi, verse 21). This hell is no less real because it is a mind-created one. Fierce illusions[12] will beset the soul and those who know not the Paths will be whirled irresistibly away. Turning their back upon the Fearless Stainless Light of the One Atman, they will embrace the seeming beautiful but horrid phantoms of their own desires. No sooner do they do so than the phantoms change. The beauties vanish, leaving only shame, through which the soul descends to birth again to tread once more the weary path of sorrow.

Much that is written in ancient tales of magic is a reality in this enchanted realm. Sir Gawain, awearied of his questing for the Grail, finds a silken pavilion in a field and merry maidens in it,

> *... but the gale*
> *Tore my pavilion from the tenting pin*
> *And blew my merry maidens all about.*

These illusions work their fell magic from behind the veil even in this daily life of ours, but after death they burst upon the disembodied mind with all the vividness of ancient myth. Those who yield to them echo the cry of Tennyson's Gawain, whose ghost cries out to Arthur at the last:

> *Farewell! there is an isle of rest for thee.*
> *But I am blown along a wandering wind,*
> *And hollow, hollow, hollow all delight.*

Two are the Paths, there is no third for human beings. Cleave to the Self in yoga or lose yourself in matter. Brief is the choice, yet endless, too, for at each point the Way is forked: one can go up or down. The choice should be made now, while yet the heart is flexible with life, for in that After-State the mind is fixed like a deathmask by its previous thoughts. There but a ghostly shade of choice remains. Sped by its former thoughts and deeds, the soul will either sink through illusions to rebirth in matter, or it will rise past heavenly realms of Light, stopping at none till it attains the Goal, the Deathless and Supreme Eternal State.

Verse 28

Notes

1   For a fuller account of this cosmic evolution see chapter 13 and appendix F; see also the diagram in appendix E.

2   For an interesting parallel in the Kabala see appendix F.

3   This dualistic "knowing" is, however, not individual but cosmic. It springs from that mysterious extra-cosmic Something called by various schools the Will of God, *lila* (the Divine play), Eternal Law, or *Maya*. All these names express some aspects of it, but, being beyond the manifested Cosmos, it is beyond the reach of words. Its nature is too mysterious to be speculated on, but its reality is proved by the fact of manifestation having taken place at all. In attempting to describe it Shankara was forced into paradox and contradiction, while the Buddha preferred to keep silent altogether.

4   Also known in some traditions as the third Logos.

5   *Ahankara*, literally the I-maker, is a term that can be applied either on the level of the personal self or on that of higher Self, the true individual. In later writings it is usually employed in the lower sense, but in the Gita, manas is generally used for the lower self and ahankara for the higher. The term higher manas is not used in the Gita, though, as previously mentioned, it is referred to in Maitri Upanishad (vi, 34) as *suddha* (pure) manas. The term *ahankara* has the same significance, but emphasizes not its cognitive but its ego nature.

6   The use of the word *kavi*, seer or poet (also applied to the poet-seers of the Vedas), shows how essentially the creative process is conceived as one of imagination. This level is the same as that of the Gnostic Ilda-Baoth. The word *Brahma* is also used in another sense (e.g. verse 16 of this chapter), where it stands for the highest level of manifested being, the plane of the Creative World, the Cosmic ideation. There need be no confusion about this double use. Both signify the creative Power, in the one case on the level of unity, the manifested unity; in the other case on the level of plurality, the plurality which is the world of beings. There is a reference in Shvetashvatara Upanishad (v, 2) to "the reddish-colored seer who was engendered in the beginning." On the five levels see appendix E.

7   Only in one aspect of course. Throughout the Gita, Sri Krishna identifies Himself with different levels at different places.

8   A lot of nonsense has been written in the West about Om and its "vibrations." The true meaning of the word should be studied in the Mandukya Upanishad.

H. P. Blavatsky, when asked by her pupils as to the correct pronunciation of Om replied: "Aum means good actions, not merely lip-sound. You must say it in deeds."

9   *Svaha* is the mantra with which offerings are made in the sacred fire. In this, the Brahma yajña, the self has been offered and consumed in the fire of the Eternal.

10 The reason that love and devotion have this power is that they have their roots in the buddhi and so beyond individuation. It is true that, as we find them in ordinary life, they manifest through and in association with the strong currents of the sub-mental desire-nature—hence their mixed and sometimes unsatisfactory nature in common experience. Nevertheless their roots are in the buddhi, and thus they have the power to pull the disciple right through the "dead-center" of the higher ego where so many others stop, subtly magnifying self with every effort to diminish it. Hence also the fact that these higher emotions, as we may call them, have a definite cognitive aspect and give a knowledge that is beyond the analytic knowledge of the mind. Compare with the words of Jung: "Intellect does in fact isolate the soul when it tries to possess itself of the heritage of the spirit. It is in no way fitted to do this, because spirit is something higher than intellect in that it includes not only the latter, but the feelings as well."

11 See appendix G.

12 A good account of the after-death illusions is given in *The Tibetan Book of the Dead*.

Chapter Nine

The Yoga of the Royal Science and the Royal Secret

"The One Swan is in the heart of the world;
He verily is the fire that has entered into the Waters.
Having known Him one crosses over Death;
There is no other Path for going there."

—Shvetashvatara Upanishad

The Royal Secret is not one that can be told in words. Throughout the world runs a tradition of a wondrous Secret sought under different names by people through all the ages. The Philosopher's Stone, the Elixir of Immortality, the Holy Grail, the Hidden Name of God, all these have been the objects of human quests, and all are one if rightly understood. Many have "followed after wandering fires," and others have sold their quest for gold or fame, but throughout all ages there have always been a few who trod the Path and found the shining Secret.

Verse 1

This Secret is written in the inmost heart of humanity and has lain there through countless ages, awaiting the day when disciples, tearing aside the veils of ignorance, perceives its blazing letters in their hearts. There is no one, however mean or sinful, in whose heart it is not written, but few there are who read its life-giving words.

Verse 2

This is the meaning of the statement that it is *pratyakshavagamam,* to be directly known. The ones who tread the Path see for themselves the Truth, not in some promised heaven after death, but here in this very life. Here are no books demanding blind unreasoning obedience, no priests waving the keys which unlock heavens and hells. The Truth, once seen, shines by its own resplendent Light, and those who drink of its waters "shall never thirst again."

No doubt faith is required to reach this Knowledge, but that faith *Verse 3* is not an intellectual belief in any set of dogmas nor in the efficiency of any priestly rites.[1] The faith required is the inner conviction that sent the Buddha on His lonely quest, the faith that "Surely at last, far off, sometimes, somewhere, the veil will lift for his deep-searching eyes"[2]; that *somewhere* there is a Knowledge that will save the world from sorrow, and a determination to rest not till that Knowledge be attained. This is the faith and this the will that has sent out the Seekers of all ages. Its life is rooted not in intellect but in the inner Knowledge itself, and from there its rays shoot out, though dimmed by matter, to draw the hearts of men towards the Goal.[3]

How far this knowledge soars beyond the reach of words is shown by the contradictory descriptions cast on the beaches of our lower worlds. The Upanishadic Seers termed it the knowledge of the Full, the Atman; the Buddhists, knowledge of *Anatman*, of the Void. Yet both descriptions were attempts to express the same transcendent Truth, Truth that was known to both but which, when clothed in words, appears in these conflicting forms.

The Gita, too, has recourse to paradox, the paradox that all *Verses 4, 5* beings dwell and yet do not dwell in the One Supreme. In order to understand this at least partially, for full understanding comes only with direct knowledge, it should be borne in mind that throughout the Gita Krishna speaks from different levels. In verse 4 He is speaking of His Great Unmanifested Form (*avyakta murti*), the *Parabrahman*, Rootless Root of all. By that Supreme all this world is pervaded; Itself rooted in naught, all beings dwell within Its bosom.

Of it Plotinus writes: "Generative of all, the Unity is none of all, neither thing nor quality, or intellect nor soul; not in motion, not at rest, not in place, not in time; It is the self-defined, unique in form or, better, formless, existing before Form was or Movement or Rest, all of which are attachments of Being and make Being the manifold it is."[4]

But yet it is not in that ultimate Brahman that beings may be said to dwell, for it is not until from that One have sprung forth the Two, the Unmanifested Self or Subject and the Unmanifested Root of Objectivity, that "the beings" come into existence at all. It is from the mystic union the *yogam aishvaram* of these Two that the beings come forth and therefore they cannot be said to stand in the One but rather in the Two. Nevertheless, it is the One who is their final support, and, though not standing in or becoming them, yet is He the cause of their forthgoing. Like Space itself, He holds them all but yet is touched by none.

Verse 6

Perhaps the best way to gain some understanding of the mystery is to remember the Hermetic axiom[5] and study the creative process in the microcosm, for, as it says in the *Zohar*, "esoterically the man below corresponds entirely to the Man above." By a Mystic Union, the yogam aishvaram of verse 5, the Unmanifested Self unites, as it were imaginatively, with the Unmanifested Nature, the Mula-prakriti. The Self leans on or "embraces" the Dark Nature, and at that embrace the seeds of plurality buried within from previous universes shoot into life and the Great Descent begins. This Descent

Verse 8

is a graded perception of increasing objectivity. As the Self "gazes" at each level a further objectivization takes place, resulting in plane after plane of being. Through the mystic union with these levels[6] the whole Cosmic Machine, down to the so-called gross objective matter, whirls and revolves with the indwelling Life, for, as Hermes says, "not a single thing that is dead hath been or is or shall be in this Cosmos."

Nor is this process one which is accomplished once and then remains forever. Again and again, as described in the last chapter, the mighty Outbreathing takes place and all the countless beings thread their tangled ways throughout the worlds, to be absorbed again at the next Cosmic Night, in which "only the One breathes breathless by Itself." *Verses 8-10*

"This is the Truth: As from a blazing fire thousands of sparks of like form issue forth, so from the Imperishable, O friend, manifold beings are produced and thither do return."[7]

All that has here been written, all that can be written, is but a web of words, a ladder by whose help we seek to scale the ramparts of Eternity. Viewed by the eye of Wisdom all this clash of world with world, the Sparks which fly from the Eternal Anvil, are but a vast phantasmagoria. Nothing is outbreathed nor anything descends to rise again. All are the visions of the Eternal Mind the changing finite centers that are us ourselves being but the countless points of view within that mighty Whole, "for there is naught in all the world that is not He."[8]

But few there are whose souls are of such stature that they can look upon the highest Truth and live. In those who see before the soul is perfect, love and compassion die, killed by that freezing Knowledge, and all the strivings of a million lives are lost, and they who might have been a lamp to suffering humanity choose Nirvana and are lost to us as though at no time had they ever been.

Let us take up our web of words again lest too much knowledge, like the Gorgon's head, should freeze us where we stand. Though the One Self projects the Cosmic Wheel and fills it with Its life-blood, yet is that Self not bound upon its whirling spokes. Filled by the One *Verse 9* Life, countless beings strive, enjoy or suffer, die and come to birth again, and yet that One Life is forever free, "seated like one indifferent, unattached to actions."

> *I saw the King of Kings descend the narrow*
> *doorway to the dust,*
> *With all His fires of morning still, the beauty,*
> *bravery and lust,*
> *And yet He is the life within the Ever-living*
> *living Ones,*
> *The Ancient with Eternal youth, the cradle*
> *of the infant Suns.* [9]

Human beings sin and suffer, act and reap the fruits, and yet the Atman seated in their hearts, the Self whose life moves all that is, impelling all to action feels not the sting of death but lives forever, free and unattached even in the very web of deeds. This is the mystery of the Divine Action; one who knows its secret comes not to birth again (chapter iv, verse 9). The Atman free though through Its life the Cosmic Wheel revolves. "He ever is at work, Himself being what He doeth. For did He separate Himself from it, all things would then collapse and all must die." [10]

Two types of people are found in the world. The first are those who unite their being with the deceitful outer nature (*mohini prakriti*), the ever-changing world of transient forms. These are those foolish ones who disregard the shining Atman, seeing only the perishable bodies which It ensouls. Therefore are they said to be empty of hope, for there can be no hope in forms that come and go; and empty of deeds, for deed can have no meaning save as the service of the One Eternal Life. *Verse 12*
Verse 11

In contrast with these are the wise ones who unite their being with the daivic prakriti, the Divine Life which flows like *Ganga* through the triple world, ensouling all the forms, the stainless living Radiance streaming from the Imperishable Source of all. Ever united with that living Light, firm in the vow[11] which offers self in service of the Self, they turn their gaze within and see the radiant Source as One beyond all forms and yet as manifold within the hearts of all. *Verses 13-15*

From that Source, the Father, Mother, All-supporter of the Cosmos, comes forth the fire of life and the creative waters of desire. All that is manifest, as well as what is still unmanifest, comes from that wondrous Treasure House (*nidhanam*). *Verse 19*

The higher up the Path of Light a person ascends the more gloriously radiant are the forms which It ensouls, and there are always many who climb a certain height only to lose themselves in heavenly enjoyments.[12] But, if this temptation is yielded to, the energy of the ascent is dissipated among those fair creations and, when it is spent, the pilgrim soul is carried down by the unresting cycles and must, in circumstances good or ill, start on this earth once more its upward climb. The seeds buried in the darkness of earth shoot up and bear their fruit in the free air, the corn seven cubits high that grew in the Egyptian fields of *Ahloo*, and then return as seeds once more to earth. *Verse 20*

Verse 21 Though this is called the Path of Darkness in the previous chapter, it is only such in contrast to the glorious Path of Light. It is the normal cyclic path of human life throughout the long ages of evolution, during which the souls lured by desire (*kamakama*) must know and suffer all before they take the Homeward Path.

It is only for the grown souls of the disciples that this path becomes a snare to be avoided for they are the ones who have renounced desire and may not without shame yield to the lure of heaven. Their duty is to offer up themselves in sacrificial service to *Verse 24* the One Great Life that is the Lord of all; all other worship is an obstacle for them. Forms in the psychic world, spirits of the blessed dead, the shining Gods themselves, all these exist beyond the world of humanity, and all have drawn the souls of human beings in worship. But the result of worship is assimilation to the being who is worshipped, and no limited, finite God can give the Soul that State which is beyond all limitations. These shining forms may serve to lead some upwards and make them blossom in the higher worlds; but blossoms fade and must return to earth, this drab but wondrous earth in which alone the plant of life can grow.

The Path of Liberation is for humanity alone. The Gods are stopping-places on the way, fair forms for most, but veritable Moloch *Verse 25* mouths for him who treads the Homeward Path, since, once assimilated to their being, there is no onward path save through the womb of earth again. The disciple at this stage must leave the forms and see the Light that shines through all, for it is by that Light that all are glorious. The worshippers of Gods are ignorant, for they see but the forms and not the Light of that Unknown Eternal without which they are nothing.

But, comes the question, how can that Light be worshipped? Stainless, serene, eternally transcendent, "that from which speech turns back, together with the mind, unable to attain,"[13] is not through any complicated rites or ceremonials but through sheer giving. The disciple must reverse that process of grasping which builds up a personal self and strive to give away instead of getting. First with symbolic gifts of leaves and flowers and fruit, but afterwards with gift of self, the consecration of all acts to Him. Nor should any think their gifts are not accepted. All gifts, however small, are "accepted," because all giving is a breaking-down and weakening of the barrier which, like some iron egg-shell, cuts off the soul from the wide life outside. The smallest act of giving is a step upon that Path and leads the soul by easy steps to that sublime stage where the whole personal life, with all its acts and thoughts and feelings, is dedicated to the service of the One in all, where acts can bind no more since self is dead, and nothing remains that can be bound by them.

Verse 26

Verses 27,28

The Way is taught, but each must tread it by themselves. "The same am I to all beings; there is none hateful to Me nor dear." No special privileges can be found upon this Path. Those who seem to climb with glorious ease today are not the favored darlings of the Gods but the ones who reap the fruit of the arduous struggles of yesterday, while those whose breath comes hard upon the mountain path may know for certain that, if they persist, a time will come when they too will gain the athletes' grace and mastery.

Verse 29

There is no other way to Krishna than giving of the self to Him in service. By their own efforts each must climb the Path, but always Krishna stands within the soul and none who seek to offer up themselves can be refused the chance. Though they must climb in weary loneliness, serve him with an undivided heart, that loneliness is a mere illusion, for there, unseen, "closer to them than breathing, nearer than hands and feet," stands the eternal Friend and inmost Self. Nothing interposes between them and their inner God except the veil of egoism which they themselves have made, and which is thinned and weakened by each unselfish act of giving.

Verse 30

Therefore is it said that even if the most sinful turns to Him and serves Him with undivided heart, they too must be accounted righteous, they too have entered on the Homeward Path. True, the self-assertive acts that constitute the evil of their past have left them with a legacy of tendencies that they will have to struggle hard to overcome, for nothing can annihilate deeds once they have been done. To seek to have their consequences washed away by any magic or by any prayers is merest superstition, but even so, no one is ever fettered utterly. Some may sin a thousand times, and by those acts so strengthen the lower self that it is almost certain they will sin again next time. Almost, but not quite certain, for in everyone shines the free Atman, and where That exists no bondage can be absolute. Always human beings *can* turn and climb the upward path, for the Divine Freedom that is in their hearts can never be annulled, and even the very power by which they sin, traced to its source, springs from the Stainless One.

Verse 31

Once the resolve is made *and kept* to act in future for the higher not the lower self, progress is speedy, and the Path is entered on which leads at last to the Eternal Peace. Though there will many times be failures, once the link with the Divine Self has been established, the disciple cannot fall again into the utter darkness. Something has awakened within which will never allow rest again in matter, and though at times there may even be a fight against it, the inner pull will ever and again be felt, and like a big fish held on a slender line such a one will eventually be brought out of the stream to land, for, as Krishna says, "know thou for certain that my devotee perishes never."[14]

The Atman dwells within the hearts of all and therefore is this *Verse 32* path open to all without distinction of race, caste, or sex. The Vedic path needed a wealth of learning and therefore was inevitably closed to those, such as women and the Shudra caste, who were debarred by social rules from Vedic study.[15] This Path, calling only for sincere self-giving, needs no scriptural or philosophic learning and so is available for all, since all the Knowledge that is needed comes of itself to those who give themselves.

Therefore the Teacher sums up all that He has said in one brief verse, a verse whose great importance may be seen from the fact that the same verse (with an insignificant variation) is used to sum up the completed teaching at the end of chapter eighteen:

"On Me fix thy mind; give thyself in love to Me; sacrifice to Me; *Verse 34* prostrate thyself before Me; having thus united thy whole self (to Me), with Me as thy Goal, to Me shalt thou come."

The disciples must with a pure mental vision see Him, the One in all, and with their hearts offer themselves in love. Their active powers they must use in sacrificial service and, as prostration, see the personal self as naught before that mighty Whole. Thus in balanced union, avoiding any one-sided intellectualism, emotionalism, or activity, head, heart, and hands all fixed on Him, filled with Him, transmuted to His nature, they tread the Royal Path on which the

Soul, dying to self, rising again in Self, knows the Eternal Swan, and, having known, crosses beyond all death.

Notes

1   In fact, as the Buddha taught, faith in rites and ceremonies as such is one of the fetters that has to be thrown off by the disciple on this Path.

2   *The Light of Asia.*

3   See the notes on the higher emotions on p. 112 of the previous chapter.

4   Plotinus, vi, 9.

5   Compare also the words of Hermes: "And if thou wouldst in practice understand this work, behold what taketh place in thee desiring to beget" (*Hermetic Corpus*, xi, 14).

6   "Having entered into union (*yoga*) with principle (*tattva*) after principle" (Shvetashvatara Upanishad, vi, 3).

7   Mundaka Upanishad, II, i, 1.

8   *Hermetic Corpus*, v, 9.

9   From A. E.'s poem *Krishna*.

10   *Hermetic Corpus*, 11-14 (Mead's translation).

11   Compare these "firm vows" (verse 14) with the vow of the Bodhisattvas, "as the chain of births is endless, so long shall I live the holy life for the well-being of all creatures." (*Shantideva*).

12   At the time when the Gita was written this gaining of heavenly enjoyments after death had come to be considered the path taught by the Vedas (verse 20 and 21).

13   Taittiriya Upanishad, II, iv, 1.

14   The symbolism of the soul caught on the line of the Divine Fisher is found in many ancient mysteries and underlies the statement of Jesus about "fishers of men." For details see Eislers *Orpheus the Fisher*. The words of Vyasa (in the *Vishnu Purana*), uttered at the commencement of the *Kali Yuga*, should also be remembered. Standing in the waters of the Sacred Ganga he exclaimed: "Women are fortunate! Shudras are fortunate!" When asked why he thus

exclaimed he replied: "Women are fortunate because self-giving comes to them by birthright and Shudras because their dharma is that of service."

15   Verse 32 must not be taken as sanctioning the relegation of women to an inferior place in society. When the Gita was written (as to a large extent even now) women were *in fact* depressed and practically deprived of the advantages of education. Sri Krishna is not supporting this but pointing out that, even with these handicaps, this Path is open for them. The phrase "womb of sin" refers to the fact that the karmic penalty for wasted opportunities is loss of opportunity in future, and so a birth in one of those sections of society which, *at that given time and place,* suffer in fact from lack of freedom and opportunity. It should not be taken as justifying such a state of society.

✳

Chapter Ten

The Yoga of the Pervading Powers

Seeking nothing, giving thyself utterly to Me. These words will serve
to summarize the teaching that has now (in Chapter 9) been given.
But who is it who thus claims allegiance from the Soul? "Worship
thou Me," says Krishna, and His words find echo in the saying of
Christ: "No one cometh to the Father save through Me." Creeds in
East and West have fastened on these sayings and urged the personal and unique greatness of their own particular Teacher, Son of
God or very God Himself, incarnate in the world to save the souls
of men. Either we must think these Great Ones were deluded in
proclaiming themselves the sole Way to the Highest, or we must
suppose, which is indeed the case, that it is not as separate individual
beings that they speak but as the unborn, beginningless Eternal, the
Brahman in which all abide, "by which all this is pervaded."

It is the knowledge of this One Eternal that, from the seventh
chapter onwards, is growing in the heart of the disciple. This is the
knowledge which "having known, naught here remains to know."[1]
It is not enough to know the individual Christ or Krishna, though
indeed, as we shall see at the conclusion of the whole teaching, there
is a secret, the most purely mystical of all, hidden in the heart of what
we term their personalities. There is a direct Path to the inmost heart
of Reality, one that proceeds straight through what may be termed

the concrete infinity of the Divine Lord who shows forth with human limbs the action of the Actionless, who utters with human speech the voiceless Wisdom of the Eternal. But the context shows that it is not with that most secret path of all that we are here concerned, but rather with the Diving Presence that stands, pervading all.

It is as that Brahman that Sri Krishna here speaks, the Brahman out of Which all beings come and into Which all will in time return. Its secrets are forever hidden in that uncreated Darkness. Nor God nor Sage can know Its rootless being, for from It all come forth, and he who plunges in to know Its utmost mystery is dissolved in a blazing Light that yet is darkness to the highest dualistic knowing. *Verse 2*

All we can know is that all separate qualities, the various states of mind, some positive, some negative, exist in unity as moments of that blazing Darkness and from It issue forth to shine in men as separate states of being. *Verses 4, 5*

The seven great Lights,[2] which are the planes of being, all issue forth as previously described (chapters 8 and 9). These seven Lights or planes are here divided into three main classes. First come the "previous four,"[3] the four high levels of being (two of them "unmanifested") beyond all individuation. These have been symbolized as four eternal, chaste, ascetic youths, the four *Kumaras*, who refused to create offspring, preferring to remain in contemplation of the One. The truth behind this symbol is that these four planes are planes of unity in which the separate individualities have not been formed. *Verse 6*

Below these come the *Manus*, here the separate individuals (*jivas*), the "points of view" within the all-seeing Light.[4] From them issued "this race of men," dying and being born on endless wheels of change.

These "Manus" are the central or, as it were, neutral points of the whole manifold creation; on them as on a pivot all is balanced.[5] The two higher levels (for we can leave aside the "unmanifested" two as no part of the manifested cosmos) are mainly inward-turned, so to speak centripetal, and hence are symbolized as chaste ascetics. The lowest two, the changing worlds of beings, are outward-turned or centrifugal in their tendency, while between both, as points of equilibrium, are found "the Manus" standing firmly in themselves. Of them, or "through" them, come the changing beings, the children of *Manu* known as *manavas* (humans). These Manus are the Children of God and no one goes to the Father save through them alone.

Verse 7   On all the planes of cosmos is the One as immanent pervading Power (*vibhuti*) united with the forms by mystic yoga (see previous chapter), and therefore it is said that one who knows in essence this pervading power and yoga of the Supreme unites with Him in firm unwavering yoga.

Verse 8   "I am the source of all," says Krishna, "by Me all revolves." As Mula-prakriti, He is the Source of all the forms and, as the One transcendent Self, it is His yoga that throws them into motion. Ordinary people see nothing but the passing forms, in them they put their hopes, in them is fixed their being. Forms come and they feel happy; they go and sorrow overwhelms their minds, for never can it be that forms shall stand forever. But disciples, seeing thus the source and life of all as one, are rooted in that One and remain blissful though all the forms around them change and pass.

Verse 10   To those who can root themselves in Him, serving Him ever with the worship born of love, He gives the buddhi-yoga, that union with the buddhi by which they go to Him. The buddhi is the wisdom which *sees* the One in All; it also is the faculty by which that vision is acquired. We have seen how the individual self is balanced between the centrifugal and the centripetal forces. United to the lower levels the self flows outwards into forms and dies, as it were, with them, while united to the higher it is carried Homewards by the inflowing cosmic tides.

"Out of pure compassion for them, dwelling within their Self, *Verse 11* I destroy the ignorance-born darkness by the shining lamp of Wisdom."

It should not be thought that this compassion is something capricious, something given or withheld at will like a Maharaja's favor. The sun's rays shine on all alike; without them all would die. But those who would feel their warmth upon their skin must leave the shut-in cave and seek the open air. Similarly, those who would experience the Divine Compassion in their soul must leave the cave of self and seek the wider being. They must strive upwards, outwards from the self, breaking the barriers till the Homeward-flowing tides are felt and sweep them off their feet.

These Homeward tides that sweep the upper planes of being, sometimes termed "grace,"[6] are the Divine Compassion which will bear the soul up to the One Eternal, but, before they can be felt, the disciples must strive desperately with all their might to cling to Krishna, and by their own unaided efforts break down the prison walls.

To one who says "show us the Lord and it sufficeth us" comes the reply "that which is highest in thyself is He, as much of Him as thou canst see as yet. Cling then to that and thou shalt go to Him."

Clinging thus to Krishna, the mind becomes irradiated by the

Light of the One Atman shining serenely through the buddhi above. The effect of this irradiation is that the intellectual knowledge of the mind is vivified and rendered luminously certain by the buddhi's direct intuition. This is shown very clearly in the Gita in the twelfth and following verses.

Verse 12   "Thou are the Great Eternal, the Great Light, the pure and stainless One, Divine, eternal Man, primal Divinity, Unborn and all-pervading."

Verse 13   All this was known before as abstract truth, testified to by all the Seers of the past, but "now Thou Thyself sayest it to me." A new and rapturous warmth whose source is in the buddhi pervades the mind which soars beyond itself. New vistas, like a landscape half-perceived, open before the mental gaze and the old words and thoughts, now shine transformed within a magic light never before perceived. Useless to try to state in words this new luminous perception. It shows in the note of ecstasy that sounds through Arjuna's words. It is as if one strumming idly on a windless organ should suddenly hear the notes sounding forth in answer to the keys. The thoughts that were but thoughts, bare intellectual concepts, greyly self-sufficient, now waken colored harmonies that echo through the arches of what seemed a void. No longer are things seen as separate unities but as the interlinked and shining web of a vast splendid pattern still but half-perceived.

Verse 15   To change this twilit half-perception into the sunshine of true knowledge further advance is needed. It is by the Atman itself that the Atman is gained,[7] or, as the Gita puts it, "Thou thyself knowest Thyself by Thyself, O Highest *Purusha*, Sender forth of beings, Light of the Shining Ones, Ruler of the World!"

Even the buddhi shines not by its own light. Beyond it is the Light of the Great Atman, the Cosmic Ideation in which the Divine archetypes of past, present and future exist in one vast interpenetrative whole.[8] Here is the splendid pattern of the Cosmos radiant with Divine Light, a wondrous unity of spiritual Beings.

"For There everything is transparent, nothing dark, nothing resistant; every being is lucid to every other, in breadth and depth; light runs through light. And each of them contains all within itself, and at the same time sees all in every other, so that everywhere there is all, all is all, and each all, and infinite the glory. Each of them is great; the small is great: stars and sun. While some one manner of being is dominant in each, all are mirrored in every other."[9]

All that is in the world is what it is because of the reflection of some portion of that glorious Being. In it the unity of all the manifold is found. It is, as has been said before, the topmost edge of manifested being, what lies beyond is all unmanifest. The soul, united to the buddhi (*buddhi-yukta*), must now ascend this snowy peak of being, must see, first by the mental eye, and at last by direct spiritual vision, those Divine Glories by which the Supreme *stands* pervading *Verse 16* all the worlds. These are the Divine Ideas spoken of by Plato, the pervading Powers (*vibhuti*) that are the subject of this chapter.

The phrase "Divine Ideas" should not mislead the reader (as it has misled many intellectuals) into thinking that they are pale abstractions, the conceptual "universals" of academic philosophy.[10] These "Ideas" are not conceptual abstraction at all, but living Spiritual Powers which, as the Gita says, "stand" in their own nature eternally and are reflected in the flux of beings, giving to each its form and its essential nature, not abstracted from beings but formative of beings, the perfect types and patterns of all things here below:

> *Out of the dark it wrought the heart of man,*
> *Out of dull shells the pheasant's penciled neck:*
> *Ever at toil, it brings to liveliness*
> *All ancient wrath and wreck*

To reach this Divine world is now the task of the disciple and therefore Arjuna asks:

Verse 17 "O Yogi,[11] how may I know Thee by constant meditation? In what aspects are Thou to be thought of by me, O Glorious One?"

The Divine Realities cannot be seen by eyes of flesh; the eye by which they must be seen is that of buddhi, the eye of spiritual vision.[12]

But though that eye is now available for the disciples they must first learn to open it and to habituate themselves to its use. Just as a person, though having as a birthright, mind, with all its powers of thinking, yet has to learn by slow and arduous steps how to unfold those powers, so the disciples who have now united mind with buddhi must slowly and with effort open up its powers of vision. The mental life in which they, for the most part, are still rooted must be transmuted by the higher vision. A person born blind, but who has gained sight, finds for some time the new sense unfamiliar and rather trusts the highly cultivated sense of touch with all its limitations than this strange power of sight which now has opened.

Therefore the Teacher now sets forth a method, a discipline by which the soul may learn to use the eye of the buddhi and to trust its baffling, unfamiliar vision more than the familiar seeing of the mind.[13]

The verses which follow (20-42) are not to be considered as the self-praise of a merely personal God. Again it must be said, the "I" who speaks is not just the personal Krishna[14] but the Great Atman, One and manifold, pervading by Its Powers all things that are. These verses contain the practical method by which the soul may learn to use and trust its eye.

The disciple is instructed to try to see in all things, not their separate being, but the Great Atman, by whose Powers all have their form and nature. Each type of being on earth is what it is because of the "reflection"[15] of some aspect of that Atman. This "reflection" is best seen in those objects which are preeminent within their class, for it is in them that the Divine Archetype has best found expression. This is the meaning of the list that Krishna gives.[16] In all things, gods or humans or sages, so-called "inanimate" objects or in mental qualities, "He" is to be sought out and contemplated in the chief of every class.[17] For He indeed is verily the Atman in all beings, their very Self, the base on which they stand.

Verses 20

What makes the gods shining and powerful? It is the Light and Power of the One. What makes the Vedas holy, worthy of our reverence? It is the ancient Archetypal Wisdom. What is it that calls forth our aspirations in the sight of mountain peaks, calms us in sheets of water, whispers to us in trees, or disturbs our hearts in animals?[18] What is it but Him shining through all these beings in spiritual Powers to which, if we give names, they are but poor translation?

Verses 21-38

Even in the greatly wicked, in one who says to evil "Be thou my good," in the fierce pride of *Duryodhana*, in such a type of monstrous wickedness as Shakespeare's *Richard the Third*, we feel His presence compelling wonder, even admiration, in spite of all the protests of our moral nature.

Verse 36

What is thus felt in beings in not a fancy but something truly, if but vaguely, seen within. The disciple must cling to these intuitive perceptions and by constant meditation sharpen them to clearness until the outer forms seem unreal things through whose translucid shells the wondrous Powers shine in their gleaming splendors.

As the disciples proceed a change will overtake their vision. Not only will they see the spiritual Power in each form, but since these Powers are united in a living Whole, they will begin to *see*, what before they could but think, the vast interconnectedness of all things.[19]

"In our realm all is part arising from part and nothing can be more than partial; but There each being is an eternal product of a whole and is at once a whole and an individual manifestation as part but, to the keen vision There, known for the whole it is."[20]

Thus to the seeing eye all things are linked to all in a great Cosmic Harmony. Flowers in the green are seen as one with the far-distant stars gleaming forever in the blue abyss of space. Within this six-foot frame blow all the winds of heaven and in the heart of humanity lie the glittering pomp, the sometimes cruel beauty, and all the hidden secrets of long-vanished empires buried now beneath the desert sands or ocean waves.

There is a story current that on certain days, if one goes out to sea from the town known as Dvarka, beneath the waves can dimly be descried the towers and pinnacles of Krishna's island city. Legend, no doubt, for Dvarka was not there. Nevertheless beneath the storm-tossed surface of our hearts the ancient wars are fought, Atlantis shines in glory, darkens with pride and falls; Sri Krishna walks the earth and Buddha leaves his home for love of others.

Nothing is lost, forever all remains, deep in the waters of eternal

Mind. He who can plunge within lives in the Cosmic Heart and sees Its mighty throbs send forth the cycling years to run their changing courses through the worlds back to the blue depths of Eternity. It is said that in a lotus-seed exists in miniature a perfect lotus. So in that Mighty Being is the seed of all that is,[21] subtle beyond all images of sense, the shining spiritual Cosmos; Infinite seeds and yet one wondrous Seed, beyond the reach of mind, yet to be seen by Mind. *Verse 39*

All that is glorious, beautiful, or mighty shines by reflection of a portion of that Being. Vainly we seek on earth a symbol grand enough to adumbrate Its glories. In ancient Egypt and Chaldea the starry heaven was Its only symbol; the heaven with its interlinked and patterned stars whirling in gleaming cosmic depths, their mind-annihilating magnitudes of time and space, symbol to all men of eternal Law and Beauty, are but a moment of the Mighty Atman; infinities ranged on the shoulders of infinities; a wondrous hierarchy of living spiritual Powers where each is each and each is All and all dance forth in ecstasy the Cosmic Harmony.[22] *Verse 40*

Vast beyond thought as is this spiritual realm, this flaming Cosmos of Divine Ideas, yet still beyond lies That, the One Eternal, the Parabrahman, Rootless Root of all.[23] Beyond all Gods, beyond all time and space, beyond all being even, flames Its dark transcendent Light. *Verse 42*

From that Eternal Brahman issue forth the Mighty Atman, great beyond all thought, and all the countless starry worlds that fill the wide immensities of space. Yet so vast is Its spaceless, timeless grandeur that all these wondrous emanated worlds are as a drop taken from out the ocean, leaving Its shoreless being ever full. Therefore Sri Krishna, speaking for That Brahman, says, "having established this entire universe with one fragment of Myself, I remain."

> *That is the Full; this is the full;*
> *From that Full has this full come forth.*
> *Having taken the full from the Full*
> *Verily the Full Itself remains.*"[24]

Notes

1   Gita, vii, 2.

2   Verse 6. In addition to the meaning of sage or seer the word *rishi* means light or ray. And it is in this latter sense that the word has been used. Here, as so often, the ambiguity of the Sanskrit language has been used to symbolize abstract truths in personal forms, the seven sages of mythology.

3   Some read "the four previous Manus," but there were more than four previous Manus according to the *Pauranic* account and commentators are reduced to various ingenuities to explain why four are mentioned. These four levels are referred to in the Katha Upanishad as the Shanta Atman, the atyakta (Mula-prakriti), the Great Atman (Mahat) and the Jñana Atman (Buddhi). See diagram in appendix E.

4   This use of the word *Manu* may be seen in the *Vaishnava Pancharatra Agana.* See Schrader's *Introduction to the "Pancharatra."* This level corresponds to manas, the (higher) mind or, in other systems, ahankara. This level is sometimes also referred to as *sthanu*, the fixed or stable, and is the same as the adhiyajña of chapter eight.

5   The desire-nature and the physical world referred to in the Katha Upanishad as the *indriyas* (senses) and their objects. This structure of the universe is one meaning of the well-known ancient symbol of two triangles standing point to point ✕ (*cf.* the *damaru* of Shiva), the upper triangle, the worlds of being; the lower one, the worlds of flux and change, reflected worlds of Maya's shifting play.

6   The term Grace, however, if used at all, is better reserved for a mysterious Power, testified to by mystics of East and West, a Power that is wielded alike by Krishna and the human guru, and which is so ultimate that it baffles all attempts at intellectual formulation. All we can say is that it is utterly free and that it is rooted in that aspect of the Supreme and Eternal One that manifests

in us as personality.

7   Compare Katha Upanishad, ii, 23, the famous words *yamevaisha vrinute tena labhyah*, which may be rendered "that very (*Atman*) which the disciple chooses (i.e. clings to), by means of that (*Atman*) is it attained."

8   Compare Plotinus vi, 9: "Thus we come to the *Nous* (Divine Mind) almost as an object of sense: the Intellectual Kosmos is perceptible as standing above the soul . . . a multiple but at once indivisible and comporting difference."

9   Plotinus, *Enneads*, v, tractate 8.

10   The latter are only diagrams constructed by the mind, and while they may refer to, can never *be* the true "Divine Ideas."

11   Note that Krishna is here addressed as "Yogi" because it is on this plane that the Wondrous Yoga, the Yogamaishwaram, takes place. It is here that the one unmanifested Self (*Shanta Atman*) unites with the one unmanifested Nature (*Mula-prakriti*). See previous chapter.

12   *Cf.* Hermes, vi, 4: "For all the things that fall beneath the eye are image things and pictures as it were, while these that do not meet the eyes are the realities."

13   The mind sees by analysis and separation, splitting the unity of life into the separate aspects named and pinned like insects on the board it calls science. The buddhi sees the unity in all and therefore Krishna teaches Arjuna how the Divine Pervading Powers are to be looked for in the things below.

14   This is made quite clear in verse 37, in which the personal Krishna, son of Vasudeva, is treated as quite separate from the "I" who is speaking.

15   "We do not mean that the Idea, locally separate, shows itself in Matter like a reflection in water; the Matter touches the Idea at every point, though not by physical contact, and by dint of neighborhood—nothing to keep them apart—is able to absorb thence all that lies within its capacity, the Idea itself not penetrating, not approaching, the Matter, but remaining self-locked" (Plotinus, VI, v, 8).

16   The various mythological beings and symbols that occur in this list, some of which have now ceased to play a very vivid part in even a Hindu mind, were all quite living to the man for whom the Gita was composed two or three thousand years ago. *Vittesha*, for instance, King of *Yakshas* (gnomes), is at best for us a hieroglyph which must be carefully translated; at worst, he is a charming old-world fancy. But long ago he was, for the many, an actual being as real as, say, the Eskimos to us, or, for the few, a living symbol needing no painful learning to decipher.

17   Compare Plotinus, vi, 9: "Things here are signs; they show therefore to the wiser

teachers how the supreme God is known; the instructed priest reading the sign may enter the holy place and make real the vision of the inaccessible."

18   In spite of our ill-treatment of and contempt for the "lower animals" we have always felt a disturbing sense of something strange and archetypal in their being. This is the underlying cause of the "totemism" of so-called primitive peoples, of the animal-gods of the Egyptians (so distasteful to both pagan Greek and Christian) and of the animal signs in the Zodiac.

19   These connections, vaguely intuited, give life to poetry and art. What the poet dimly senses and dares not take for more than metaphor is clearly seen by the awakened seer. It may also be added that the use of these affinities is an essential part of Kabalistic and other forms of magic, white or black.

20   Plotinus, v, 8.

21   Gita, x, verses 39-42. Compare this with the so-called Naassene document. "Accordingly they (the Egyptians) declare concerning the Essence of the Seed which is the cause of all things in the world of generation, that it is none of these things, but that it begets and makes all generated things saying, 'I become what I will and am what I am.' Therefore that which moves all is unmoved; for It remains what it is, making all things, and becoming no one of the things produced" (Mead's translation). Also compare the seed principles (*logoi spermatikoi*) of the Stoic philosophers.

22   This Cosmic Harmony, known to Pythagoreans as the music of the spheres, was in the Vedic tradition termed *rita*, the cosmic order in which all the gods exist. Those who find in the Vedas mere chaotic polytheism and those who find incipient monotheism are alike mistaken. Unity indeed there was, but it was not the unity of a personal being but of Divine impersonal Cosmic Order within *Indra*, *Varuṇa* and *Agni*, the whole pantheon of Gods, all shone and had their being.

23   Strictly speaking, between the Great Atman and the Parabrahman are the unmanifested Two. For convenience they are here included in the Supreme Unmanifested One.

24   *Shanti* to *Ishopanishad*.

Chapter Eleven

The Yoga of the Vision of the Cosmic Form

With the opening of the eleventh chapter we find the disciple on the brink of a tremendous experience, one so great that many have thought it to be the final Goal beyond which nothing remains. If that were so the Gita would have ended with this chapter; nevertheless, one who has seen this Vision has attained to the third stage, called by the Buddhist *Anagamin*,[1] from which but one last stage remains to tread.

The three great Secrets have been learnt so far, at least as far as buddhi-aided mind can grasp them. First, the great Secret of the transcendental Atman, the source of all that is and yet Itself unmoved forever. The universe of finite beings streams forth under the gaze of that unchanging One, coming and going in never-ending change; while between both, the link between the two, stands the Imperishable Greatness,[2] the Spiritual Cosmos, changeless in change, changing in changelessness.

Verses 1, 2

The dawn has come, the shades of night have vanished; in a short while the Sun will rise. Eager for yet more Light, the disciple stands straining his eyes towards the East, aspiring to that Teacher in the heart who is, Himself, the Soul of all the world. Not knowing of the terror that the Vision holds for all that yet remains of self, the disciple longs to look upon that Face which nothing that is mortal may behold.

Verse 4

"If Thou thinkest that by me it can be seen, Lord of the Cosmic Yoga, then show me Thine imperishable Self."

Verse 8

No fleshly eye can see that Sovereign Form. Only the Atman's never-closing Eye can see the Atman's self. But, for the disciples "who have made the thought in them a stranger to the world-illusion,"[3] who can pass through themselves into the Life beyond, that Divine Eye is now available and flashes into dazzling, all-revealing vision.

Verse 12

A splendor bursts upon their gaze "as though ten thousand suns were blazing in the sky," and in that spiritual Light, which, though so brilliant, dazzles not the Eye, they see the myriad Powers of the Great Atman. There in the body of that boundless Being are all the

Verse 13

living Powers that human beings have worshipped as Gods, not as if standing side by side in space, but each a facet mirroring the Whole, so interfused in being, each with each, that those who see know not indeed whether it is one Being that they see or many Powers.[4]

All who have seen the Vision, for to this day, as in times past, it dawns upon the gaze of all who tread the Path, know the astonishment, the rapture mixed with terror, that fills the soul as the Great Atman flashes into view.

Dead to all worldly things, standing outside themselves, the disciples see the great Expanse all blue with quivering supernal Light like lightnings massed in some world-ending cataclysm, the storm-tossed Ocean, glittering with souls, dizzily spinning in the Vortex Whirl, the terror of the Sound, throbbing in awful power through the vast Space like some great engine pulsing forth the Cosmic tides to ebb and flow throughout the Universe, and yet beyond the storm the changeless Peace, massively shining in a bliss beyond all words.

All this they see and more that none can tell, with a vividness past all mere human seeing; yet all are symbols cast on the background of the Fathomless, wherein is neither Sound, nor Space, nor Sea, nor Vortex Whirl, nor any form at all.[5]

Filled with great wonder the disciples see and in their souls well up the mystic Knowledge which burst forth from their lips in an ecstatic hymn.

Within that boundless Form they see the Gods, Brahma, the *Verse 15* great creative Power, and archetypes of all things here on earth. They see the upward Path, the contemplative Rishis, also the Serpent's Way spiraling downwards in divinely urged desire.[6] Mouths, all-consuming, eyes of the infinite, all-seeing vision, arms wielding *Verses 16, 17* all things, bellies containing all; the Mace of time's all-dominating power, the shining Discus of its ever-circling flight, the Crown of sovereignty, all these are seen in a great blaze of boundless, world-consuming Light.

Perishing not throughout creation's ages, this Being stands forever as the Treasure-House in which are stored the jewels of the *Verse 18* Cosmos. As Cosmic Order, It maintains eternal Dharma, the Principle by which all things are linked to all in faultless harmony:

> *It seeth everywhere and marketh all:*
> *Do right—it recompenseth! Do one wrong—*
> *The equal retribution must be made,*
> *Though Dharma tarry long.*[7]

This is the immemorial Heavenly Man, the *Adam Kadmon* of *Verse 19* the Kabalistic wisdom; His eyes, the Sun and Moon, are life and form[8]; His mouth, a burning Fire, consumes the worlds, life feeding on itself in ceaseless sacrifice.

Verse 20 The consciousness that streams through three great Halls, the waking, "dreaming," and the "deep-sleep" states,[9] is agitated in its ceaseless ebb and flow by the immortal "Fourth," the Flame which all may see but none can touch.

Verse 21 The *Maharshis* and the *Siddhas*, mighty Teachers of the past, exist inscrutably within that radiant Being. Christ, Krishna, Buddha, all are there, and he who worships one draws near to them all.

Verse 24 Spanning the Void, leaping from earth to heaven, gleams the great Rainbow Bridge whose substance is composed of all the Gods. Upwards and downwards flash the waves of Light, weaving the many-colored garment of the One. Here are the calm *Adityas*, shining in their golden Light, and there the stormy *Maruts*,[10] thrusting downwards with their flame-tipped spears.

Verse 25 But there is terror in the Vision too, for in that Light all forms are seen to pass. Only the Divine can live in the Divine: all that is human dies upon the threshold. All that in us which fears the so-called cruelty of nature, which trembles at the ruthless ocean waves, all that which clings to form and personality, sees doom approaching it on flaming wings.

As in an earthquake when human beings are filled with panic terror, not so much by the actual physical dangers as by the feeling that the solid earth, unconscious symbol of stability, is rocking beneath their feet, so in this Vision, self is seized by terror, seeing its old familiar landmarks vanish in the Void. Nowhere can self find any standing-place; all is dissolved into an ever-changing fiery flux.

Verse 26 The hundred sons of Dhritarashtra who are the facets of the lower self, Bhishma and Drona, faith and old tradition, Karna, the mighty warrior, nobly clinging to ideals but finding them in matter, all these are swallowed up in the great teeth of never-resting Time. These selves of ours, to which we cling so fiercely, are streams of psychic states linked each to each by changeless causal law; and all *Verse 28* these streams wind through the fields of Time like rivers flowing swiftly to the sea.[11]

No forms are permanent; all come and go according to their *Verse 29* karma. Even the worlds, circling around the sun, are but as moths which flutter round the lamp; their age-old rocks and "everlasting hills" melt into nothing like the down on the moth's wings. Nothing remains but karma's subtle streams, invisible to human sight, yet stronger than fine steel, linking each pattern of the universe to all that went before.

Terror unutterable fills all self in us as we behold this world-devouring Fire. The image of a human-like, extra-cosmic God, Creator of the worlds, is seen to be a dream of our weak hearts, a dream that serves to hide from human eyes the awful depths of Being's shoreless sea. "This world order, the same for all beings, neither any of the Gods hath made, nor any man; but it was always, is and shall be ever-living Fire, kindled in measure and quenched in measure."[12]

If one of unfirm heart should see this Vision such a one would *Verse 31* recoil within the self, not daring further question of the Infinite; but the strong soul of the well-tried disciple, not rooted in the self but in the buddhi, goes out in aspiration for yet deeper knowledge, seeking the One beyond these flaming ramparts. What is this ever-flowing Emanation, this Cosmic Fire that beats in flaming waves upon the heart?

And with the aspiration comes the answer; a Voice is heard *Verse 32* where there is none to speak; letters of Light float on the waves of Fire. A sudden insight comes and the disciple knows that what is seen is the great flux of Time,[13] Time that is death to all things save the Soul. "Thus at the roaring loom of Time I ply, and weave for God the garment thou seest Him by."[14] All forms are seen to come and go, over-mastered by the cyclic waves of Time, but this insight brings no tragic sense of loss such as inspired Villon's *Where are the Snows of Yester Year?* Rather, there comes a sense of great deliverance, a sense of standing on the Eternal Rock around which the surging waves forever beat in vain. As from a mountain height the travelers see the road winding on towards their destination, so, from this vantage-point of insight, the disciples see a Path and know for certain that the obstacles will pass.

From the Goal issues forth the Path; to It the Path returns; both are within the Soul. Coming and going, bondage and liberation, all are illusions which the light of jñana dispels. Forever shines the Goal, shining in golden glory; seen from another angle It itself becomes the Path. The Goal, the Path and one who treads that Path are all the same; nothing is there anywhere except the One Being that, breathless, breathes eternally within Itself.

It is impossible to state in words this wondrous insight. All things remain the same yet all are changed. Time flashes bodily into Eternity; the streaming Flux itself is the Eternal, which, though It moves unceasingly, moves not at all.

This is the insight which makes the disciple what the Buddhists termed an Anagamin, one who comes to birth no more. Life and death have vanished in the Light of the Eternal, and though a portion of the Path remains to tread, it will be trodden with the knowledge that by Krishna Himself "already are the foes all overcome" and

that no separate treader of the Path remains.

Crowned with the diadem of insight,[15] the initiated disciple gazes into the awful Mystery of Light in rapt adoration of the Eternal, and the mystic Knowledge that now floods the soul pours forth in yet a further hymn of ecstasy.

These Hymns, parallels to which may be seen in the *Poemandres* and *Secret Sermon on the Mount* of the Hermetic books, are the natural outflow of the mind seeking to give expression in mental terms to the great Knowledge that now streams upon it, the ferment that takes place as all the lower undergoes alchemical transmutation at the touch of the Higher. The difference between the two Hymns should be carefully noted. The first expresses chiefly awestruck terror as the disciples see their universe dissolve into the Cosmic Fire; the second gives expression to the rapture with which they see, within the waves of flame, the shining spiritual Cosmos.

Gazing within, the disciples see that all is ruled by living spiritual Law. Two mighty tidal urges rule the world and both of them are living spiritual Powers. One is the movement of the *Rakshasas*, fleeing as in fear to all the quarters of the Universe. This is the great outgoing Creative Breath by which not only is the universe spread forth in space, but all the inner life of thought and feeling flows outwards seeking whom it may devour.[16] This is the urge of self-assertion, self-expansion, survival of the fittest, "nature red in tooth and claw." Here is the inner cause of war and all the selfish life of competition, each for himself and devil take the hindmost, but here, as well, the force behind the human mind, wheeling in ever-widening circles to receding frontiers.

Verse 36

The second movement, symbolized by hosts of Siddhas, is the nivritti, Homeward-flowing Tide. By this all the rich treasures of experience, the Fruits of the World Tree, are gathered in once more to the One Life like mighty rivers flowing homewards to the sea.[17]

Here is the Mighty Atman, source of both these Tides, the Primal Man of all the ancient Mysteries, the Cosmic Treasure-House, the Realm of shining Light, Knower and Known both fused in unity.

Verses 37, 38

Glimpsed through the robes of Cosmic Ideation stands the unmoved Eternal, poised aloof, Being, Non-being, *That* beyond them both, the Nameless One, worshipped alone by silence of the mind.

Verse 39

The seven great Cosmic planes, here symbolized as Gods, are all within that One, and though the disciples seek to pour forth all their soul in utter reverence, they know not where to turn, for now they see that even the very earth on which they stand is holy, and that

Verse 40

around, above, below, within, without, everywhere is the One and only One, containing all, from lowest earthy clod to that unmanifest, transcendent Self whose Light forever shines beyond the worlds.[18]

No longer can they think that He whom they have worshipped,

Verses 41–43

the Teacher in their hearts, Friend of their nights and days, is any personal being, human or superhuman or God. Rather they see that it was the Light of the Eternal which, shining through loved but yet symbolic eyes, has led them on the Path and is both Path and Goal.

But yet, while they are human, there must still be Forms for

Verse 44

them. They cannot bear for long the blaze of Light that floods upon them, shattering all their being. No human mind and body can for long endure upon the summits of eternal snow-clad peaks. They must return once more to lower levels, the dazzling Light be veiled in the familiar forms of Father, Lover, Friend; for still the fourth stage of the Path remains to tread and, while they need a body, they must see the Light in human form.[19]

Therefore they see once more the Form of their loved Teacher in their own hearts and in the hearts of all, though, as reminder of the glorious Vision, the Form is Crowned and bears the Mace and Discus, symbols of the Lord of Time. They know that He who sits within their hearts is throned beyond all Time and that, however the fight may press upon them, their final victory is sure, since He who rules their hearts rules all the worlds. *Verse 46*

Thus ends the Vision seen by union with the Self (*atma yogat*), ends as a vision though its Knowledge will remain forever in the heart of the disciples. Henceforth that inner Knowledge must be the master-light of all their seeing, must make "the noisy years seem moments in the being of the eternal Silence." Never may they forget what they have seen; always must they realize "the voidness of the seeming full, the fullness of the seeming void."[20] For them, not as a poet's intuition, but in sheer fact, will it be true that *Verse 47*

> . . . *in a season of calm weather*
> *Though inland far we be,*
> *Our souls have sight of that immortal sea*
> *Which brought us hither;*
> *Can in a moment travel thither—*
> *And see the children sport upon the shore,*
> *And hear its mighty waters rolling evermore.*[21]

Not Gods, the great impersonal waves of Light, nor the separate selves of mind and body, "none but thyself," the immortal soul, has ever or will ever see this Cosmic Form. No mystic rites, no study of philosophy, no harsh austerities, no alms or offerings, can show It, *Verses 47-54* for all these are of the mind alone. Only the power of love, the Soul's own power, love that forever seeks to give itself, straining towards Eternity, can bring about the union of the self with the One Self by which alone the Cosmic Form is seen and ultimately entered. There-

Verse 55   fore the chapter ends with a reiteration of the Path, a purely spiritual Path, one quite distinct from all the rites and outer pieties that most people term religion:

"Giving the self in love to Me, with Me as Goal, doing all actions for Me (the One Life in all), devoid of all attachment to the forms, free from hostility to any being, one comes to Me, O Arjuna."[22]

Notes

1   *Anagamin* literally means one who does not come again (to birth). The common view is that the Anagamin attains Nirvana direct from some higher world after death. Actually the meaning is that having attained to the *Alaya Vijñana* (the Mahat Atman) the disciple is the one with all and thinks no more "I die or I am born."

2   The Mahat Atman.

3   Hermes, xiii, 1.

4   Compare Plotinus, v, 8: "He who is the one God and all the gods, where each is all, blending into a unity, distinct in powers but all one god in virtue of that one divine power of many facets."

5   This is true not only of these visions but of our ordinary experience as well. All perception is symbolic through and through. When we see a wooden door we see a symbol of a moment of the Brahman.

6   See verse 5 in the Vedic Creation Hymn given in Appendix F.

7   *The Light of Asia.*

8   See Prashna Upanishad, i, 5.

9   See Appendix C.

10   See Glossary for both *Adityas* and *Maruts*.

11   Compare the experience of the Buddha on the night of attaining the *Sambodhi*:
     "With the Divine eye which far surpasses human vision I saw beings in the act
     of passing hence and of reappearing elsewhere—beings high and low, fair or foul
     to view, in bliss or woe; I saw them all faring according to their pasts" (*Majjhima
     Nikaya*, sutta iv).

     Compare also the Buddhist term for the individual self, *santana*, meaning
     "continuous flow."

12   Heracleitus, Fragment D 30.

13   The Time here spoken of is not the same as the abstract time of mathematical
     physics. The latter is a mere mode of measurement of certain relations between
     phenomena, and no very clear reason seems to be given for the fundamental
     character of real time—namely, its irreversibility. The Time here referred to
     is the great prime mover of the universe. It has its root in Consciousness, of
     which, indeed, it is the active aspect. The mental construct of a four-dimen-
     sional Space-Time continuum seems to have little relevance here. To gain an
     understanding of real Time the best starting-point is the power of selective
     attention found in consciousness.

14   Goethe.

15   Note that the disciple is now (verse 35) referred to as "the Crowned one." This
     is a reference to the Crown of Knowledge given to the Initiate. A parallel is to
     be seen in the *Atef* crown worn by *Osiris* in the Egyptian Mystic Ritual and,
     according to Marsham Adams, placed on the head of the Initiate after he has
     passed through the pylons and stands before the Throne.

16   Compare the *Pauranik* accounts of creation in which Brahma first created Rak-
     shasas who promptly attempted to devour him. That is to say, the outgoing
     forces would, if left to themselves, dissipate the universe at once. The technical
     term for this outgoing is Pravritti.

17   For further discussion of these two movements see chapter 16.

18   Compare the magnificent hymn of Hermes Trismegistus:

     "Whither, again, am I to turn my eyes to sing

     Thy praise: above, below, within, without?

     There is no way, no place is there about Thee,

     nor any other thing of things that are.

     All are in Thee; all are from Thee,

O Thou who givest all and takest naught,

For Thou . . . art all and there is nothing else which Thou art not."

Hermetic Corpus, v, 10.

19 The *chaturbhuja* form of verse 46 should be translated "four-limbed" (*i.e.* two
arms and two legs) and not, as usually done, "four-armed." The word *bhuja*
means limb as well as arm, and verses 49 and 51 clearly show that the form
in question was a *human* one, four-limbed in contrast to the thousand arms
and legs of the symbolic vision. The Vishnu form, no doubt, has four arms; but
in the earliest texts, such as the Mahabharata, Krishna has always the normal
human two. For this interpretation I am indebted to my friend Pandit Jagadish
Chandra Chatterji, Vidya Varidhi.

20 *The Voice of the Silence.*

21 Wordsworth's *Ode on the Intimations of Immortality.*

22 This verse has been described by *Shankaracharya* as giving the quintessence of
the whole Gita.

Chapter Twelve

The Yoga of Devotion

It has already been pointed out that the Vision of the Cosmic Form is not the same as the attainment of the final Goal. To interpret this or the Beatific Vision of Western mysticism as the Goal would be to ignore the whole structure of the Gita. The Vision is a vision, not the attainment, and we have seen that at its end disciples return to the lower level, the level of form, once more. Before the Goal is reached they will have to learn to live entirely in the Reality, to transmute their whole nature so that not an atom of the lower shall remain unredeemed. This subject, however, will be referred to again later. In the meanwhile we have to deal with a certain problem that has arisen out of the experience of this Vision.

The disciples have seen the great Cosmic Form, the Mighty Atman, the One Life manifesting in the world of beings, and they have been told (xi, 54) that by devotion alone can that Form be seen and entered. At the same time, they have also caught a glimpse (xi, 37) of the unchanging Unmanifest behind the Cosmic process and the doubt occurs to them whether this devotion to the manifested Form, this acting for the One Life in the hearts of all, can ever lead beyond the manifest. Doubtless, devotion to the Life of all will take them to that Life; but will it take them further? Will it not leave them there, just as devotion to the Gods strands some in the enjoyment of heavenly bliss, knowing that beyond even that Mighty Atman lies the indestructible Unmanifest, should not they rather resolutely turn their back on all manifestation, abstract themselves from every trace of form and bend all energies on one supreme attempt to bring about the flight of the alone to the Alone? Are these two separate Paths and, if so, which is better?

To this question Krishna replies that both the one who is devoted to Himself as the One Life in all, and the one who worships the Ineffable, Unthinkable, Eternal attain to Him, but that the latter is a Path of surpassing difficulty for those who are embodied—that is to say, for those who have the slightest trace of self-identification with their bodies.

To understand this answer we must remember that in chapter three, verse 4 *et seq.*, the attempt to win through to the Unmanifested Goal by a process of pure abstraction and inactivity, the method of some Sankhyas, has been condemned as utterly impracticable. Certainly it is not by turning one's back on all activity and refusing any commerce with form of any kind that the Unmanifest is reached, for such a process is impossible. It may be possible to toy in thought with such a path but in reality it is scarcely a path at all. The Homeward Path must be a gathering-up of all the cosmic Fruits, not a retreat, negating all experience, as if the cosmic process were a cosmic blunder which never should have been.

There is, in fact, but one Path, and if we compare verse 4 of the present chapter, which defines the character of him who worships the Unmanifest, with verses 13-19, which give the character of one who is devoted to the Life in all, we see that they are, in effect, the same.

Not by attempting an impossible rejection of the world of

sense-experience but by "restraining and subduing the senses," not by trying to turn their back on all forms but by "regarding all forms with an equal vision," not by achieving a stony indifference to the joys and sorrows of the world but by being "devoted to the welfare of all beings," do the true worshippers of the Unmanifest Eternal attain their Goal.

Verse 4

If, then, both Paths are essentially the same, wherein lies the special difficulty of the Path of the Unmanifested? It lies in the fact that the worshipper of the Unmanifested has nothing to fasten the mind to, for that One is beyond all objects of sense, beyond even all concepts of the mind. The point has been excellently stated by Plotinus: "The main difficulty is that awareness of the Principle [*i.e.* the One] comes neither by knowing nor by the pure Intellection [*noesis*] that discovers the Intellectual Beings [the Spiritual Powers seen in the Vision], but by a presence overpassing all knowledge.... Our way takes us beyond all knowing; there may be no wandering from Unity; knowing and knowable must all be left aside; every object of thought, even the highest, we must pass by, for all that is good is later than This and derives from This as from the sun all the light of day."[1]

Verse 5

Even if the disciples think of It as God or as the Eternal Mind they still, as Plotinus says, "think of It too meanly," for "God" connotes ideas of personality and the Eternal Mind Ideation. Into that Silence how shall the disciples soar, what steps are there to help them on their way? Not only is the One beyond all thought but also the great wings which bear the soul upon its upward flight, the wings of love, beat vainly in that Void and the bruised soul falls back in desolation, losing the forms but finding not the One beyond all forms.

Fatally easy is it for the soul to sink back on the earth, loveless and sterile. Appearances may be preserved but yet the heart within is eaten all away and the disciple treads the *false* unmanifested Path, rejecting forms as maya, fearing even to do an act of mercy lest some bondage for his soul be the result. "To perish doomed is one, who out of fear of Mara refrains from helping another lest he should act for Self."[2]

Therefore Sri Krishna recommends the other Path, the manifested Path through the One Life. The One is the same One, the Goal the same, but on this path that One is manifest within the hearts of all. This is the way that Plato, too, has mentioned, rising from love of one to love of many, from love of form to love of spiritual beauty, and so by steps to That which is beyond. This also is the Path the *Gopis* showed, first loving Krishna in His sensuous beauty, then feeling Him in their own hearts and, lastly, with all selfhood gone, rising to union with His Eternal Being.[3]

Verses 6, 7

On this Path the disciples do all actions not for themselves but for the one loved figure. For love they act, for love they speak and think, and so by love they rise swiftly to the Goal. Where there is love no sacrifice can be too great to be performed with joy. Even animals will give their lives for love and countless men have gladly gone to hideous deaths, counting their pains a privilege that so the loved one, humanity, or God, be served thereby.

> *In this is seen why there is hope for man*
> *And where we hold the wheel of life at will.*[4]

Here is the power lying in all hearts by which to scale the peaks of the Eternal. But, as its place within the Gita shows, there must first be some knowledge, some desire to tread the inward Path and reach the Goal. Without this knowledge, faith, or aspiration there is no urge to soar beyond the body, and love itself, dragged in the dust by self, turns to desire and works ruin.

Nevertheless, if guided by knowledge and aspiration, there is no force which will so powerfully bear the soul upwards as that of love. This can be seen by its power to transmute and render beautiful, if only temporarily, the lives of even quite ordinary people. A selflessness which may take the yogi many years of effort to attain along the path of conscious mind-control and which, even then, may be a hothouse plant, constantly menaced by the cold wind which comes from fancying oneself a being apart from others, may grow quite healthily like a great forest tree in the rich soil of love.

It is only the absence of knowledge and aspiration that makes the transmuting power of love so short-lived as a rule. Love which has power, when guided by true knowledge, to carry even the body upwards with it in its soaring flight, is blinded and its wings are clipped by the dark ignorance that sees no reality but that of outward things. Thus it falls down upon the earth, only to share the fate of all things earthly:

> *And or ever the garden's last petals are shed,*
> *In the lips that had whispered, the hearts that had*
> *lightened, Love lies dead.*

Therefore Sri Krishna urges disciples to place their mind, united   *Verse 8*
with the buddhi, in Him and thus to live in the immortal Life that is in all.[5] This "Him" will be at first the human form that draws in love

the heart of the disciple. That Form, idealized by love and worship, will be a symbol of the Eternal Mind and will transform into Itself the human soul. Once more to quote Plotinus: "We shape ourselves into the *Nous* (Eternal Mind); we make over our soul in trust to Nous and set it firmly in That; then what That sees, the soul will waken to see; it is through Nous that we have vision of the Unity." Thus, *if the eye of knowledge has been opened*, the Form will seat itself within the heart and be a window through which the soul takes flight into the blue.

Verse 9   The power to center all the being in the Eternal Mind will not, however, be attained at once. *Abhyasa*, or constant practice, is required. The process is described in Shvetashvatara Upanishad with the aid of a metaphor taken from the production of fire by the friction of two sticks: "Having made one's body (the lower self) the lower fire-stick and the Pranava (the symbol of the Light of consciousness) the upper, by the friction of continued practice (*abhyasa*) of meditation, one should see the God hidden within."

In plain words, the practice is one of constant withdrawal from the desire-nature and constant self-identification with the higher levels. This effort is twofold. In the first place there must be the effort to churn out the fire, as it were, the attempt to isolate by analytic meditation on experience the watching Self from the participating self. In the second place there must be the effort of the will to identify one's being with the former and from there to rule the latter. If this twofold practice is persisted in it will inevitably culminate in the ability to center oneself permanently in the Eternal Mind.

Verse 10   If, however, the disciples find themselves as yet unable to perform this meditative practice, they should devote themselves to Krishna's service. All life, whether in human beings, in animals, or plants, is a manifestation of the One Eternal Life which in a thousand forms seeks to express Itself in mastery of matter. Behind the struggling forms, behind the petty human personalities surge the great tides of Life, beating in tireless power against the narrow confines of the forms. Let the disciples live in such a way that all their acts will help that Life to manifest. Let them "help Nature and work on with her," striving incessantly with all the obstacles that thwart the beauty, bliss, and power that are, even now, within the hearts of all. And thus, forgetful of themselves, a time will come when they will find themselves one with that Life to which their hearts are given. Performing all their deeds for Krishna's sake, they will attain the Goal.

If even selfless, love-inspired action is out of reach yet one way *Verse 11* still remains: they may perform actions for themselves but renounce the fruits. Unable to attain the level of action for the welfare of all beings, let them act for themselves but from a sense of duty. Let them do what is right, resigning all the fruits into the hands of that disposing Power which some call God, others, Eternal Law.[6] In order to achieve this duty-prompted action they must take refuge in the Yoga of Krishna, the *Sovereign Yoga* in which the Eternal Light unites with forms and yet is never separate. In practice this means that they must be refuged in the buddhi, the faculty which gives decisive knowledge. In still earlier stages, when the buddhi is as yet out of reach, it means that they must unite the lower mind with "Sañjaya," the voice of the higher speaking as conscience, and make that voice the guide and ruler of all his acts. The voice of conscience is, as we have seen before, in some sense a "reflection" of the buddhi, the chief difference being that, while the buddhi sees the truth as an all-embracing whole, the conscience, as befits a principle on the hither side of individuation, sees but a single point, the point needed at the moment, and speaks with certainty concerning that alone.

The buddhi is a faculty that all possess though few make use of it. It is the Light that shines between the eyes, the Voice that speaks in silence in the heart. To see that Light the fleshly eyes must close, to hear that Voice the fleshly ears be deaf. Only when, for a time at least, the clamor of desire is stilled can that internal monitor be heard which is the Voice of Krishna. Guided by that Voice the disciples will see before them the clear path of duty and, if they tread it, find themselves beyond the conflict of the heart's desires.

Verse 12   This is the easiest path. To clamor for an easier one than this is to cry, child-like, for the moon, to ask for what has never been nor, indeed, ever shall be. Renunciation of the fruits of action to follow duty's path has thus been praised as best because it is the easiest of all paths, and from its practice all the rest will follow. Renouncing fruits, the heart will fill with peace and in that peace the yoga of practice will be possible. From practice follows knowledge of the Truth and that unchanging state of meditation in which, waking or sleeping, in action or repose, the inner Self will live in the Eternal.

But some will ask why, at this stage, is all this talk of inability, why this insistence on the easier path? Surely the earlier stages have been long ago accomplished; has not the glorious Cosmic Form been seen? Such a question shows a lack of knowledge about the way of climbing on this Path. Great heights, indeed, have been attained, but not by the whole being. Climbers on a mountain face first reach for a hand-hold on the rock above and, that having been securely grasped, pull with great effort their whole bodies upwards. Just so the climber of the Path aspires with all that which is best within, attains a hand-hold on the heights of vision, but then must pull the lower nature upwards till the whole being stands firmly on the summit.

Plotinus too asks the question how it is that the soul cannot keep the level it has achieved, and answers that it is "because it has not yet escaped wholly: but there will be the time of vision unbroken, the self hindered no longer by any hindrance of body. Not that those hindrances beset that in us which has veritably seen; it is the other phase of the soul that suffers, and that only when we withdraw from vision and take to knowing by proof, by evidence, by the reasoning processes of the mental habit."

Hence all the recapitulation in the teaching. That which was done for part must now be done again for the whole being that all may be regenerate, so that the flashing light of vision may change into the steady blazing of the sun shining beyond the darkness.

Sri Krishna now goes on to set forth, in verse thirteen to the end, the characteristics of the follower of the path of bhakti. It has already been stated that these characteristics are the same in sub-stance as those of the follower of the *true* path of the Unmanifested. Too often is the path of bhakti mistaken for an abandonment to a frothy, uncontrolled emotionalism. What the real path of bhakti is may be seen from a study of these verses. The qualities enumerated must be built into his character by the disciples.

Bearing ill-will to none, they look on all with love and great compassion, for they know that He who smiles as friend and He who frowns as foe are One, the One great Life struggling to mani-fest through countless passing forms.   *Verse 13*

Knowing that all joy or grief that comes is but the fruit of their   *Verse 14* actions in the past, they are content and strive for nothing finite but, with the mind clinging through buddhi to the One Eternal, they stand like a rock amidst the surge of Time. To none are they a source of grief nor do they let themselves feel grief at other's words or deeds, for they know well that pain inevitably returns to those who caused it and they care not to be the cause of pain, even the unwitting cause, to those who are in fact his own true Self. Those who feel grief at others' words are like a wall reflecting back that grief upon the causer, but the ones who put aside all fear, elation, or impatient anger make themselves like the sea, which buries all in peace. By this means the sum of pain and hatred in the world is actually decreased, and thus we understand the meaning of the Buddha's words: "Not by hatred but by love does hatred end; this the eternal Law."

Seeking nothing for themselves, renouncing every undertaking, that is to say, renouncing the fruits of all their actions, for, as will be shown later,[7] the renunciation of action itself is neither fitting nor even possible for those who are embodied. Acting solely for the One who is in all, their acts are expert, passionless, and pure. Note the word "expert" (*daksha*). There are some who in the name of devotion give up their grip on life and muddle through all things, making spirituality an excuse for unpracticalness. True disciples are no mere ecstatic dreamers, so dazzled by the white eternal Light that they see not the way among the shadows here. Rather, since "yoga is skill in action," they show by the fact that they perform all actions better than others, that this Path leads to mastery of the world, not to a weak withdrawal.

If skill in action is one of the definitions of yoga, balance of mind (*samatva*) is the other.[8] The ordinary person is ruled by the pairs of opposites, cold and heat, pleasure and pain, friendship and enmity, attraction and repulsion. Then life is one perpetual oscillation between these pairs, but yogi's are those whose minds are balanced beyond their sway and whose lives are guided, not by the blind forces of attraction and repulsion, but by one deep-seated urge to give themselves in service of the one great Life of all.

Even ideas of good and evil, as those words are understood, no longer sway their acts. Those two great words, which all invoke so freely to justify their acts or to condemn their enemies, are, at best, constructions of the mind, and now rooted in realms beyond, they thus transcend both and know but one great Law, to help the play of the Eternal Life as It shines forth or hides Itself in forms.

Whether these actions bring praise or blame, whether they harmonize with ideas of moral law or, as may sometimes happen, they depart entirely from what most think right, is a matter of indifference to him. This may seem dangerous doctrine but it is the truth. What most call ethics is an affair of actions and their consequences and, as we have seen, the disciples have renounced all concern with personal consequences. They are not lawless for they know one all-transcending Law—obedience to the voice of the great Teacher in the heart.[9] That Soundless Voice, speaking within their hearts, drowns for them all the clamorous judgments of the world. Listening ever to the Voice of that inner Lord, they pursue their way "unperturbed as the earth is unperturbed, firm as a pillar, clear as a waveless lake."[10]

Verse 19

Like the pure mountain air that blows among the pines, fertilizing all and yet attached to none, the disciple moves about, amidst the human throng. Whether he lives in crowded cities or on lonely

Verse 19

mountain peaks he is a Homeless One, for though he may fulfill all social duties, yet neither family, nor caste, nor race holds him in bondage. In the words of Hermes, he is "one who has struck his tent," and though he may not wear the outer garb of a sannyasi, yet of no place in all the world does he feel "this is mine; here I belong."

Verse 20   Such is the path of bhakti. Those who follow it, not for the sake of their own soul's salvation, but as the service[11] of that one Eternal Wisdom which gives true Life to all who drink its waters, they, the beloved disciples, shine like lights amidst the darkness, servants of the Eternal Krishna, crest-jewels of the world.

Notes

1   Plotinus, vi, 9, 3; the parts in brackets are for clearness.

2   *The Voice of the Silence.* Thus in the original edition but "Self" should no doubt read "self."

3   For substantiation of this view, one which runs counter to some accepted ideas, read Srimad Bhagavada, x, 29, v. 12; x, 47, v. 9 (and many others); x, 82, v. 48, which clearly set forth these three stages. For the middle stage many references might be given.

4   *The Light of Asia.* The original reads "thee," not "this."

5   It must be remembered that love is rooted in the buddhi. See footnote 10 in chapter 8, p. 117.

6   The difference between the former type of action and this is that, while the former disciple acts with the thought of service of the Life in all the latter acts without any such definite thought but does what seems to be right for the self. The former feeds the hungry out of love, the latter because he knows that it is right to be charitable.

7.   See Gita, xviii, verse 2 and 11, where the subject is treated in full.

8.   Gita, ii, verse 48.

9   This should not be taken as supporting ordinary amorality: these words apply *solely* to the disciple who is selfless enough always to hear the Voice of the Teacher, balanced enough always to discriminate it from other voices, and devoted enough always to obey its commands. Till then, no merely intellectual insight into their limitations should justify a man in disregarding the accepted moral laws. The fate that overtook Nietzsche stands as a solemn warning.

10   Dhammapada, 95.

11   The word *paryupasana* has the primary meaning of "to attend upon, to serve." The usual rendering as "worship" is a secondary one, and obscures the meaning here.

❋

Chapter Thirteen

The Yoga of the Distinction between the Field and the Knower of the Field

We have now reached the beginning of the third section of the Gita. The Path is the path to mastery of the world, and now that the disciple has a firm hand-hold on the heights of vision, it is necessary that his intellect, suffused by the Spiritual Light, should have a clear grasp of the principles of the cosmos in which he is to work. Hence the effect of slight anticlimax that some readers of the Gita find in these chapters.

The first thing that has to be understood is the division between consciousness and the objects which that consciousness observes. If we examine our experience we find that it is composed of a number of concrete forms all lit up by the light of consciousness.[1] This is the distinction between the Field—that is, the field of consciousness—and the Knower of the Field, the clear light of awareness itself. Reflection will show that the physical body which the ignorant suppose to be the self is but the focus in which the forms or data of our sense-experience are, as it were, collected.

But the analysis of experience does not stop here. If the disciple abstracts the light of the witnessing consciousness from all the witnessed forms—the forms of sense, of feeling, or of thought—he will perceive at once that the light is not something

164

which is different in different beings, but something like the sun-shine which is the same whether illuminating the blue sea or the red earth. That light of consciousness, though associated with an individual point of view, is something which can only be described as all-pervading, something which, however different may be the Fields which are illumined, is the same in an ant as in a person, the same even, though science may not yet be ready to admit it, in a piece of rock as in a living being.

The disciple is now in a position to understand why Sri Krishna *Verse 2* says that He, the Atman, the all-seeing Consciousness, is the Knower of the Field in all Fields. If he will follow up this distinction between the Field and its Knower in his own heart, the disciple will find himself on the highroad to an understanding of the Cosmos; he will have a clue to guide him through the mazes of this world.

The beginning lies here in the midst of our sense-experience, for it must be emphasized that the Gita's teaching is not concerned with wondrous far-off things but with what lies right here to hand, would we but open our eyes and see. Again it must be said: "What is There is here; what is not here is nowhere." So clearly shines this truth that he who has seen it once cannot understand why he was blind so long. He has lit his lamp and truly the effect is like a sudden shining of a light in a dark place. "Within you is the Light of all the world": so all the ancient Seers have always said and now their words blaze with a vivid light in which all false belief and superstitions fade like candles in the sun. "Knowledge as to the Field and the Knower of the Field, that in my opinion is Wisdom."

The Field, or content of experience, has been analyzed by the *Verse 5* ancient Teachers into twenty-four *tattvas*, or principles. First come the five great elements, known symbolically as earth, water, fire, air, and space.[2] Connected with these are the five contents of our sense-experience, smell, taste, visual form, touch, and sound. Next come the eleven senses, five the faculties by which we gain knowledge of the external world, five by which we react upon that world, and the eleventh the (lower) mind, the mind which functions as the common inner sense. Then comes the ego center (*ahankara*), elsewhere called higher manas, the buddhi (here, as often taken with mahat, being the intuition which gives knowledge of that Cosmic Ideation), and lastly Mula-prakriti itself, the great unmanifested matrix of all forms.[3]

These principles constitute the frame or skeleton on which the universe of forms is built. It should be noted that only the lowest of them are what we call material and that the other levels are what we would class as mental. Their modifications are known to us in the form of desire, aversion, pleasure, pain, thought, feeling and so forth, but nevertheless all of them are objective to the light of consciousness and make up in totality the content of experience, for it is to be observed that the feelings and thoughts, no less than the sensations, are analyzable into a content-form and the awareness of it.

Verse 6

There follows a list of qualities which are said to constitute Wisdom in the sense, that is, that they are the qualities which lead up to Wisdom. They are all calculated to cause a perception that all these objective forms are not the Self, or, in the Buddha's words, "this is not mine, I am not this, this is not my Self."[4] Thus is brought about a cessation of that process of projection by which the Light is bound within the passing forms, and the eternal Wisdom is attained, the knowledge of the ever-changeless Self, witnessing all and yet attached to none.

Verses 7-10

Verse 11

For that eternal Self is what is to be known, "which being known *Verse 12* immortality is enjoyed." It is the great transcendental Atman[5] which, being unmanifest, is neither being nor non-being. It is the one Subject of all objectivity whatever, everywhere having hands and feet, everywhere ears and eyes. When it is said that "It standeth enveloping all" it is but a plain description of that wondrous *seeing* Light, *Verse 13* that great "awaring" holding in Its bosom each grain of dust in all the countless worlds.

One of the greatest difficulties in understanding such books as the Gita lies in the fact that we have got used to reading them in a special "holy" mood, thus placing them out of relation with the actual world of life. But this is fatal; we must learn to see that what is being described is what is here around us and can be seen just now even though long ages may elapse before we plumb the shoreless Sea of Light.

The Ancient Wisdom is inscribed in glowing letters in the *akasha* of the heart: let the disciples plunge within and read its message for themselves. They will find that the deathless Consciousness within, though separate from all the organs of sense, yet shines with their power. In fact the apparent power of the eye to see depends entirely *Verse 14* on the power of vision inherent in that Light which sees through the eye but which the eye does not see; which hears through the ear but which the ear does not hear; which thinks through the mind but which the mind does not think.

"It is the unseen Seer, the unheard Hearer, the unthought Thinker. Other than It there is no Seer, no hearer, no thinker. It is the Self, the Inner Ruler, the Deathless."[6]

It supports everything in the sense that It holds all forms within Its embrace, and were Its support withdrawn, even for a moment, all things would collapse at once. Witnessing all, It is attached to nothing, so that experiences of pleasure and pain are as one to Its impartial gaze. Although It is the enjoyer of all qualities It itself is free from quality (*nirguna*). In fact, this qualitylessness or "neutrality" is one of the first aspects to be noticed.

Verse 15
Though the Light shines within the our hearts and it is in the heart that It is first perceived, it would be a mistake to suppose that It is only there and not in the outer world as well.[7] The heart is a focus through which It shines but It is equally "outside" us, for the entire content of experience floats in Its all-supporting waves:

> *"As a cloud that hides the moon, so matter veils*
> *The Face of Thought."*[8]

So subtle is It that, though all-pervading, It is unperceived by us and, though "nearer to us than breathing," there is no cosmic depth so far away but It is farther still. From Its profound abyss this universe in which we live and all the island universes in the Cosmos are seen to shrink into a starry cluster no bigger than a hand.

Its firm immovability supports the universal "changeless" laws of science and yet that firmness is a living one, and gleams with *inner* motion whence arises all the movement in the Cosmos.

Verse 16
Just as the sun, or, better still, the daylight, is one and yet is, as it were, distributed in all reflecting objects, so is the Light a perfect unbroken unity though It appears divided by self-identification with the separate forms. In speaking of It we cannot avoid the language of paradox. It has already been said that a certain "neutrality" is one of Its most characteristic features, and yet it would be entirely wrong

to think of that neutrality as something dull and featureless; rather, it is a calm and shining bliss.

Similarly, it is only too easy to misunderstand Its actionlessness which, together with the neutrality, is one of the first characteristics to become clear to the disciple. In spite of this fact, and that it is a fact no one who has experience will deny, and notwithstanding the categorical statement in verse 29 that all actions spring from the Mula-prakriti, it remains true that the creation, preservation, and destruction of the forms are rooted in the nature of the Light.

Verse 16

Words fail us here: we must plunge deeper yet within the heart and see that in that mystic inactivity, within this very being, lurks divine creative power. It gazes and the forms spring into being; gazing, It holds them fast; ceasing Its gaze, they fall back in the matrix once again. Here lies the mystery of the Will both in the macrocosm and the microcosm. The Will, even the individual will, is not the creature of mere outward forms. A Divine freedom is its very essence: the Light has an inherent power to gaze or not to gaze, also to change the level of Its gazing.[9] This cannot be described; it must be seen and known within the heart. Failure to understand this mysterious actionless activity has disastrous consequences, for it transforms the central Fount of joyful, radiant Light into a static Absolute, an eternal Futility, throned in the heart of being.

No worship of the Gods, no outer ritual, no mantras, prayerful pieties, or magic touch of saints can be a substitute for the heart's Knowledge by which alone that Wisdom can be reached. Only the clear, far-shining light of Mind can mingle with that Light, the Light of lights, and pierce beyond the Darkness to the Goal. "By the Mind is It to be gained," says the Upanishadic seers and Hermes, too: "this human Mind is God and for this cause some of human-kind are Gods and their humanity is nigh unto Divinity."

Verse 19

So far we have been studying the Field and its Knower chiefly with a view to their separation[10]; we have now to glance at the mode of their interaction. In the first place it is to be noted that, if not the Field itself, its source the Mula-prakriti is, like the Knower, the Purusha, or Shanta Atman, beginningless. These two are, as we saw in chapter eight, the two unmanifested moments of the Parabrahman.

On account of the mysterious selective gazing of the Self the Mula-prakriti manifests in a graded universe of forms and qualities. The following quotation will perhaps be of interest as showing that modern physics is feeling its way to a substantially similar view:

"The physicist's world is a spatio-temporal flux of events whose characteristics are limited to severely mathematical (i.e. *abstract, ideal, non-sensory*) properties. Upon them the mind imposes, or from them it selects (accounts differ) certain patterns which appear to possess the quality of comparative permanence. These patterns are worked up by the mind into continuing objects and become the tables and chairs of daily life. . . . Different minds with different interest, selecting different patterns, would perceive different worlds."[11]

The last sentence is of particular interest as throwing light on the nature of the different levels or *lokas*, for the hypothetical different minds of the writer have real existence as the different levels of consciousness.

Verse 20

The Mula-prakriti, then, is the root of the causally inter-linked series of spatio-temporal events, but that that series manifests as *living* sequences of sensation, feeling and thought, pleasant or painful, is due to the Light of Purusha, the witnessing consciousness.

The latter, gazing on the flux, draws out from it the patterns which on any given level are to achieve significance as objects and in so doing identifies itself with them.

Just as a spectator at a cinema experiences joy and sorrow through self-identification with the patches of light and shade that make up the pictures on the screen, so the free, blissful nature of the Self is or appears to be stained by joy and sorrow arising from the purely neutral flux. Birthless and deathless, It is born and dies with forms Itself evoked and gazed Itself into.   *Verse 21*

This union of the seeing Self with forms takes place not all at once but on five levels[12] which are enumerated here from below upwards, but which it will be more convenient to consider in their order of evolution. Beyond all levels is the Parabrahman, here styled the highest Purusha, in which seer, seen, and seeing are all merged in one. In that inconceivable Abyss a movement of limitation takes place as a result of which, abstract, unmanifested Selfhood, here termed the *One Enjoyer*, the *Great Lord*, the *Transcendental Atman*, as it were settles out and contemplates with calm aloofness the other moment of the Parabrahman appearing as the unmanifested Matrix.[13]   *Verse 22*

Gazing selectively on that Matrix, a process of self-identification with various aspects takes place, and thus we have the second level, here termed the *Supporter*, the One Life. Out of the infinite potentialities of the first level a certain number have been selected (in accordance with the *sanskaras* or karmic tendencies remaining over as seeds from the previous manifestation) to form the basis of a universal manifestation and are hence known as the Cosmic Ideation.

The third level, that of the buddhi, is not separately mentioned here. Buddhi and Mahat are often taken together and in later books they came to be completely identified. The former may be considered as the purely cognitive aspect of the latter. The difference between the two is not easy to explain; attaining the level of the buddhi, one is in touch with the Mahat.

The fourth level is here termed the *Sanctioner* or Inner Ruler. It is the level of the Higher Mind in which, out of the all-grasping, all-uniting levels of *buddhi-mahat*, the Light selects a given point of view and thus becomes the individual Self. Hence arise the countless separate individuals. The "content" of experience on this level is, though grouped with reference to an individual viewpoint, of a non-sensory nature, what some would, perhaps wrongly, term abstract. It is what the Buddhists term the *rupa loka* as opposed to the *arupa loka* of the buddhi-mahat and the *kama loka* of the fifth (and sixth) levels.

The fifth level is that of concrete sensing, feeling, and thinking. Out of the "abstract" possibilities of the fourth, the Light (the same Light, it should be noted) selects the concrete patterns which it works up into the objects of sense and feeling which are the content of our ordinary consciousness. This is the level of the sense- or desire-life and on it the Light is known as the *upadrashta*, Overseer or Watcher.

Strictly speaking this fifth level may be divided into two according to whether the concrete patterns are the "inner" ones that we term dream images, fantasy images, or merely images, or whether they are the "outer" sense-data from which we infer physical objects. As they are both of similar nature the Gita does not count them as separate levels though sometimes they are so counted. If reckoned separately they would form a sixth level. Similarly the seven of some traditions are accounted for by taking the buddhi as separate from the mahat.[14]

The so-called physical objects, tables and chairs, as opposed to the colored and other sensory shapes of perception, are but inferred or imagined causes with which we explain to ourselves the observed regularities in the data of sense, the data of the upadrashta level. They form a sort of underworld, an eighth world of pure Maya, peopled by ghosts with no reality. And yet it is these "ghosts" that are the basis of the materialism which vaunts itself as rooted in reality!

The importance of this knowledge cannot be overestimated, for it enables the disciples to see that even on the lowest levels the Self is one in all. They will be able to see with perfect clarity what they were taught long ago in chapter two—namely, that the Self cannot be pierced or injured, cannot be born or die. The separate self, that burden on their back for which they have felt anxieties, hopes, and fears, is seen to be illusion and with calm heart they can address themselves to the great Work with its two aspects: first, of climbing up the Ladder of the Soul by identifying with higher and ever-higher levels by irradiating them with the Light of the higher. *Verse 23* Although it may be several lives before the Heights are scaled yet are they born no more, being the birthless Light.

Several methods exist to reach this Knowledge. Some by the mind's *Verse 24* clear vision see the Self within the self, within the body even. They see that even the lower is what it is because drawn forth and upheld by the Light and thus they meditate upon that Light within all forms. Others follow the path of the Sankhya and reject the forms as not the Self. Unable to escape from dualism, they analyze away all content of experience as forms of Prakriti. Rejecting thus the lower, what remains is Self, or Purusha, not in the world but, star-like, far apart.

Others attain the same result by the Yoga of Action, tran- *Verse 25* scending self by acting for the one great Self of all. Still others hear the Truth from teachers or, in modern times, read of it in the writing of great Seers and, as they read, some inner feeling wakes telling them of its truth and they adhere with faith to what they hear. These also tread the Path of Life.[15]

Thus it has now been seen that all beings arise from union of the Light with forms. Those who allow the mind to sink the Light into the illumined forms, to feel "this form is me, these forms are mine," turning back on immortality, they slay their own Self. Let them open the eyes of the heart amidst the surrounding blackness and *see* the mighty Ruling Power, the wondrous Light seated within all beings. Let them *see* that It is unperishing within the forms that perish; see that It is the same in all and *see* that all the fret and fume of action is but the interplay of form with form and has no power to soil the stainless, all-supporting Light which, actionless, draws them forth from the great Matrix.

Verses 26–29

When they have seen all this (and even here and now it can be seen) a calm liberation will come to their spirit. They will perceive the great diversity of forms standing together in one mighty Being. Anyone who has served in a regiment knows the sense of being set free from the burden of self that comes from feeling oneself a part of a larger whole. There, however, the absorption is only partial and is often mixed with much that is undesirable. The perception of the great Unity gives such a wonderful liberation just because the self is completely and absolutely absorbed in That of which it is a part and because it is not something alien in which the self is lost but one's own Self.

Verse 30

Without beginning, parts, or limitations, untouched by actions even though seated in the body, the Sun of Consciousness irradi-

Verses 31–34

ates the Space of Thought. Those who have seen Its calm, immortal shining feel no more fear in all the triple worlds. They know that all the whirling flux of sense has its sole being in that radiant Light: They know the Light the Stainless, the Serene. For them—

> *In the wind of the hill-top, in the valley's song,*
> *In the film of night, in the mist of morning,*
> *Is it proclaimed that thought alone*
> *Is, Was and Shall be.*[16]

Notes

1   See appendix A.

2   See appendix H.

3   Space forbids more than the merest enumeration of these tattvas. For a detailed study of them the reader is referred to any book on the Samkhya, and especially to the excellent account given in J. C. Chatterji's *India's Outlook on Life* (Kailash Press, New York).

4   *Majjhima Nikaya*, i, 135.

5   The Gita here uses the term *param Brahma* but what is meant is the Unmanifested Self (see the chapter on Gita viii), what the Katha Upanishad terms the Shanta Atman, for the parabrahman itself is not strictly speaking an object of knowledge at all. For most purposes, however, the two may be taken as one and, indeed, are often so considered. See appendix E.

6.   Brihadaranyaka Upanishad, iii, 7, 23. See also Kenopanishad, where the Gods (sense-powers) find themselves unable to perform their functions without the help of Brahman (the Light).

7   Compare *The Secret of the Golden Flower*: "The Light is not in the body alone, neither is it only outside the body. Mountain and rivers and the great Earth are lit by sun and moon; all that is this Light. Therefore it is not only within the body."

8   *Nō Plays*. Trans. by Arthur Waley.

9   See *ante*, the end of chapter 3.

10   Compare this with the *Manichaean* doctrine that it is the duty of the faithful to separate out all the particles of Light that are entangled in the darkness of matter. In Mani's hands, however, the doctrine seems to have stopped at dualism.

11   *Return to Philosophy*, by C. E. M. Joad. The italicized portion has been added.

12   Compare Gita, viii, verse 9. See also diagram in appendix E.

13   See appendix F.

14   See appendix E.

15   This "faith" is not the same as blind belief. Discussion of its nature is postponed to chapter 17.

16   From a Japanese *Nō* play. Translated by Arthur Waley.

Chapter Fourteen

The Yoga of the Division of the Three Gunas

Having set forth the distinction between the Field and its Knower (in Sankhyan terms, the Prakriti and Purusha) the Gita now turns to the further analysis of the Field. The Root or Mula-prakriti, termed in verse 3 the Great Brahman, is characterized by three moments known as *gunas*. The word *guna* is usually translated as quality, but it should be borne in mind that there is here no question of a substance-quality relationship between the Mula-prakriti and the gunas. The gunas are the Mula-prakriti and the latter is the gunas in a state of equilibrium. For this reason some have preferred to speak of the three Strands, the totality of which make up the twisted rope of manifested being.

In order to understand something of the nature of these gunas it is necessary to remember that the Mula-prakriti is not a substance standing in its own right but a dark matrix full of unlimited potentialities, the appearance of the Parabrahman to the abstracted Light of Consciousness. Its potentialities are unlimited because it is the whole objective aspect of the Parabrahman and it is "dark" because the Light has been abstracted as the Atman. While it would be a mistake to equate it with the collective unconscious of Jung, the comparison will give a truer understanding of its nature than any study of those neatly intellectualized diagrams to be found in most books on Sankhya.

Under the contemplative gaze of Consciousness, three tendencies manifest themselves within the Matrix. One moment of it reflects the Light and is irradiated by It, itself becoming, like a fluorescent substance, an apparent source of light. This is the moment known as sattva guna and it has the characteristic of radiance (*prakasha*).[1]

A second moment as it were transmits the Light, not reflecting it back towards the Source but ever speeding it onwards and outwards. This moment is known as the guna of rajas, having as its characteristic outward-turned movement (*pravritti*).[2]

The third moment neither reflects nor transmits but absorbs the Light that falls upon it. This is the gunas of tamas, characterized by a stagnant inertia, a heedless indifference.[3]

The operation of the gunas can be observed in the microcosmic matrix of unconsciousness from which we wake each morning. First from the dark background of dreamless sleep arise a set of memories which by reflecting back the consciousness proclaim: "I was, I am." Next rajas comes into operation and the contemplative self is swept away along the crests of associated ideas into desire-filled plans of: "I will do." Still later the fluid universe of thought ossifies under the veiling power of tamas into the outer world of rigid objects which, though in truth sustained by consciousness alone, yet seem to be hard lifeless things existing in their sheer inert material right and amongst which the planning self of dawn only too often passes from itself under the dull compulsion of the outer.

In the macrocosm we see the same processes at work. First by the operation of the Light on sattva arise the calm and light-filled worlds of mahat-buddhi, the Cosmic Memory which is the Cosmic Imagination. The radiance and harmony of those worlds arise from their sattvic nature, and Krishna's direction to stand firmly in sattva (*nitya sattvastha*, chapter ii, v. 45.) has the same meaning as his counsel to be ever united with the buddhi (*buddhi-yukta*).

As the Cosmic manifestation proceeds we find the mobility of rajas coming into play. Out of the Light-filled unity of the spiritual worlds arise the many points of view which form the mental (*manasic*) level. The movement of the Light as it is transmitted through the Field gives rise to point-like individual selves from which the Light radiates in a network of intersecting lines of experience.[4]

In the upper worlds, the attributes and modes shine forth in a majestic and impersonal unity, rising and falling like the ocean swell beneath the Moon of Light. But in the mental world of *rajasic* plurality we pass into a world of monads in which each monad mirrors the universe from a given point of view and thus, though separate from its fellows, is united with them in the ideal unity of all.

But the effect of rajas does not stop at pure plurality, or, rather, in plurality itself is found the basis of the next tendency. Once the unity has been lost, the separate parts strive to complete themselves by a passionate outward-turned seeking. This is the *trishna* (Pali, *tanha*) of the Buddhists, the "constitutional appetition" by which they tend to pass from state to state. If not identical, it is yet related to what Jung terms libido and, stripped alike of Sanskrit terms and of the jargon of philosophers, it is that burning thirst which drives the soul out from itself to range throughout the world, seeking its food, devouring all it meets.

From this tendency arises the great natural law that life must feed on life, but metaphysically we should observe that this most terrible of all the laws of nature, by which the tiger rushes on his prey is also a manifestation of the unity of all. Under the outward-rushing impetus of rajas, the soul no longer sees the unity within. But since, even though unseen, that unity can never be denied, the soul goes forth in passionate desire to seize and grasp whatever lies outside, subordinating others to its will and even, on the lowest plane of all, devouring their material envelopes that so itself may grow. Thus all the horrors of the world we know arise from ignorance, which turns the soul to seek without what is already there within; desire is based on love and strife on unity.

As soon as the plurality has been established, the sinister power of tamas begins to make itself felt. Once the division between self and other has been made, the veiling power of tamas drains that "other" of all Light. It is no longer "me," instinct with life and movement, but something dead, inert, passively hostile, a death-hand gripping with a cold inertia the human soul that struggles to be free. Thus is the outer world of objects formed. Our Self has drawn them forth and given to them "a local habitation and a name," and now they turn upon that Self, denying It reality.

It is tamas that veils the mind's creative power so that it quails before its own creation. Even religion, which should have taught the Path of Light, has ended, for the most part, in succumbing to the deadly drag of tamas, taking all power from humanity to bestow it on the Gods.

But, as Hermes says, "if thou lockest up thy soul within thy body and dost debase it, saying: I nothing know; I nothing can; I fear the sea; I cannot scale the sky; I know not who I was, who I shall be; what is there then between thy (inner) God and thee?"

These three gunas, sattva, rajas, and tamas, are, as has already been said, the strands of which the twisted rope of being is woven.

All things, from grossest "matter" to subtlest cosmic thought-stuff, are the manifestations of one or more of these three tendencies, and it is one of the tasks of the disciples to analyze all phenomena in terms of these gunas. Their effort is to be able to stand firm in sattva for, as we have seen, it is sattva alone that can reflect the Light. They must therefore be able to say of any phenomenon: "this is *sattvic* for it brings increase of Light and harmony and so will lead me upwards; this is rajasic for it leads but to motion and is founded on desire; this is tamasic for it fills the soul with darkness, taking it captive to an outer Fate."

This division applies to all things in the Cosmos, food (see chapter 17), recreations, companionships, or books; all may drag downwards, outwards, or lead upwards. But above all the disciples must watch the gunas as they manifest in their own minds, for the mind is the gateway to the Real and the disciples must, in Hermes' words, be one "forever living at the Inner Door." At that Door they must constitute themselves as doorkeepers, letting all sattvic tendencies pass through, checking all rajas, overcoming tamas.[5]

Therefore the Gita gives some indications whereby the move- *Verse 11* ments in the mind may be marked down. "When the light of knowledge is born in all the gates of the body, then it may be known that sattva is increasing." In other words, a state of mind that fosters clear, unclouded knowledge, that brings a peace and inner harmony, stilling the lake of mind till it reflects the stars, bringing a sense of calm eternity, that state is sattvic, and all outward things, food, friends, or occupations, that help forward such a state also partake of sattva.

The rajasic state, on the other hand, is characterized by passionate *Verse 12* mobility. The mind is restless, occupied by greed, full of desire for things outside itself. Bright dreams may fill it, dreams of great things to be done, yet all those things are for the sake of self though they may sometimes wear the glittering robes of altruism and service of the world.

This rajasic restlessness is often confused with the Divine activity. There are many who cannot sit still for a moment, who think that to be always up and doing, no matter what, is to be full of life, and they bow down before activity in any form whatever. But this rajasic lust for movement is not the same as the Divine action, for it will be found, if analyzed, that it is always tainted by some personal desire, always in bondage to some personal gain, while the Divine activity is free, calm, and majestic in Its selflessness.

Verse 13   *Tamasic* states of mind are dark and stagnant, the mind is overcome by lethargy or broods in dull depression. Nothing seems worth doing, nothing can be done; all things oppress the soul, which sinks in sheer inertia. The Path is nothing but an empty dream or else a task beyond our feeble powers, while cynicism lends its dagger to cut the very root of worldly action. "All things are shows, and vain the knowledge of their vanity."

This tamasic despondency is the greatest obstacle to one who seeks to read the Path. The soul "flags wearily through darkness and despair."[6] It is a state which must be fought off at all costs, for not even the fierce, burning winds of rajasic passion are so fatal to all progress.

Unfortunately, just as some mistake the restless urge of rajas for Divine activity, so others mistake the dull indifferentism of tamas for spirituality. Mealy-mouthed cowardice is called "turning the other cheek," lazy inefficiency is termed indifference to material circumstances, shallow fatalism is confused with wise acceptance of the karma of one's past, cold indifference to one's fellows becomes a rising above love and hate, and that dull poverty of spirit that ignores all art and literature becomes transcendence of the lures of sense. All is Maya! All is *Shunya*! All is the Play of God! What does anything matter? This is not spirituality but tamas.

The disciples must thus keep constant watch upon the mind so that when tamas makes itself felt therein, if they cannot at once rise to sattvic light, they will at least be able to overcome it with the outward-turned activity of rajas. In general it may be said that sattvic states will lead them upwards to higher levels of being, for their transparent luminosity allows a reflection of the next higher level to show itself, suffusing the lower with the light of higher manas, or manas with the buddhi.   *Verse 18*

Rajasic states will leave the disciples stationary, since, though they fill the world with activities, they move but outwards and can never leave the plane whereon they stand. Tamasic states will drag them downwards till they lose all they have and sink into a less than human, mindless state. The phrase "sinks downwards" should not, however, be interpreted, as in sometimes done, to mean that the ego enters on an animal incarnation. That is impossible, though it may sometimes happen that a process takes place which is best described as the ego's having to watch over one or more animal lives with which it will feel itself bound up. In general, however, the meaning of the phrase is that they sink gradually into the lowest grades of human existence.

Another characteristic of the gunas is the constant interplay of action and reaction that goes on between them. The world, "the moving thing" in Sanskrit, is never still. Sattva gives place to rajasic activity, which, carried to extreme, provokes a tamasic rebound.[7] Everyone knows how states of elation pass without apparent cause   *Verse 10* into a dull depression. This instance, alone, will show how important it is for the disciples to gain an understanding of the operation of the gunas, passing and repassing as they weave the web of life.

Because of its power to reflect the steady poise of the eternal Light, sattva alone is relatively stable. Yet even sattva has its binding power. Stainless and sorrowless, its light is still reflected light and binds the soul to the happiness and knowledge that are in manifestations. At any time the love of happiness, the sacred thirst for knowledge, may, through the touch of rajas, degenerate into lust for pleasure and mere curiosity.

Therefore the disciples must bend their energies upon transcendence of the gunas altogether. They must strive to see that all their play is objective: they are the *seeing* Light. Refuged within that Light, the Heavenly Ganga wherein who bathes is rendered pure and sinless, "they drink the nectar of eternal Life." The movements of the Cosmos, shining with knowledge, passionately active, darkly inert, they see with steady vision. Theirs is the calm immortal

gaze of Spirit, cool as the moonlight on a tropic lake. Nothing that comes can be unwelcome; nothing that goes can be a source of grief. Sorrow and joy, honor and evil fame, are one and, though they act quite freely, the fatal thought "I am the doer of these actions" can find no entry in their Light-filled hearts.

Torn is the threefold Web of Fate. The gunas have been crossed and the one-time disciples stand on the edge of the Eternal Brahman. Their light can merge in the transcendent Flame and blaze in bliss beyond the human world; the Stream is crossed, the great Reward is theirs. But Krishna tells us of another Path that opens as a possibility before them. They may elect not to withdraw their Light

to the Unmanifest Eternal but to stay and serve the one Eternal   *Verse 26*
Life that is in all. This freedom won, they may devote themselves
to freeing others, silently guiding pilgrims of the Path. There is
no shrinking from the final plunge, for Krishna says that they are
"worthy of becoming the Eternal," implying that they stay by their
own choice to serve the One Great Life that is the manifested basis[8]
of the Parabrahman. Nor are they human beings, but a great Power
which, by Its presence, though unknown, unseen, lightens the bitter
sorrows of the world.

Notes

1   Verses 6, 11, 22.

2   Verses 12, 22.

3   Verse 13.

4   There are many interesting references to this symbolic net in ancient mystical
literature. In Shvetashvatara Upanishad I'shvara is termed the Wielder of the Net
and in the Egyptian *Book of the Dead* (chapter cliiiA, Budge), under the vignette
of a net occur the following interesting words: "Hail, though 'god who lookest
behind thee' (manas united with buddhi), that 'god who hast gained the mastery
over they heart,' I go a-fishing with the cordage of the (net), 'uniter of the earth'
and of him that maketh a way through the earth. Hail, ye fishers who have given
birth to your own fathers (manas in which the Divine birth has taken place)."

5   Compare the four exercises in recollectedness (*satipatthana*) of the Buddhists.

6   These lines of Shelley were written of Coleridge, who, it will be remembered,
composed an "Ode to Dejection."

7   The extreme illustration of this is to be found in the alternations which char-
acterize the so-called *manic-depressive* type, perhaps with lucid intervals which
are (relatively) sattvic.

8   *Pratishtha.* Compare the phrase "the Nest of Brahman" in Maitri Upanishad, vi,
15, which is there identified with the samvatsara—i.e. the great Cycle of Time,
the Mahat Atman, whose discus Krishna carries.

✺

Chapter Fifteen

The Yoga of the Highest Spirit

The subject of the last chapter was the analysis of the Field, and that of the present one is the analysis of the Knower, the Consciousness, especially in its threefold aspect as individual Self, Cosmic Self, and Supreme Reality.

The chapter commences with an account of the World-Tree. This great symbol, mentioned in the Rig Veda and Upanishads,[1] was known to all the ancient peoples. The Scandinavians knew of it as the sacred ash-tree, *Igdrasil,* with its roots in the death-kingdoms and its branches in the sky. In his poem to Hertha, the Norse nature-goddess, Swinburne writes of—

> *The tree many-rooted*
> *That swells to the sky*
> *With frondage red-fruited,*
> *The life-tree am I;*
> *In the buds of your lives is the sap of my leaves:*
>   *ye shall live and not die.*

The Egyptians worshipped the sacred sycamore fig-tree, the Aztecs of America had the sacred agave-plant and the ancient Sumerians of Eridu tell of a wondrous tree with "Its roots of white crystal stretched towards the deep, its seat the central place of the earth, its foliage the couch of the primaeval Mother. In its midst was *Tammuz*."[2]

The Tree was a symbol of the great World-Mother, the Goddess of Nature who nourishes all life with the milk of Her breasts. The choice by the Egyptians of the sycamore fig with its milky juice derives from this, as does the fact that the three most sacred trees of the ancient Indo-Aryans were the *ashvattha*, the *bat* (banyan), and the *udumbara*, all of them being species of the fig-tree.

The name *ashvattha* is usually derived from *a-shva-stha*, "not standing till tomorrow," and while this is an appropriate description of the world which is ever passing away before our eyes, there is an earlier account which tells how Agni, the desire-consciousness, hid in this tree for a year (the cycle of manifestation) in the form of a horse (*ashtva*), the well-known symbol of the desire-mind.[3] This myth is of great significance as it links up with the statement already quoted that Tammuz was in the midst of the Sumerian World-Tree and also, perhaps, with the growth of an erica-tree round the coffin of the dead Osiris,[4] for both these "dying Gods" were, from the inner point of view, symbols of the Atman, dismembered and imprisoned in the world.

The authors of the ancient Indian tradition introduced, however, one modification into the symbol which is not, so far as I know, *Verse 1* found elsewhere. The other World-Trees all have their roots in the underworld and branches in the sky, but the Tree of the Gita, following that of the Veda "whose root is high above," is rooted in the unmanifested Brahman and sends down its branches, the various levels of objectivity, the evolutes of the Mula-prakriti,[5] to form the worlds of manifested being. The Tree as a whole is termed the Veda as it is the content of all knowledge and the leaves, the individual selves, are the separate verses (*chandansi*) of that cosmic Veda. "He who knoweth it is a Veda-knower."

Nourished by the three gunas of which all phenomena are made (compare the three roots of *Igdrasil*), the branches spread both upwards and downwards, referring to the Cosmic Tides which flow upwards in the upper worlds and downwards in the lower.[6] The sprouts, peculiarly sticky in this tree, are the ensnaring objects of the senses and the root, the karmic tendencies from the past universe,[7] grow downwards to generate "the bonds of karma in the human world."

While in the world, human consciousness is absorbed in the forms it perceives, and it is impossible to see the Tree as a whole. Still

less can be seen that fundamental Light which has drawn forth the forms, holds them in being and, in the end, will dissolve them once more in the Matrix.

"Now then the inquiry into Brahman," says the author of the Brahma Sutras, "That from which the origin, by which the preservation, and in which the end" of the whole world of forms is found. The answer is there, lying close at hand, but the inquiry will lead to nowhere unless certain preliminary qualifications are present in the inquirer. These qualifications are usually given as four: *viveka*, discrimination between the constant and the transitory; *vairagya*, a turning-away from what is transitory; *shat-sampatti*, a group of six attainments comprising control of mind, control of sense, endurance, a turning-away from the outer (whether in experience or in religion), faith (in the Gita's sense) and mental balance; *mumukshutva*, desire for liberation from the bondage of ignorance.

The Gita, however, mentions only one supreme qualification, which, if truly attained, includes all the rest, the qualification of non-attachment. This is the axe that will cut down the firmly rooted Tree, but non-attachment means a great deal more than ascetic refusal of commerce with the world. The latter may strengthen personal willpower but, as the Buddha found, will take the ascetic no nearer to the Goal. In fact, by strengthening the personal will, it may even bind more tightly. *Non-attachment can never be attained while standing in one's personality,* nor even while standing in the individual ego, the separate Jiva. The disciple must see the personality as something separate from the self, like the personalities seen in dream, and must take refuge in the impersonal Light. Then alone will non-attachment flower in the heart because the Light is ever unattached.

"Destroy all sense of self," said Buddha; "come unto Me," said Christ; "still all the movements of the mind," said Patañjali, that mind which, by attachment to all outward things, produces the false self. These and all other Teachers of the Way were, in their different languages, saying but one thing: that human beings must come from self into the Self, from death to Life, from darkness into Light. Established in that Light, cohesive power will leave the Cosmic Tree and it will fall to pieces like those fabled ships which, on approaching the magnetic mountain, lost all their nails and sank into the sea. "Not by traveling is the world's end reached. Verily I declare to you that within this fathom-long body with its perceptions and its mind lies in the world, its arising and its ceasing and the Way that leads to its cessation."[8]

Detaching themselves from the union with the objects of both *Verse 4* outer and inner senses, the disciples must soar upon the trackless Path of Light towards the Primal Consciousness from which in ages past the Cosmic Energies streamed forth.

Verse 6   That Consciousness, however, being Absolute, is far beyond all that we know. Knower and Known exist as one in It as, in another way, they are at one in absolute matter, if any such exist except as abstraction. It is in fact no consciousness for us, being beyond the Fire of manifested life, the Moon of Mula-prakriti, the Sun of the unmanifested Atman. It is the Void; It also is the Full. Having gone thither, none return again. That, Krishna says, is His supreme Abode;[9] That is the Goal; That is the final bliss.

Verse 7   But now the Gita turns to lower levels and deals with the mystery of the incarnation of that One. A constant moment of that partless Whole stands in the "matter" of the mental world uniting with its forms. As it turns outwards under the urge of rajas it becomes the lower, the desire-infected mind. The integral power of knowing that is inherent in its light, in the attempt to grasp the various aspects of the world around, manifests as the five organs of sense-knowledge. These are at first the inner senses but they exteriorize into the so-called physical organs under the pull of tamas, as explained in the previous chapter. Moreover, from our point of view, the physical body belongs, not to the subjective, but to the objective side of experience. It is in fact only a specialized portion of what is actually environment, as it is merely a part of the content of consciousness upon the lowest level.

It should always be remembered that the sense-powers are differentiations of the integral illuminating power of Consciousness and are by no means something belonging to the material manifestation. This explains the fact noted by biologists that the senses are formed by differentiations from one primitive sense and the fact that under certain conditions one sense-organ can be made to do the work of others. The sense of touch can even be made to manifest at a distance of several inches from the surface of the skin.[10]

When the Ego, the inner Lord, takes a body it manifests these *Verse 8* senses as powers of gaining experience of the outer world. Here we must be careful not to confuse the scientific with the metaphysical account. Scientifically, or from the point of view of form, the process of incarnation may be described as the actual entry into a suitable organized vehicle (the embryo) of a subtler but still "material" body, the body of desire.[11] Metaphysically, the process is to be viewed as a hardening-out of the forms with which the consciousness identifies itself, their so-to-speak de-illumination under the veiling power of tamas, so that the fluid form of the desire-mind crystallizes into the relatively rigid material body.

Once it has come into being, the physical body is battleground for the opposing forces of rajas and tamas. There are two sets of processes, known to biologists as *anabolism* and *catabolism* respectively, which go on simultaneously in the body from its first formation till its ultimate decay. One set, under the urge of the rajas of the desire-nature, are always building up the organism and repairing any damage, while the other, under the tamasic pull of "matter," are as busily engaged in breaking down whatever is built up. During the first half of life the former are in the ascendant, but gradually the destroyers assert themselves more and more, until the body refuses to obey the promptings of the ego and desire-nature and forces them to withdraw and leave it to disintegrate in peace.

The sense-powers, however, as we have seen, are no property of the material body but belong to the Ego itself, and therefore the

Verse 8   latter is said to seize them and return with them to its own plane "as the wind takes fragrances from their retreats." As it withdraws it of course leaves behind, not only the doomed physical body, but also the desire-nature, which is, as we have seen, intermediate between the Ego and the body. The *essence*, therefore, of our sense-experience is taken up by the ascending consciousness to be assimilated in that purely mental form which is built up around the central point throughout the age-long alternations of physical life and death.

There, as the Gita says elsewhere, the Ego on its purely mental plane "enjoys the spacious heavenly realm," reaping, as the Egyptians put it, the heavenly corn in the Fields of Aahlu until, when all fruits have been reaped, a process that may last centuries or even thousands of years, the downward pull of mingled rajas and tamas asserts itself once more and the Ego seeks a further incarnation.

The deluded do not perceive the Self as it departs nor even as it
Verse 10   stands within the body. "How shall the Seer be seen?" asks the Upanishad, and those whose vision is engrossed in outer forms, with all their scalpels and their microscopes see naught but forms. Even the would-be yogis, absorbed in outward practices with breath, or even struggling to subdue their minds, unless they make the inward turn
Verse 11   towards the Atman, detaching themselves from forms, will gain no more than psychic powers. Only the wisdom-eyed, those few who, seeking immortality, turn their gaze inwards, behold the individual Self, seated within the heart.[12]

Nevertheless, that individual Self is but a moment of the Cosmic Self. The Light which shines within the ego (as opposed to the latter's
Verse 12   built-up form) is the same Light that shines within the other Selves as well, and one who sees It rightly sees the unity of all, founded on

that great Unity of Brahman, beyond Sun, Moon and Fire.[13]

That Parabrahman in the form of Its Light-Energy (*ojas*), entering the "earth" of Its objective aspect (Mula-prakriti), supports all beings and then again, having become the desire-natured immortal one (*rasatmaka soma*), It nourishes the "plants" of personal life (*aushadhi*).[14] Lower still, It becomes *Vaishvanara*, the Fire of the desire-life which burns throughout the world. Organized around, though not itself the Ego, its fierce, impersonal but living flames, in union with a living, breathing body, grasp and digest the food of the four elements of matter.   *Verse 13*   *Verse 14*

In all these manifestations on the various levels it is the one Divine Krishna that is to be sought, He who is "seated in the hearts of all." It is His presence there that sustains the entire flow of life, microcosmic as well as macrocosmic. Because of His presence the images of all past experience cohere as memory, a memory which extends throughout the whole series of his past lives. Without His vision, embracing as it does past, present and future, the past could not persist before our mental eye.   *Verse 15*

From Him, too, comes the power of perception (*jñana*), the link between subject and object, by which we are able to perceive what is "really there" and are not limited, as some have thought, to "ideas" in our own minds. True perception is possible only through His presence in the heart as it is He who holds subject and object in one unity.

From Him, also, comes absence, or loss of memory and knowledge (*apohanam*), since it is only by a limitation of the all-pervading knowledge, by a shutting out of the images of the "future" which form the other half of "memory" and which are equally present to His gaze, that the movement of life is made to flow in a given direction. That which we fail to remember determines equally with what we remember the direction of the life-flow at any given period, whether of individual or of social life.

He, also, is that all-transcending and yet all-pervading One Being whose rich unity is set forth in the many-faceted harmony of the Vedic symbols, and, in a more directly "philosophical" manner, in the Vedanta (Upanishads). Were He not present in the heart, the Vedantic Knowledge could never arise. He is the secret Fount from which well up its life-giving waters.

Verse 16   The next verses are concerned with the very important teaching about the three modes in which Spirit or Consciousness (*purusha*) manifests. Sri Krishna first sets forth the two well-known modes

Verse 16   which He here terms the flowing or mutable and the immutable or flowless. The Flowing is that consciousness which, as it were, flows along the stream of time from a given focus. In other words it is the consciousness that manifests as the countless beings, as individuals, extending indefinitely in the mode of temporal succession. It is the basis of all finite selves, flowing, stream-like, through the universe.

Beyond it, however, is a vast and Flowless oceanic Consciousness that, with an equal, and, as it were, neutral vision, embraces the entire realm of manifested being. It is the *Kutastha*, seated on the summit of the World-mountain, and, in Its calm, impassive gaze, all things are equal, all yesterdays are one with all tomorrows, action and flowing movement can exist no more. This is the unmoved Witness of the Cosmos, the stainless Light that nothing can ever move. Many have viewed It as the Goal of all and sought a refuge in Its changeless peace beyond a world of constant change and sorrow.

These two modes of Consciousness are the two birds of the

Upanishad, fast friends, perched on one tree. One, the changing individual self, eats the sweet fruits of dynamic experience and is bound thereby; the other, the changeless Witness, watches but does not partake.[15]

Beyond these two is yet a third, the Consciousness that is the Supreme Self, highest and most excellent of all.

The Purushottama, this Highest Purusha, is not a merely tran- *Verse 17* scendent Being, throned in isolated grandeur beyond the limits of all universes. The second or Immutable Purusha could scarcely "enter" the play of manifestation without beginning to "flow" and so losing Its own nature. But that Supreme Consciousness is within as well as beyond the Cosmos, for Sri Krishna says that it is as Purushottama that He sustains and rules the entire triple world, having without any loss of poise entered into the heart of manifestation.

It is this Consciousness, indeed, which is Sri Krishna's Essen- *Verse 18* tial Being to which He has so often referred. Beyond the finite but yet dynamic changing Selves, beyond also and more excellent than the changeless stasis of the Cosmic Witness, beyond the opposites of personality and impersonality, form and formlessness, He is the highest and most excellent of all. His is the Consciousness which stands, sustaining all; His too the Consciousness which, from its minute heart, moves every tiny atom. Movement and rest are both as one to Him, freedom and necessity are but as His two hands. The changeless Sun and ever-changing Moon are His two eyes; He sees with both at once. Fearing no limitations, He enters in the heart of every form; fearing no bondage, He is the secret Power who moves each moving thing.

It was because of its knowledge of this ultimate Divine poise that the *Bhagavada* or *Pancharatra* teaching (to which we have already referred in chapter four, footnote to verse 1) was known as *Trisauparna*, the teaching of the Three Birds, to distinguish it from the teaching of those schools who knew only the Two Birds referred to above. It is by this marvelous poise of the Purushottama that the two aspects of being, the changing and the changeless, the world and Nirvana, are held together in one firm embrace and that the former is redeemed from being.

It is, moreover, this same supreme poise of the Ultimate Spirit that is manifest as the "personal" Krishna, enabling Him to speak with such transcendent authority, to act with such all-dominating power and freedom, to stand serene beyond all loves and hates and, *at the same time*, to be the passionate Lover of those who gave themselves to Him in love. In all things He mingled, in love, in war, in politics; and yet in all was He utterly unperturbed. First of all lovers, teachers, warriors, statesmen, He was yet the friend of simple cowherd boys, the lover of the cowherd girls of Braja. To all He was the same, and yet forever on the side of those who loved Him. Kauravas and Pandavas were one to Him, but, though He strove with all His eloquence for peace, yet His word was pledged to Draupadi for war.

That is why He goes on to say in the concluding verses of the chapter that only he who knows Him thus as Purushottama is a knower of the All, and he alone is able to serve Him with his *whole* being. Others can serve Him only with what is best in them; he alone serves with fully integrated being. This is the most secret teaching of all and to it Sri Krishna will return at the conclusion of the entire dialogue. To understand its profound mystery is to accomplish all.

Notes

1   Rig Veda, I, xxiv, 7, and Kathopahishad, vi, 1.

2   D'Alviella, *The Migration of Symbols*, p. 157.

3   Taittiriya Brahmana, III, viii, 12, v. 2. See Tilak's *Gita Rahasya* on this verse. The myth also occurs in Mahabharata, Anusgasana Parva, s. 85. It may also be noted that one of the meanings of *Ashwa* is "seven" (see Apte's *Dictionary*), that a vignette in the Egyptian *Book of the Dead* represents the sacred sycamore fig-tree with seven branches, that the same is true of some representations of the Assyrian Tree of Life, and, finally, that the trunk of the famous many-breasted statue of Artemis of Ephesus is divided into seven levels, five of which are filled with representations of living creatures. See Mackenzie, *The Migration of Symbols*, pp. 162-169, for drawings of these.

4   See Plutarch's *Isis and Osiris*. The ramifications of this subject would take us all over the world.

5   See Gita, vii, 4. There is also a microcosmic correspondence with the cerebral nervous system, rooted in the brain, the seat of consciousness, and ramifying downwards to the sense organs all over the body.

6   See chapter 11.

7   Or, microcosmically, from past lives. It is a peculiarity of the ashvattha that its roots, instead of merging into the trunk at ground-level, often maintain a semi-independent existence for several feet above ground till they finally merge into one. Many explanations of this verse are vitiated by confusing the ashvattha with the banyan, which sends down aerial roots, whereas the former does not.

8   Buddha, Samyutta Nikaya, ii, 3, 6.

9   Note that the word *Dhama* means Light as well as abode.

10 See *L'Exteriorisation de la Motricite*, by de Rochas; also *Eyeless Sight*, by Jules Romains. The interchanging of the sense-function is also a practice of certain types of yogi in India.

11 The "stuff" of this subtle body may perhaps be identified with what in spiritist circles is termed ectoplasm. But all references to matter or stuff should be taken

in the light of what is written in appendix B.

12   Katha Upanishad, iv, 1.

13   See above for explanations of these terms.

14   The *aushadhi* are plants like corn, etc., which wither after bringing forth their fruits and spring up again from seed the following year. Opposed to them are the *banaspati* which, like trees, remain from year to year. The former symbolize the transient personal selves; the latter the relatively permanent egos or jivas.

15   Mundaka Upanishad, iii-1, also Rig Veda, I, clxiv, 20. Similarly, on the highest branch of Igdrasil was perched an eagle while other creatures occupied the lower branches.

Chapter Sixteen

The Yoga of the Division between the Bright and Dark Powers

Literally translated, the title of this chapter would read "the division between the divine and demoniacal endowments," but such a rendering suggests to Western readers a dualism which is far from what is meant by the Gita. The word *deva* and its adjective, daivic, come from a root meaning "shining," while *asura*, though originally a title of Indra and other Vedic Gods, came to have the sense of "not-divine," hence "dark." There are two natures in this world, the Bright *Verse 6* and the Dark. This is not an arbitrary division into good and bad based on the will of some personal God or Teacher, but one which is rooted in the very nature of the Cosmic manifestation.

Mention has already been made of the two great tides or movements of the Cosmos, technically known as pravritti and nivritti. The former is the great outgoing breath by which the universe comes forth from Brahman; the latter is the inflowing counterpart by which all things return towards the One.

We must be on our guard against any introduction of ordinary ethical ideas in giving the names Bright and Dark to these two movements. The former is dark because it is characterized by an ever-increasing absorption of the Light within the forms, while the latter is bright because its tendency is towards the liberation of

Light. Mental states that aid or manifest the outgoing movement are also called dark, and those that express the movement of return are termed bright.

This is the real basis of the ethical dualism that we find in the world. The dualism of the Cosmic Tides is inevitable in *any* universe whatever. It is no more possible to have a universe based on one movement alone than to have a gun that will fire without a recoil. Action and reaction are the conditions of all manifestation and not even the great Machine of the Cosmos can escape the operation of this law.

Most so-called ethical science is an attempt to find intellectual sanction for the prejudices and customs of the society in which the particular thinker has been born. Certain actions are labeled good, others are termed evil. But this labeling not only raises the problem of evil but also leads to the discovery that other societies have no cognizance of these particular labels, or even apply them in an opposite sense. Since, moreover, the universe as a whole shows no sign of acting in accordance with the labels, the conclusion is reached that the universe is non-ethical and a further dualism between human beings and nature is set up, so that the former find themselves in the unenviable position of being concerned with good and evil in a universe that is profoundly indifferent.

Such a conclusion is extremely unsatisfactory, since it leaves humans either worshippers of the image that their hands have made, one that they know has no reality behind it, or else drives them into the arms of unregulated desires.

Our ethics must in fact be based upon the twofold Cosmic Movement and therefore must be relative. Buddhist philosophy speaks of two types of *kalpa* (period of manifestation), termed respective *vivarta kalpas*, or periods of "unrolling," and *samvarta kalpas*, or periods of "rolling up," and when, on the eve of Enlightenment, the Buddha saw the whole series of His past lives, He remembered having lived through several of these alternate periods of evolution and involution. The universe is not then to be regarded as a perfectly straight unrolling followed by an equally straight rolling-up but as a cyclic process, spiraling downwards through many alternating ages and then reascending in the same spiral fashion.

From this it follows that, if ethics are to have any foundation in the Cosmos, we must define good and evil in terms of the processes that aid or hinder the cosmic tendencies that are dominant at the time, and these will be different according to whether the age we are living is in one of unrolling or one of rolling-up. The qualities that are of assistance during an outgoing period of further descent into matter and which therefore must at that time be termed "good" are precisely the opposite of those which will be of use during a period of ascent or involution. Thus the virtues of the one period will become the vices of the other.

This ambiguity or relativity can be avoided by the use of the ethically neutral terms Bright and Dark, for they express simply the characteristics of the period in question without passing ethical judgment upon them.

Traces of this alternation of values have been preserved in Hindu mythology. We read in the Puranas how, at certain early periods of the world, certain egos were entrusted with the work of generation of the species and ordered to produce offspring. They, however, refused to do so and became chaste ascetics, a course considered meritorious at other epochs but here evidently considered a "sin" since we read that they were cursed in consequence of their refusal.

The reversal of meaning that came over the word "asura" is perhaps a further indication of the same sort. Originally, as has been said, the word was a title applied to the great Gods, *Varuna*, *Indra* and *Agni*—a sense which has been preserved in the *Ahura Mazda* of the Iranian tradition—but in later times it came to signify the "dark" enemies of the Gods. The same may be said of the process by which Lucifer, "Son of the Morning," whose very name of Lightbearer shows him to have represented the downward movement of the Light, becomes in later times the Christian Devil, the enemy of God and righteous people.

When we leave theory and come to practice we find ourselves at once confronted by the question how we are to know whether the period in which we are living is one of evolution or of involution. The answer is primarily to be found in our hearts, which, reflecting as they do the whole of Cosmos, are able to know which tendency is operating at a given time. But that still small voice within us is reinforced by the words of the great spiritual Teachers of the epoch who, being Seers, teach in accordance with the voice of Cosmic Law.

Now it is noticeable that all the great Teachers of the historic epoch have inculcated an ethic of a definitely ascending or nivritti type. The ascending character of the ethics of the Gita, the Buddha, Christ, and Shankara, is so obvious that we are apt to identify such teachings with ethics pure and simple and to assume that teachings of the opposite sort are evil for all time.

But there are definite indications that such a conclusion is erroneous. If we look back to the earliest cultures of which we have any historical knowledge, the civilizations of the five or six millennia preceding what we call our era, we see that the religions of those civilizations were of a fundamentally different type. I have written religions but perhaps the singular would have been more appropriate, for, just as there is a certain uniformity about all modern religion, so there was a similarity between all the ancient religions.[1] Comparison of Babylonian, ancient Egyptian, or Cretan religion with the religions founded by "historical" Teachers shows that a fundamental difference of attitude prevailed in the ancient cults.[2]

There is in all of them an emphasis on pravritti, especially as manifested in the great forces of sex, and an inculcation of practices that seem to us of very dubious morality. The Great Mother was then the chief object of worship. To the type of religion represented by the Gita she has become the great World-Tree that is to be cut down with the axe of non-attachment. It is easy to gloss over such a difference with talk of the evolution of a religious sense, but such a phrase only masks a real change in the values appropriate in the two epochs.

Orphic and kindred movements in Greece, "Hermeticism" in Egypt, Buddhism in India and Christianity in the Near East and Europe were not simply religion *par excellence* coming into a new age, and, by reversing many previous values, directed human hearts along the path of nivritti, which is the tendency at present ruling, not, indeed, in the sense that it yet dominates humanity but in the sense that the values for the present epoch are the spiritualizing ones of the ascent.

But it is time to return more directly to the Gita. The teaching about the bright and dark tendencies which, like the *anabolic* and *catabolic* processes in the body, go on simultaneously in all ages, has been deferred till the disciple was at such an advanced stage of the Path because the effect of such teaching upon immature souls is always to make them identify their own party with the bright and their opponents with the dark forces. They are themselves the "chosen people of God," while their opponents are the people of the Devil! Each of the nations fighting in the last war was, in its own opinion, fighting for Justice and the Right.

In studying the lists of bright and dark qualities enumerated in the Gita we should be careful to disinfect them somewhat of the atmosphere of "holiness" and "sinfulness" that centuries of popular ethical thinking has surrounded them with. *Dana*, for instance, must be divested of its associations with almsgiving, charitable institutions and sanctimonious merit-mongering, while "study of the scriptures" (*svadhyaya*) has little connection with the Bible classes of the West or with the futile mechanical intoning of the Gita that is so popular in orthodox circles in India. Dana is the process whereby the good things of the universe are made to circulate and penetrate the whole instead of being locked up in stagnant individual centers, and is thus obviously a means of breaking down the barriers of egoism, while svadhyaya signifies the pursuit of knowledge by study, not necessarily the study of "holy" books.

It is not necessary to go in detail into all the other qualities enumerated; all that is needed is to sound a warning against taking them in their conventional sense, for, in those senses, they often become vices, accorded lip-service by the great majority but instinctively rebelled against the heart. It is not without significance that the conventional virtues of the conventional saint are objects of dislike to healthy-minded people. The task of thinking out the real meanings of these qualities and of divesting them of the accumulated holiness of centuries is a useful and important exercise for the disciple of this Path. Only those who have made the attempt know what valuable results it yields and what a profound ethical enlightenment comes from the discarding of the copy-book conceptions. Above all, the disciples will be cured of the almost universal habit of judging by appearances, for they will learn that apparently identical actions performed by two different people have very different values from the inner point of view.

It will be noticed that all the qualities which are described as bright are ones which help the liberation of the Light. In themselves, of course, they are qualities, not of the Light itself, but of the psycho-physical vehicles in which it is entangled, but, just as it is easier to extract water from a sponge than from a brick, they are such as make it easier for the Light to detach itself and dominate those vehicles.

Thus, *ahimsa* (harmlessness) involves a checking of the outgoing   *Verse 2* forces of rajas, which, as we saw in connection with chapter fourteen, are what lead to the transformation of the unity-based love into a Nature "red in tooth and claw," and worse, into humanity red with sword and bayonet. Similarly, *teja* (vigor) is the means of overcoming   *Verse 3* the tamasic drag which sinks the Light in the stagnant inertia of matter.

In dealing with the dark qualities one difficulty appears at first sight. Contrary to what we should expect from the foregoing conclusions, a certain moral odium appears in the phrases which are used to describe them. "Dark" people are not even allowed to have   *Verse 7* a proper knowledge of pravritti, which one might have thought was their special province. They are "ruined selves" (*nashtatmanah*), that   *Verse 9* is to say, those whose Light is sunk in matter, and they "come forth for the harming of the world."

But this condemnation is explicable when we reflect that the Gita is written for an epoch of nivritti[3] and that therefore the dark qualities described are not the outgoing (*pravritti*) tendencies in their own proper forms but, as it were, the aftermath of those qualities, the distorted and ugly forms in which they manifest themselves when prolonged beyond their proper time into an epoch of nivritti. They have the same relation to the qualities of pure pravritti that the sexuality of old age has to the normal passion of youth.

The pravritti of a nivritti age is not the healthy and vigorous outgoing that it is in periods when it has the backing of the Cosmic Law but a sporadic, disruptive and harmful manifestation comparable to that unwanted cell-activity which produces the growth of tumors in an organism. That is why it is said that "dark" ones (in an age of nivritti) "know neither right pravritti nor right nivritti."

Verse 7

It is in that sense too that we must understand verse eight. "The universe, they say, is without truth, without basis, without any Ruling Power, brought about by mutual union,[4] caused by lust and nothing else." Conscious as they are that their own activities are without any underlying harmony or truth, and that they are motivated by sheer desire and have no sanction in the Cosmic Law, they naturally erect philosophies which deny the presence of those attributes in the Cosmos as a whole. We can see nothing in the universe which we have not first perceived in our own hearts, and if the heart is given over to "insatiable desires" the person will be able to see nothing in the Cosmos but the wild strife of untamed forces. This lack of vision will seem to justify self-indulgence and abandonment to the gratification

Verse 11

of all desires, "feeling sure that this is all."[5]

One particular consequence of this yielding to desires must be noted. We have seen that the forces of desire are not really personal forces seated in the Ego but great impersonal tides that sweep a person away. Just as someone experiences a rather fatuous sense of gratification and power when traveling at high speed in a motor-car, even though that power and speed are no attributes of that person, who may be the merest weakling, so we experience an exhilaration in yielding ourselves to powerful currents of desire quite oblivious of the fact that they are neither us nor ours, but swirling tides that bear us to destruction.

Verses 13, 14

We need only examine ourselves when carried away by violent anger, passion, or grief to realize how much we are enjoying the swift rush and how reluctant we are to allow its luxurious ecstasy to come to an end. Although most (though apparently not all!) modern societies will not allow us to exult in the naive fashion of verse fourteen over the enemies we have slain and are about to slay yet we can all recognize the desire-born thrill of the next verse: "I am wealthy, well-born; who is there that is like unto me? I will sacrifice, I will give alms, I will make merry. Thus, deluded by ignorance."

Verse 15

The ignorance in question is ignorance of the fact that the current of desire is something quite outside the Self, its exhilaration being that of the Gadarene swine as they "rushed down a steep place into the sea." For, truly, the end of such wild careering is, as the Gita puts it, "in a foul hell." The fire and brimstone of the mediaeval Christians and the ingenious tortures of sadistic hell-makers in India are mere superstitions, but for all that, there are hells enough, both in this world and after death, the hells of unsatisfied desire which are entered by "the triple gate of lust, anger and greed." Equally true is it

Verse 16

Verse 21

that these hells are "destructive of the Self," for the Light of the Self is dissipated among the objects of desire.

Verse 19, 20

In chapter eleven, verse thirty-six, we read of the Rakshasas fleeing in fear to the uttermost boundaries of the universe. That was the cosmic aspect of the process and here we are told how the "dark" ones who are its actual embodiments turn from the Light within and are carried by the fierce abysses of materiality and Self-loss. For, once a Soul has attached itself to these currents, it is not easy for it to stop and reverse its course. "Easy is the descent into hell," as Virgil wrote; it is the return that is difficult and laborious.

Yet it must always be remembered that underlying all the moral indignation of the text is the knowledge that those who follow the path of Darkness do so because they are those who have not yet plumbed the depths of matter, depths that those who love the Light have also plumbed before. The Soul Itself perishes never; all movements, Dark and Bright, take place within the One, and so from every depth there is return. As Plotinus expresses it: "It is not in the soul's Nature to touch utter nothingness; the lowest descent is into evil and, so far, into non-being; but to utter nothing, never. When the soul begins again to mount, it comes not to something alien but to its very self."

Verses 23, 24

Before concluding this chapter it is necessary to say a few words about the last two verses, which, with their command to refer all matters to the authority of the Shastra, have been and are the delight of orthodoxy. But to take Shastra here as meaning merely the traditional scriptures is to misunderstand the whole tenor of the Gita, with its reiterated counsel to take refuge in the buddhi (e.g. chapter ii, verse 49) and its constant teaching that all knowledge is to be found in one's own heart.

The fact is that the Shastra in its highest sense means the Three-fold Ruler (*shasaka traya*),[6] the manas united with the buddhi and mahat, or, in plain language, the inner knowledge that is revealed in the heart by the spiritual intuition. This is the meaning of the Upanishadic counsel to sink the senses in the mind, the mind in buddhi and the buddhi in the Mahat Atman or Great Self, and it is to these Inner Rulers that one should always submit. Following the dictates of that inner Light one should perform all actions in the world, and one who ignores that inner Voice, "to follow the promptings of desire, attains neither success nor happiness nor the highest Goal."

Notes

1   I am not referring to the thin stream of "mystery" tradition reserved for the few who, at all times, have been treading the upward Path, but to the great exoteric cults designed for the masses of men.

2   It would be easy to controvert this by the selection of appropriate instances, but a sensitive study of the popular ancient religions will, I think, reveal profound *qualitative* differences of value and of general "atmosphere." Notice how D. H. Lawrence, for example, in revolt against accepted spiritual values, was attracted to old-world cults such as that of Etruscans, and notice also his worship of "dark Gods." Writing about Saturnalia and kindred festivals, Sir James Frazer says in his *Golden Bough*: "All these things appear to hang together; all of them may, perhaps, be regarded as the shattered remnants of a uniform zone of religion and society which at a remote era belted the Old World from the Mediterranean to the Pacific."

3   This is implied by Sri Krishna's assurance to Arjuna, the individual Soul, that he is born with the bright endowment (verse 5).

4   In using the words "mutual union" the author was probably thinking of sexual union, but the words would apply equally to the theory that the world arose, in the last resort, from a "fortuitous concourse of atoms."

5   It is not proposed to point a moral by applying these verses to current societies, East or West. Readers must judge for themselves whether or not they constitute an indictment of their particular society and whether the ways of their civilization are "bright" and "dark."

6   It is only fair to state that this is not the accepted etymology of the word *shastra*. I am quite aware that many will consider it a fanciful one. Nor is it at all intended to make light of the Shastra in the outer sense. The inspired writings of sages are our greatest heritage and their value arises just from the fact that they are transcriptions of the inner Shastra as it revealed itself in the hearts of men of great inner attainments. At the same time, it must not be forgotten that they were not delivered in the void but in definite conditions of time, place, and society—which change.

Chapter Seventeen

The Yoga of the Threefold Faith

The seventeenth chapter begins with a question that is often asked: *Verse 1*
what is the status of those who set aside the injunctions of Shastra
(inner or outer) not in order to follow the promptings of desire but
full of faith that what they are doing is right? But this question is
based upon a misunderstanding of the nature of faith.

True faith is something of a much higher nature: it is the reflection in the lower mind of *knowledge* already possessed by the higher
and the buddhi. We read in chapter thirteen, verse twenty-five, of
those who on hearing of higher truths at once give themselves up to
them. They are able to do so because of this irradiation of the lower
mind by the knowledge of the higher, an irradiation which gives a
sense of certainty akin to that which someone feels on understanding
a geometrical proposition. Therefore it was that Hermes said:

"My word doth go before thee to the truth. But mighty is the
mind, and when it hath been led by word up to a certain point,
it hath the power to come before thee to the truth. And having
thought over all these things, and found them consonant with those
which have already been translated by the reason, it (the mind) hath
believed and found its rest in that Fair Faith."

It is important to understand this. The world is full of people
seeking to persuade others to believe in this or that doctrine, book, or

teacher, but the blind belief which they demand is, if given, nothing but the inert response of a tamasic mind and has no connection whatever with the Fair Faith of which Hermes speaks. Blind beliefs are perpetually coming into conflict with ascertained truth and it is for this reason that the believers are so fanatically propagandist, for they seek to silence their own doubts by the shouting of many voices.

Truth must be all-inclusive and harmonious. It cannot form into little eddies and closed systems. The only safe course is, as Hermes says, to think over all things and to accept those which are found to fit in with what is already known in one harmonious whole. If it be asked in what way this differs from the procedure of the so-called rationalist, it must be answered that the latter accepts only the data of the sense and the logical conclusions of the mind upon them, while the follower of the Fair Faith accepts the data coming from above and then proceeds to work over their interpretation until it can be expressed in a form consonant with reason.

Verses 2, 3

The necessity for this "working over" arises because the mind in which the knowledge is reflected is a thing of many colors, being made up of the gunas. "The faith of each is shaped to his own nature." If any can rise to the true Self they are no more concerned with faith for they have knowledge, but as long as that knowledge is reflected in the lower mind it is inevitable that it should take on the colors of that mind.

The turn which is given to it by their mind is also the lower, personal self, for the expression of their faith depends on which of the three gunas is dominant in their personality. A sattvic person will give faith a sattvic expression, and so with the other types. This comes out very clearly in the objects of worship. The only object of worship to the person of knowledge is the Atman within and in all beings, but those who live by faith alone will feel that unperceived Atman as a wondrous Power, sensed in external things and worshipped accordingly. Sattvic people will feel Its presence in the great awe-inspiring forces of Nature, in Sun and Wind and Water, and so will "worship the Gods." As their faith becomes purified they will turn more and more to the spiritual power behind those forces and leave the outer form.

Verse 4

Rajasic types will sense the same Power as it rushes fiercely in the desire-currents and so will worship *yakshas* and rakshasas, the personified consciousness behind desire for wealth and angry violence respectively. Those in whom tamas predominates will feel their imagination captivated by the fact of death and so the shades of the dead will draw their worship.

In modern civilization, too, these types appear in the nature-mysticism of a Wordsworth, in the all-too-common worship of wealth and power that show itself in a morbid interest in the lives of the wealthy and powerful, and in the devotion to the so-called spirits of the dead who are the Gods of spiritist cults, though in this last case there is also an admixture of rajasic curiosity.

It is not only in the objects of worship that the influences of the gunas make themselves felt; they show also in such things as the type of food eaten. Western readers may be inclined to see very little connection between faith and food, and on the other hand, in India, there is a tendency to see only too much connection. The true course, as always, lies in the middle. Since the body is built up of the food that is taken into it, and since, also, the taste of food forms an important and regular portion of our sense-life, it is obvious that both the quality and taste of food will have a significance for one

Verses 7-10

who is trying to follow the Path, though by no means the excessive significance that is sometimes attached to it in India. No amount of merely sattvic eating will suffice to make anyone spiritual.

Verse 11   The sacrifice (*yajña*) which the Gita mentions next must not be limited to the ceremonial sacrifices of ancient India. The yajña of the Gita means sacrificial action in general, the dedication of one's goods and deeds and self to the service of the Life in all. Sattvic people will do this, not out of any desire for personal reward, even in the shape of their own salvation, but because their sattvic nature reflects the knowledge of the Cosmic Sacrifice and impels them to participate therein.

Verse 12   The sacrifice of the rajasic person is, as might be expected, tainted by desire, and so this type sacrifices in order to gain some benefit for themselves, and usually denies the possibility of action that is free from such desire. In inferior types the mainspring of their actions is to be found in the wish to be known as religious, philanthropic or patriotic.

Verse 13   Tamasic sacrifice is still lower type, in which only the semblance of sacrifice is shown. It is not governed by any rule or principle (*vidhi*) nor has it any sanction in the inner Shastra (*mantra*). No actual giving away is involved (*asrishtanna*) and the whole performance is carried out without any skill (*dakshinam*). The motivation of such so-called sacrifices is usually mere instinct for social conformity.

It would be tedious to comment at length on the other ways in which faith may manifest. Worship, food, sacrificial action, self-discipline and charity are all important aspects of the spiritual life, and it is for this reason that the Gita has gone into such detail about them.

Verses   Some words must, however, be said about tapasya, usu-
5,6,19   ally translated as austerity, but better rendered as self-discipline. Tapasya does not mean standing on one leg in a forest nor piercing

the body with sharp spikes. Such torture of the body, common both in mediaeval Europe and in India, is the tamasic person's idea of tapasya. Identifying with the physical body, this one can see no way of making spiritual progress but by forcing that body to be passive under torture,[1] and so goes about naked or wears hair-shirts, or else starves the body and then mistakes the hallucinations of a weakened brain for spiritual visions.

Discipline of the body is quite a different thing from its injury by such practices. The body is the field in which we have to work and, later, will be needed for the service of the One. To weaken or destroy it by injudicious austerities is to destroy a valuable instrument. It is sometimes urged that the body is unreal and transient and that the person of knowledge will not care whether it functions well or badly, whether it lives or dies. But such a view is based on misunderstanding. Those who are practicing self-discipline do not have knowledge but, rather, are trying to gain knowledge. A weakened body, as the Upanishad has taught,[2] means a weakened mind, and if the body is unnecessarily abandoned before the Goal is reached, it only means that valuable years will have to be spent in educating a new one and in bringing it to the point at which the Path was left. The true attitude to one's body should be to treat it as one treats a riding horse, something to be intelligently disciplined, adequately cared for and properly used, and not to something either to be allowed to wander off at its own free will or else to be beaten to death or uselessness.

There is a further consideration that is equally powerful. The outer senses are but the manifestations of the inner or mental ones. The mortification of the outer leaves the inner ones quite intact.

Indeed, the sense-powers, forcibly suppressed without, are driven inwards and revenge themselves in a riot of imaginative fantasy within, which will disturb the spiritual life far more effectually than ever the outer sense-life could have done.

Self-discipline must begin, not with the senses, but with the mind. In the enumeration of the six mental endowments that form part of the fourfold qualification for knowledge of the Brahman (see chapter 15), *shama*, or control of mind, precedes *dama*, the control of the senses. The disciples must bend all their energies to the task of controlling their unruly minds, and when that is accomplished they may be sure that the outer senses will offer no serious obstacles to being brought under control.

Trying to control the senses without having first subjugated the mind is like trying to bail water out of a sinking ship without first stopping the leak. Even in cases of definitely inappropriate sense-indulgence, the inner fantasying about the objects of enjoyment does far more damage to the inner life than the actual outward gratification.

Another point that must be noted is that the mind cannot, under ordinary conditions, be treated as something separate from and independent of the body. It is true that the mind is the crux of the whole discipline, but it is also true that ordinary disciples are quite unable to rise to the level of functioning in their true or higher mind and that the mind in which they do live is very closely bound up with the physical body. It is easy to talk about being indifferent to bodily sensations, but nevertheless, to say nothing of severe pains, a few hours in a stuffy room will destroy almost anyone's power of clear thinking, and a few days of overwork or loss of sleep will cause self-control to vanish in gusts of irritability. This being so, it is obviously foolish for ordinary disciples to attempt a fine disregard of the bodily and external aspects of life when, all the time, the mental life is intimately bound up with them. "The contacts of matter come and go," as we read in chapter two, but while the disciples should "endure them bravely," they will not, in the earlier stages,[3] be able to disregard them altogether without disastrous results.

So much for the negative side of tapasya. On the positive side *Verse 14* what is needed is harmonious control of body, speech, and mind. The body is to be disciplined by being used for the service of the Gods, the Twice-born (of the genuinely spiritually illumined, that is, not of those who merely arrogate the title to themselves on the strength of outward ceremonies alone), of Teachers and all Knowers of the Truth, and further, by the practice of cleanliness, straightforwardness, harmlessness to all beings, and brahmacharya.

The last word connotes control and not suppression of the sex-forces. A neurotic celibacy with the so-called unconscious mind full of thwarted sex, issuing in a welter of more or less disguised fantasy, is the very worst condition to be in for one who seeks the inner life. Such a condition may, like extreme bodily weakness, give rise to strange experiences and visions, but it will quite effectually prevent any real treading of the Path. Sex can be transcended; it cannot be suppressed—with impunity.

It is important to note that a mere renunciation of sex by the conscious mind and will is not enough. Many would-be sannyasis in India, and I suppose some people in the West, having heard or read of the virtues of brahmacharya attempt a renunciation of all sex. The inevitable result is that the unsatisfied sex-desires are repressed into what psychologists term "the unconscious." However we may phrase it, the fact remains that these desires, with the psychic energy that is locked up in them, prevent all peace of mind, and, if denied attention, manifest as disturbing dreams and in other ways, such as bad temper. The only remedy is to bring them once more into the focus of attention; but in such cases—namely, where sex-desires have been repressed—this is usually impracticable, since to do so involves tormenting the mind with thoughts of having fallen from the Path or with division in the will.

A mind at peace with itself and a unified will are absolute essentials on the Path. The disciple should therefore be content to grow harmoniously as a flower grows, and not try to force development by renunciations which spring from the will alone and not from the whole being. The sex-desires must be de-energized by withdrawal and not pushed away by mere will. Only when they are drained of their energy is it safe to "renounce" them and then, indeed, renunciation is no longer needed.[4]

Of harmlessness (*ahimsa*) it is quite sufficient to say that one who seeks to serve the Life in all must certainly abstain from killing living creatures for his "sport" or even, in ordinary circumstances, for his food. "All beings tremble before punishment; to all life is dear. Judging others by yourself, slay not, neither cause to slay."[5] To cast eyes of greed at the flesh of a fellow-being is no act for disciples of this Path. Better to remember the perhaps legendary story of how the Buddha in a previous life gave his own flesh to feed a starving tigress and her cubs.

In addition to the above-mentioned discipline of the body they will discipline their speech, taking care that it is always truthful and helpful.

> *Govern the lips*
> *As they were palace doors, the King within;*
> *Tranquil and fair and courteous be all words*
> *Which from that presence win.* [6]

While being truthful they must avoid the common egoistic fault of making a devotion to the truth an excuse for inflicting pain upon hearers. This control of speech is by no means easy, as all who have tried to practice it are aware. In any case it is not possible to bring it to perfection until the mind is also disciplined.

The mental discipline is in fact the most essential of all, since it is in the raising of the mind to its true nature and in bringing about its union with the buddhi that the essence of the inner life is found. The mind must be tranquil, gentle, and free from wandering thoughts. The word for the last quality is *mauna*, which literally means "silent," but, as the context shows, the silence in question is a mental one and signifies the ability to remain calmly still in the face of those outer stimuli which usually make the mind jump about like the monkey to which it is often compared. *Verse 16*

In addition, it must be *Self*-controlled, able to direct or check its course of thought by its own inherent power, depending neither on the demand of physical necessity, nor on the lure of some outward gain; in the later stages it should not even depend for stillness upon the hypnotic rhythm of mantra repetition. Lastly, it must be pure in feeling too, free from all fear and hatred, filled with love and great compassion for all beings. It need hardly be added that if this discipline is to bear spiritual fruit it must be carried out harmoniously, without any one-sided exaggerations or fanaticisms, and with the sattvic characteristic

Verse 17 of disregard of any personal gain. Love of the Atman, not fear of the world, must be the motive force behind the effort.

Verse 23 The chapter ends with the threefold designation of Brahman, *Om Tat Sat*. This well-known mantra is intended here to show the Path along which a sattvic faith will lead the aspirant, thus indirectly answering the initial question of the chapter. *Om*, as is well known, signifies Brahman, but also stands for the three great states of Consciousness[6] which lead up to the Fourth or transcendental state. With Om the acts of sacrifice and discipline that constitute the

Verse 24 treading of the Path are commenced. That is to say, the attainment of the true Self, the Consciousness, though in its separated, individual form, is the task of the first stage.

Verse 25 The next stage, marked by what we have seen to be the typically sattvic characteristic of abandonment of all desire for fruit, is the bringing about of the union of that individual Self with the unindividuated buddhi, the cognitive aspect of the Mahat Atman, the One great Life. This stage is referred to by the word *Tat* (That) because it is through union with the Light Ocean of the buddhi that true knowledge of That, the transcendental Reality, is gained.

The last stage is symbolized by *Sat*, which stands for Being, also for Goodness and Reality. This stage is the attainment of the Brahman and this attainment is the "praiseworthy deed" which the text mentions as yet another meaning of the word.

But we have seen in the fourteenth chapter (verse 26) that, instead of withdrawing their Light from the world and merging it in the unmanifested Brahman, it is possible for those who have won the Goal to stay and serve the One, crucified in the countless suffering forms within the bitter Sea. Therefore the Gita adds that steadfastness in sacrifice, austerity, and gift is also Sat; meaning thereby that those who maintain a life of Sacrifice and offer up their dearly bought Salvation as a great Gift of Light to those who walk in darkness have no less attained than those who go beyond to the other Shore. Their Sat is "action for the sake of That" in all. Hence is it said that by this mantra of the triple Path have been brought forth the Teachers,[8] Knowledge, and the Sacrifices—the Sacrifices, namely, of those liberated Souls who find Nirvana in the very midst of Sorrow.

Notes

1　It is no answer to this to urge that such self-torturers often hold an extremely dualistic theory of the relationship between soul and body. Theory is one thing and perception quite another. It is just because they know nothing but the body that they imagine that bodily torture will liberate the soul.

2　Chandogya Upanishad, vi, 7.

3　It should be remembered that these last six chapters are inevitably to some extent recapitulatory.

4　The above should not be interpreted as urging a free yielding to sex-desire. That too is fatal for the Path. As always, it is the Middle Path which is to be followed. What is meant is that the desires should be kept in the field of attention, *there to be dealt with* by detachment of the self from them and consequent de-energizing of them. To push them out of sight of the mind is not to deal with them at all. One of the absolute essentials of the Path is that the disciple should face fearlessly whatever is in him, no matter how much his higher nature resents its presence. Self-ignorance and self-deceit are absolutely fatal.

5　Dhammapada, 130.

6　*The Light of Asia.*

7　Jagrat, svapna and sushupti. See appendix C.

8　The word *Brahmanas* in this verse is usually taken to refer to the books of that name. It seems more appropriate to take the word as referring to the Brahmans—i.e. Teachers of the Knowledge.

Chapter Eighteen

The Yoga of the Renunciation of Liberation[1]

This chapter begins with a question about the nature of true renunciation that arises out of the conclusion of the last. There it was taught that it is impossible for the liberated soul to remain steadfast in service even after its liberation. The intention of this chapter is to show that this idea is not correct and accordingly Sri Krishna starts by *Verse 2* making a distinction between sannyasa (renunciation) and *tyaga*. The former, he says, means the renunciation of desire-prompted actions. The mind, united with the buddhi, no longer flows outwards into the desire-currents but acts from the buddhi-determined knowledge of what is right. It is possible for the sannyasi to enjoy the fruits of his right action and when, in the course of time, his knowledge brings him to the threshold of the Brahma Nirvana there will be nothing to prevent his passing forever from the manifested world.

Sri Krishna goes on to teach that there is a further stage which he terms *tyaga*.[2] Tyaga consists in the giving up or dedicating to the One Life all of the fruits which accrue from even right and desireless *Verse 3* actions. In spite of the views of some teachers that all action should be abandoned as leading to bondage, He asserts most categorically *Verse 6* that acts of sacrifice, discipline, and self-giving (the action of the Path, as was pointed out at the end of the last chapter) should *not* be abandoned, for they are purifiers.

Even these actions, though, should be performed without attachment, without, that is, the feeling of doing them for one's own personal purity. The fruit which accrues from such action also is to be set free for the service of the One Life, in the spirit that prompted the Mahayana followers of the Bodhisattva Path to dedicate the merit of their actions to the welfare of all beings. Some object that such helping of others is mere illusion and would involve an infringement of the law of Karma. It will be time to listen to that objection when the objectors themselves deny ever having received any help through the medium of books or living teachers. Others are kept back from this Path by a false humility. It will be time enough, they say, to think of such service when we ourselves are liberated and it becomes a real possibility. But that is a mistake. It is only the ones who from the very start have accustomed themselves to the idea of treading the Path for the sake of all who will be able to be certain of being steadfast in sacrifice and of giving up their bliss to serve their suffering brothers when face to face with the actual bliss of the Brahma Nirvana.

This is the luminous sattvic tyaga as opposed to renunciation that springs from laziness, sense of inferiority, or desire to avoid the pain and suffering of life. Such "sour-grapes" renunciation is definitely inferior. It is a foul slander (whether ancient or modern) to represent the renunciation of the Buddha as having been of that sort. Truer insight was shown by the author of *The Light of Asia* when he attributed to the Buddha these words when about to leave his home:

Verses 6, 7, 8

> *This will I do because the woeful cry*
> *Of life and all flesh living cometh up*
> *Into my ears, and all my soul is full*

Of pity for the sickness of the world,
Which I will heal, if healing may be found
By uttermost renouncing and great strife.

Love, not fear, is the mainspring of all true renunciation.

Verse 9

The doing of actions because they are in harmony with the Cosmic process as revealed by the buddhi, and so are "what ought to be done," but without the pride of agency and without the desire for personal fruit, is the highest renunciation. The abandonment of the actions themselves is impossible as long as the would-be renouncer

Verses 11, 12

has a body and is unnecessary under any circumstances, for the actions that are performed without any desire for fruit can bring no bondage to the Soul at any time.

When desire has been renounced and also personal gain there is nothing left in action which can bind. To show that this is a plain fact, the Gita proceeds to give an analysis of the five factors that are

Verse 14

involved in all action, whether bodily, verbal, or mental. These are the physical body, the "doer," that false self which is produced by the union of the Light with the psycho-physical vehicle, the various sense-organs, the vital energies (*cheshta*) within the body and, lastly, the forces accumulated by the karma of one's past lives (*daiva*).

Verses 16, 17

That being so, the one, through not having united with the buddhi (*akritabuddhi*), sees the self, the Atman, as bound up in actions is quite deluded. If the self does not project itself into the forms by the notation "I am the doer," it can no more be affected by actions than the moon can be entangled in the ripples of a lake. As a Chinese sage has expressed it: "The moon is serenely reflected on the stream, the breeze passes softly through the pines. . . . When this is understood, the karma bonds are by nature empty. When not understood, we all pay for the past debts we have contracted."[3]

To further elucidate the point, the Gita shows that besides the nature of the action itself we must consider the actor and the knowledge of the actor. All these factors are shown to be threefold according to the guna that is predominant. If the action is not to bind the Soul, all three of these must be sattvic. The actor must be one who is unattached and free from the sense of "I"; the knowledge must be that pure knowledge which sees one indestructible Essence pervading all, "undivided in the separate beings," and the action itself must be appropriate, sanctioned by the inner Ruler and skillfully performed with regard to the actor's capacity and to the consequences for others.

Verse 19

Verse 26

Verse 22

Verses 23, 25

This last statement is sufficient to show that, in advocating renunciation of the fruit of action, the Gita is not sanctioning irresponsible acts. The consequences of actions *upon others* must always be considered; it is only the personal gains that are to be renounced. It is true that there are certain verses in the Puranas and elsewhere which represent liberated souls while still on earth as going about laughing and crying and behaving irresponsibly "like children or idiots." But these verses must not be taken literally. People of Knowledge are not idiots, nor do they manifest their liberation by childish behavior. It is true that personal thinking will have come to an end in them, but in its place the Cosmic Ideation manifests through them, and though their actions may not accord with established social conventions they are in harmony with the great Cosmic Order.

It is not necessary to follow through in detail the threefold nature of reason (*buddhi*), firmness, and pleasure. The account given

Verses 29-32

in verses 29 to 39 is perfectly straightforward and needs no comment, except to say that the word buddhi here signifies the ordinary intellect and not the higher *buddhi* of which so much mention has been made. The latter is sattvic in nature and is beyond the mind, while the former comes under the influence of all of the gunas and is a mental function. It has, however, this in common with the higher buddhi that, when sattvic, it is able to determine truth upon its own level and, in so far as intellectual truth is one, is the same in all.

With verse forty-one, as Shankara has pointed out, a new section begins. Up to this point the chapter has formed an integral part of the last block of six chapters and has been concerned with setting forth in detail the principles underlying Sri Krishna's teaching in the earlier chapters. From the point of view of the disciple they represent the effort to assimilate and express in intellectual terms the Divine Knowledge revealed in the Vision of the Cosmic Form. From verse forty-one onwards the Gita turns to the task of summing up the whole.

Reference has already been made (chapter 4, v. 13) to the fourfold order of society. The Divine foundation there claimed for the classification of human beings into Brahmans, Kshatriyas, Vaishyas, and Shudras must not be interpreted as sanctioning every injustice and prejudice of the orthodox Hindu caste system. It is not necessary to point out that there is plenty of evidence that the caste system itself in ancient India was not always the rigid and lifeless institution that it now is.

In any case, what the Gita is concerned with is not any particular sociological system, however ancient, but something far more universal. It is expressly stated that the classification in question depends upon the gunas manifested in the natures of those concerned. Not only in India, but all over the world there are four great human types. There is the Brahman, the teaching, priestly, legal, or "professional" type; the Kshatriya, the ruling, warrior, statesman type, the "hunting and shooting type" of the West; the Vaishya, or banking, merchant, agricultural type; and, lastly, the Shudra, the servant, manual laborer type. Each of these great types has certain well-defined characteristics, sometimes, though not at all necessarily, inherited by their offspring, and, though some overlapping undoubtedly occurs, they are at least as well-marked throughout the world and in all ages as, say, the modern psychological division into introverts and extroverts.

It must be noted that the qualities by which human beings are classified under one of these types are, in the case of the Brahman and Kshatriya at least, of a moral and intellectual nature. A person is not a Brahman because he is the son of a Brahman, nor even because he performs professional priestly functions. A Brahman is one who possesses certain qualities, such as control of mind and senses, self-discipline, forgiveness, straightforwardness, and wisdom. In this the Gita agrees with the Buddha, who also said: "Not by matted hair, nor by lineage, nor by birth is one a Brahman. He is a Brahman in whom there are truth and righteousness."[4]   *Verse 42*

The four types have also an important symbolic significance for the inner life. The Brahman, detached and pure, seeing the One in all, stands for the sattvic buddhi. The Kshatriya, ruler, fearless and much-enduring, is the pure rajasic manas, the higher mind. That is why Arjuna, the individual Self, is represented as a Kshatriya. The Vaishya, concerned with the getting of wealth, symbolizes the desire-nature (rajas mixed with tamas), always flowing outwards, while the Shudra, born to serve, stands for the tamasic physical body, instrument of all.

The verses which follow describe how perfection is to be won by being intent on one's own duty (*dharma*). The word *dharma* signifies the quality or natural function of a thing or person. Thus, the dharma of fire is to burn and the dharma of a Kshattriya is to manifest the qualities mentioned in verse 43. In these verses we must bear in mind the inner as well as the outer significance of the fourfold system.

Perfection is to be attained by using one's own characteristic functions in the service of That "from which this manifestation has proceeded." The attempt to perform the dharma of another is fraught with danger since it will be an attempt to build one's life on the basis of an undeveloped, and so inferior, function. It is like the successful comedian who aspires to take a tragic part, the result being usually a complete failure. The dharma to which one is called may seem by human standards a defective or inferior one but, on deeper analysis, it will be found that the same is true of all dharmas, just because they are relative and perfection is only in the Whole. Nevertheless, all are necessary to the working of the Cosmos and one can "see Infinity within a grain of sand."

From the inner point of view an equally important meaning attaches to this performance of duty without regard for the fruits, this worship of the One through one's own natural function. Human beings are not creatures of this physical plane alone, and perfection will be attained when all the various levels of their being, as symbolized by the four types, fulfill their natural functions in perfection. Even the desire-nature, the most troublesome part of human beings, has its work to perform in the Cosmos and, once again, the Gita is teaching that instead of the Light's being withdrawn from the manifested universe in the manner of the Sankhyas, it should function free and unattached on all levels. The tamasic inertia of the physical body and the fierce rush of the desire-mind are to be transmuted by non-attachment into stability and energy respectively. Thus controlled and mastered they, no less than the luminous buddhi, are fit instruments for the service of the One.

This yoga by which all the levels are transmuted is the Path to *Verse 51* mastery of the Cosmos. The disciples must be united to the One Life by the pure buddhi, the wasteful rush of the mind (*atmanam*) must be checked by firmness so that it moves by its own power and is no longer pulled and pushed by the blind forces of attraction and repulsion. The objects of the senses, no longer considered as objects of personal enjoyment, must be dedicated[5] to the service of the One Life. Studiously detaching themselves (*vivikta sevi*) from the forms, *Verse 52* constant in that *inner* meditation which needs no special time or place or posture, they will cut the knot of egoism so that the dis- *Verse 53* torted movements of lust, hate, violence, and greed to which that knot gives birth will cease and die.

Then are the disciples ripe for becoming the Eternal Brahman. Those who were human have become the Cosmic Man, their feet firmly based on earth, their heads high in the cloudless sky above. Of all the levels of the manifested world they are master. Nowhere is anything they need reject, for all that is, is verily the Brahman. *Verse 54* Serene in their true nature, they now, if they have come along the path of Love, attain to that supreme devotion which has no care for any conceivable personal gain, not even for the greatly coveted goal of Liberation. Caring not for the intense bliss of personal liberation, the bliss of sheer self-loss in the absolutely blissful Brahmic Being from which there is no return, they seek only to serve Sri Krishna, the Purushottama, in whatever sphere their service is required.

"Neither the bliss of heaven, nor yet world empires, no sway in Brahmic spheres, nor in the magic Land of Heart's Desire, no yogic powers, nor freedom from rebirth are sought by those who have found refuge at Thy feet."[6]

Verse 55

By this great love they know Sri Krishna in His essential being, the Purushottama of whom we have written in chapter 15. They are

Verse 56

the true *advaiti* or non-dualist, for they know no dualism of "this" and "That," no opposition of Nirvana and the world. They have no need to flee from one into the other, for in all states they see the one Eternal Krishna and, by their utter self-transcending love, they see His inmost heart and dwell therein.

Thus through their love they throw away liberation, to find it where they stand. They may and do perform all actions freely: freely they serve Him who is ever-free. And ever in their hearts they see Sri Krishna's feet. Through His grace, the calm and blissful Light that streams from Him,[7] wherever they may be, whatever they may do, they dwell eternal within the Great Abode.[8]

At this point Sri Krishna drops the general exposition and speaks directly to His disciples' hearts. He promises them that if they put aside all selfish fear and cling to Him, the inner Lord, His power, the power which sways the universe will carry them past all the obstacles and dangers that confront them on the way. At the same time, He adds the warning that the treading of the Path, the fight against the embattled Powers of Darkness, is, in the end, inevitable. The ego-

Verses 58, 59

istic desire for enjoyment and fear of suffering may hold them back from the flight for the time, but in the end the remorseless pressure of cosmic evolution will force their feet along the Path they shrink from now, and that same egoism that held them back, fatted like a beast for sacrifice, will be remorselessly destroyed.

For that great Ruling Power which guides the Cosmos is seated in the heart of every being. Whirling as though upon a potter's wheel, none can escape "the Spirit's plastic stress." However much we may proclaim ourselves as independent egos existing for and in ourselves, the Ruling Power of Spirit is within us and will not let us rest. We are, as it were, bound to the Center of our being by an elastic cord; the more we strain at it, the greater will be the reaction. This is why an exaggerated movement of materialism is followed by an equally exaggerated religiosity, an age of license by an age of Puritan restraint.   *Verse 61*

Sooner or later, all must tread the Path; but there is no compulsion. The human will, a spark of the Divine willing, is ineluctably free, and no true Teacher ever forces the disciples even for their good. Having revealed the Secret Path of Wisdom, all that He says is, "having reflected on it fully, do as thou wishest." The Path is free to all; each has the right to enter but none will compel him or trespass in the least upon his will.   *Verse 63*

But why await the age-long grinding of the cycles, when all the while the Middle Path exists, and may be trodden by whoever will? Avoiding the lures of sensual desire on the one hand, and of reactionary asceticism on the other, let the disciples consecrate their *whole being* to the service of the Divine Power dwelling in their hearts. Prefacing His words by the statement that what He is about to say is the ultimate Mystery, the supreme teaching, Krishna repeats the verse with which He has concluded chapter nine: *Verse 62*

"Fix thy mind on Me, give thy heart's love to Me, consecrate all   *Verse 65* thy actions to My service, hold thine own self as nothing before Me. To Me then shalt thou come; truly I promise for thou art dear to Me."

Verse 66

> *Abandoning all supports,[9] take refuge in Me alone.*
> *Fear not; I will liberate thee from all sins.*

Who is this "Me," refuge in whom is thus proclaimed to be the ultimate secret? Sri Krishna has here returned to the final teaching that He divulged in chapter fifteen, the secret of the Purushottama, the highest Divine Spirit, poised beyond all opposites, supporting all opposites and yet involved in none. He states that this teaching is even more profoundly secret than that of verse sixty-two which spoke of the great Ruling Power which dwells in the heart of all, a Power which He spoke of in the third person while now He uses the first.

For this ultimate Being of His is not to be approached through the philosophic knowledge that leads to the experience of Him as undifferentiated Brahman nor through the yogic meditation that leads to the experience of a Consciousness that dwells, luminous but yet impersonal, within the hearts of all. Rather, it is to be approached by a power which dwells in that most apparently limited and entangled of all things, the human personality.

Torn by our personal passions, weary of our personal complexities, bewildered at our inability to manage our personal relationships, we escape with relief into the liberating experience of nature and a marvelous calm descends upon our hearts. Yet who can hold with mountains, sea, or sky that spiritual dialog that person holds with person. It is only against our personal background, only because we stand all the time on a firm basis of personal feeling, that we are able to enjoy the adventure into impersonality. A world devoid of personality would be, not merely a poorer world, but an infinitely poorer world. Hidden in the very heart of our personal failings is the mystic Jewel, unknown to the impersonal being of Gods, who covet human birth. The innermost human treasure, Sri Krishna's richest and intensest being, is approachable through personal surrender and personal love alone.

It is not true that personality is mere illusion to be dissolved in impersonal vastness. The greatest of those we meet in the spiritual world shine with more, not less, personality than do common folk, and, when we pass beyond them to the great Divine Incarnations, Sri Krishna, Rama, Buddha, Christ, we find the same personal quality raised, as it were, to an infinite intensity. The calm, compassionate gaze of the Buddha, the burning intensity of Christ and the laughing intimate glances of Sri Krishna's dancing eyes are all infinitely personal, and it is just these qualities that draw our hearts and draw them with a strength that is far beyond the power of all "teaching."

Nor does this innermost Divine value vanish away into an ocean of impersonality on the withdrawal of the visible Form. As the Gita itself has told us, "that which is real never ceases to be." Deep calls to deep in a language far transcending all philosophy. "Our most precious Stone," as the alchemists said, "has been cast upon the dunghill," and those who have so cast it have been the abstraction-loving philosophers.

It is this that is the final secret, the indefinable essence that is hidden in and gives its value to personality, a strange and magical something which eludes all intellectual analysis, and, indeed, which vanishes before the gaze of the philosopher like the *Yaksha* before the eyes of Indra in the Kenopanishad.

Therefore Sri Krishna, having in these eighteen chapters prepared, as it were, the setting, now puts into place the central jewel, the glowing heart of the whole. He drops all else and speaks in these concluding verses of Himself alone, of His richest and most secret being, knowable only by the human heart.

Not to any giving up of personality and personal feeling does He urge His friend, but to a combing out of its tangles, a reorientation and centering of it so that he may behold the central marvel that none who has ever even dimly seen can ever again forget, a glowing Lotus blooming in the Void, in its heart the precious Stone that shines with a Dark Light more lovely than all colors of the world.

"Fix thy mind on *Me*; give thy heart's love to *Me*." To such a one, giving himself in ecstasy of love, there comes the free response of love, the pressure of the hand, the strong support, as unfettered and as free from all thoughts of "deserving" as is human love at its best. "To Me, then, shalt thou come; truly I promise, for thou are dear to Me."

This is the mystery of what is termed Grace, *Kripa*, something that is beyond even the all-pervading Divine Compassion (*karuna*), that shines alike on all who open themselves to it, something utterly incalculable and unpredictable, the mystic power that flashes from heart to heart, the final undeterminable power of love.

The one thing necessary is that we should abandon the supports (*dharman*) on which we have hitherto based and propped our egos in the attempt to enhance their sense of value and security—the supports of caste and *ashrama*, of wealth and social position, of learning or of virtue—all those supports that have enabled us to say: "I am I, a person not without importance in the world." All these trumpery pedestals we must abandon and base ourselves on Him alone who is the Support of all the worlds. Then to the Soul freed of its entanglements with self, freely placing its hand in the hand of the Ever-free Krishna, comes the free gift of love: "fear not; I will liberate thee from all sins."

Those who attempt to stand on the basis of their own personal merits, good deeds, yogic skill or philosophic insight, must stand the test of having them examined in the fire, and, if they fail the test, they are still bound. But the ones who in the very depths of their heart, stand on love and friendship for Sri Krishna, stand on something that existed before the universe was born and is therefore not subject to its karmic accounts. Not "alone to the Alone" but free for the Free they live, giving forever the service that love asks of love and friend of friend.

The actual fighting they must still undertake: Krishna is charioteer and bears no arms. Nevertheless, His inexhaustible power will flow through all the vestures of the dedicated Soul, His faultless counsel will guide in all perplexity, and, at the moment of supreme peril, when the resistless magic weapon is hurled by Karna's unerring aim, His hand will press down the chariot into the solid earth so that the blazing missile passes harmlessly overhead. With Him as charioteer the victory is sure.

This is that taking of refuge in Krishna which, when accomplished, frees the disciples from all other duties. No longer have they to think of any duties of their own, worldly or unworldly, nor of any master of their separate vehicles, for their whole life on all levels is consecrated to Him and belongs to Him alone. Gradually as they proceed, the beloved Krishna becomes more and more the heart and focus of their life until no thought or action is performed except in relationship to Him.[10] In the place of their separate individual lives there flows through them the One Divine Life of all beings, "the Light that lighteth every one that cometh into the world." United in their heart with Him who is the heart of that One Life, all "sins" drop from them like things that never were; in losing self all sins are lost as well. Henceforth the free Divine Life alone acts through what human beings in ignorance will still call "them."

Verse 67   The Gita adds a warning against communicating this Mystery to anyone who is undisciplined, without love, without desire to serve (*ashushrushu*), or speaks evil of the Teacher. This prohibition is not prompted by any spirit of exclusiveness but by the desire to prevent harm being done. The above-mentioned types would assuredly fail to understand its inner meaning and, grasping at the letter of such promises as that in verse 66, would harm themselves and others.[11]

The next two verses make this entirely clear, for they set forth the praises of those who impart the mystic teaching to such as are ready to profit by it. They are the renouncers of personal salvation to whom the chapter title refers, they who out of transcendent devotion (*para bhakti*, cf. verse 54) set aside their bliss till every living being *Verse 69*   can share it with them. It is for this great Sacrifice that Krishna says of them, that none either are or ever will be dearer to Him. They are the calm Great Ones[12] spoken of by Shankaracharya who, having themselves crossed over the Ocean, devote themselves unselfishly to helping others to cross.

Little remains to say.[13] The Path, the Goal and the Great Sacrifice have been set forth and understood and the Soul breaks out in triumphant ecstasy:

Verse 73   "Destroyed is my delusion. Memory has been regained. By Thy grace, O Unfallen One, my doubts are gone. Thy bidding I will do."

Once before,[14] after the first inner perception of the spiritual Pervading Powers, Arjuna has proclaimed the vanishing of his delusion, but now the further steps have been accomplished. He is established in Reality; he has regained his Memory of That Eternal One from which he came, to which he now returns. All Knowledge now is his and, with the alternatives before him of eternal changeless bliss or of unwearying service of his suffering brother-men, he chooses the latter and cries out to the Unfallen Changeless Being that he will do His bidding and will serve Him to the end.

Thus ends the dialogue between the Soul and its eternal Source. It is the Soul itself that is enlightened, but the illumination is brought down to the level of the ordinary waking personality by the mediation of Sañjaya, the link between the two. "Remembering, remembering" the glories of that Divine Enlightenment, he floods the heart with joy and proclaims the undying truth, that when the human Soul is united with the Divine, victory, welfare, and righteousness are eternally assured.

Verses 76-78

Notes

1 In some editions this chapter is entitled simply sannyasa yoga, but that is the title of chapter five. A few also give it as *moksha* yoga, but the full title is moksha sannyasa yoga.

2 In popular usage "sannyasa" and "tyaga" are more or less synonyms, but in addition to the meaning of "relinquishiment," tyaga has also the meaning of donation, of giving away (see Apte). I cannot think of any one English word which combines the two concepts of renouncing and giving except, perhaps, the word "dedication." My friend Pandit J. C. Chatterji pointed out to me that the past participle, *tyakta,* is used of offerings made to the Gods in the sacrificial fire.

3 *Yoka Daishi.* Quoted from Suzuki's *Manual of Zen Buddhism.*

4   Dhammapada, 393.

5   *Tyakta.* The sense of dedication is dominant here.

6   Srimad Bhagavada, x, 16-37.

7   The word *prasada* means both grace and also tranquil clarity.

8.   This is the meaning of the Vaishnava doctrine of the rejection of liberation: it is also the Bodhisattva doctrine of the Buddhists, the teaching of the *apratishthita* Nirvana.

9   *Dharman.* The word *dharma* has many meanings, but ultimately it comes from the verb *dhri*, meaning to support.

10   What is said here of Sri Krishna is true also of the relationship with the human guru when rightly understood.

11   The use of the Gita to justify war and the futilities of sentimental pietism are instances of what can result from a disregard of this prohibition.

12   *Shanta Mahantah—i.e.* those who, though realizing their nature as the Shanta Atman, beyond all manifestation, remain on the level of the Mahat Atman, the cosmic Ideation or Divine Wisdom (Viveka Chudamani, verse 39).

13   The reference to the results of simply hearing with faith (verse 71) must be understood in the light of what has been said about faith in the previous chapter.

14   Gita, xi, 1.

APPENDICES

Appendix A

Consciousness and Form

The two terms, "consciousness" and "form", are in constant use throughout this book and an understanding of the sense in which they are used is of vital importance.

If any experience is analyzed—say for example, the visual experience of a blue disc—two aspects can be distinguished. There is the content, a round, blue shape in this instance, and the "awareness" of that shape. The content is what I have termed *form* and the awareness *consciousness.*

It must be carefully noted that form does not here mean outline, but filled-in content-shape, and the term must also be understood in the same way of other elements of experience, sensuous or non-sensuous. For instance we have the "form" of a sound, a taste, a feeling, or a thought, which must be understood by analogy with the forms of visual experience.

In contrast with these forms, which are all different both as regards individual forms within one class and as regards different classes of forms, there is the awareness or consciousness, which is of the same sort throughout.

There are many drawbacks to the use of the word consciousness. In the first place, it is used in half a dozen different senses by philosophers and psychologists; and, in the second place, it suffers from the great drawback that it has no active verbal form. One can say "to be conscious of" but not "to conscious" such-and-such an object. There is the word "awareness" and the dubious coined derivative "awaring," which I have also occasionally pressed into service, but it is ugly and not very current. The best term is one that was coined by E. D. Fawcett in his *The World as Imagination, Zermatt Dialogues*, etc. the term in question is *consciring*— i.e. "knowing together"—and has as its correlative, for the content-form, the word *conscitum* (plural, *conscita*). I should certainly have availed myself of these coinages but, unfortunately, they are not as yet sufficiently widely current to be generally understood and, moreover, a great deal of this book had been written before I came across Fawcett's writings.

It should be clear from introspective meditation that all forms are sustained in consciousness, and that, apart from consciousness, we know nothing and can know nothing of forms. It is in fact meaningless to talk of forms as existing apart from consciousness.[1] The objects supposed by some to exist behind the forms are mere mental constructs devised for dealing with experience in practice. No one knows them, no one can ever know them; to believe in their existence is a pure and quite uncalled-for act of faith.

It should not be supposed that by the forms are meant sensations, camera pictures of reality located somewhere in the brain. The brain itself (as an "object") is one of the constructs of which mention has just been made. The usefulness of such constructs in certain realms of thought and study is not at all denied, but they are irrelevant here.

The primary bedrock of experience is not sensations in the eye, ear, or brain, but visual and other forms *in space*. All the rest is inference and construction. Materialistic science begins by abstracting consciousness from the forms in order to deal with them more objectively and impersonally and then, when analysis fails to reveal any life or conscious principle in those forms, triumphantly exclaims that all is mechanism, nowhere is there anything of a spiritual nature. Behaviorist psychology is an example of the same procedure applied to mental life. If you start by abstracting consciousness from phenomena it is obviously absurd to expect to find it as a term in your concluded analysis. For this reason no one should feel disappointed that science (as nowadays practiced) does not know anything of the existence of "the soul." It is the old story of looking for one's spectacles when they are on one's nose.

To go into this subject fully would require a volume and not an appendix. Here I am only concerned to indicate the sense in which the word consciousness has been used in this book. It follows from that sense that the modern term "unconscious" mind can have no meaning. There is not the slightest reason for supposing that anything whatever, physical or mental, exists or can exist save as the content of consciousness. Hence we can talk of a sub- or a super-conscious mind, meaning by those terms mental processes that are sustained in consciousness below or above the level at which it is normally focused, processes which are not attended to by normal consciousness, but we cannot talk of an unconscious mind, for that would have no meaning.

It only remains to add that the Sanskrit term for what is here termed consciousness is *chit*, as distinct from *chitta*, which means the mind. The Buddhists, on the other hand, speak of *Vijñana* (Pali-*viññana*). Thus consciousness illuminating visual forms is called *caksuh-vijñana* (eye-consciousness), illuminating thoughts, *mano-vijñana* (mind-consciousness), and so on. Beyond the sense and mind consciousness (at least in Mahayana systems) is the Alaya Vijñana or store-consciousness, corresponding to the Mahat Atman as used in this book. The Mayanists also use the word *chitta* to do duty for consciousness as well as for mind. For instance they will speak indifferently of *chitta-matra* or Vijñana-matra, meaning by both terms pure consciousness.

Note

1.   This position must by no means be confused with that of subjective idealism. The consciousness spoken of is not "your" or "my" consciousness, in fact "you" and "I" exist only as constellated form-sequences brought to foci in that consciousness which, in itself, is neither human nor individualized, but a pervading Light.

Appendix B

Soul and Matter

The word "Soul" as used in this book does not refer to a separate entity within the body but to the inner center of the linked streams of experience that make up a personality. That center is a focus in consciousness, not any individual's consciousness but the all-pervading sea of Light. As such it is not a separate "entity" any more than the focus to which light is brought by a lens is a separate entity. That focus primarily exists on the level of the higher or pure manas, but a projection of it is to be found functioning as the desire-mind or personality lower down. It is that lower or projected center that is the core of the empirical personality. It does not exist in any objective way, but comes into being as a center to which our experiences are referred. That is why a very young child has no sense of self and that, too, is why, when in certain pathological states the experience-content gets organized into two instead of one constellation, we get two selves instead of one—the so-called dissociation of a personality.

As for the higher Self, the true ego, that too is not a "thing-in-itself." It is however a focus which lasts through ages. Itself not born, it yet emanates that projection which forms the self of any given life. Its own content when outward-looking is the accumulated fruit of the experiences gained by its repeated projections, and when inward-looking the universal knowledge of the buddhi.

In a still higher sense the Self is the One Life in all (Mahat Atman), seeing through all the foci but beyond them all. In the highest sense it is the transcendental Self, the Shanta Atman. Beyond that is the Parabrahman, no self at all.

It will be seen that Soul and Self have been used synonymously.

When the former word has been used it was because the context needed a warmer emotional tone than is conveyed by the more philosophic term Self. In particular it refers to what has been termed the true Ego, backed by the feeling-knowledge of the buddhi.

The Sanskrit word, Atman, of which "self" is a translation, is used in just the same way of any level with which the Light is identified. Sometimes the body, more often the mind (e.g. Gita, vi, 5), sometimes the buddhi (e.g. *jñanatman* in Katha Upanishad), sometimes the transcendental Self (Shanta Atman), sometimes, though only symbolically, the Parabrahman (*Paramatman*—e.g. Gita, xv, 18). In this last case the term should be taken as signifying That which is the reality behind all self. It will be seen from this that Atman is not a thing, but a Light or, as was perhaps the earliest meaning of the word, a "breath."

Throughout this book self with a small "s" signifies the empirical or personal self, Self with a capital the true ego or higher Self. Qualifying adjectives are added to denote the still higher levels.

Turning now to the word "matter" it is necessary to point out that it is not used in the sense of "stuff" existing in its own right. It has been shown in the course of the book that there is not the slightest reason to suppose that any such "stuff" exists at all. It is a mental construction and under the eye of modern physics it is evaporating more and more with each new advance. There is nothing beyond or behind the sense-data—except the Brahman, which, if the word must be used, is the only "stuff" that exists. The billiard-ball atoms of the nineteenth century, the miniature solar systems of the early twentieth century, and the waves of probability of the present are all alike—pure mental constructions evolved for the explaining, measuring, and predicting of experience—and have no more reality in themselves than mathematical concepts such as the square root of minus one.

Where the word "matter" has been used in this book it is in the sense of objectivity, of content standing over against the Light, of self-projection into that content and of the Self-loss, separation, and pluralism that result. The descent of the Soul into Matter signifies the going-out of the Light into its content, its self-identification with it and the consequent increasing objectification of the latter. This should be born in mind throughout.

Appendix C

Four States of Consciousness

Throughout Hindu philosophic and symbolic writings, frequent references are made to the three states of Consciousness—*Jagrat, Svapna, Sushupti*—and the fourth transcendent state known simply as *Turiya*, or "the fourth." Translated as the waking, dreaming, and deep-sleep states, this scheme seems to many merely a rather naive attempt at classification of psychological states. To those who have more vision it is a key to unlocking many locks. The "dreaming" and "deep-sleep" states are not to be identified with the states commonly known as such. Rather, the latter are species of those genera. The *Jagrat* or "waking" state is that of ordinary consciousness, a state in which the Consciousness illuminates the field of outer sense-data. It is the world of outer objectivity, or, more strictly speaking, it is the world in which the division of subject and object is most clearly apparent. In this state we think of the "world" as something quite outside us and quite independent of ourselves. It would exist, we feel, even if we did not. That is why *The Voice of the Silence* refers to it as the *Hall of Ignorance.*

The second or Svapna (literally, dreaming) state is felt as an *inner* world. Its content is made up of the data of the inner senses and of the thoughts, and it reaches up as high as the manas. Though the distinction between subject and object is not felt to be so hard and fast it still persists, as, of course, does the illusion of plurality. In the *Jagrat* state the world was felt as a hostile or at best neutral environment in which we are arbitrarily plunged, but in the Svapna state it is felt even by us that the content of that world is a projection of our own psyche. However unpleasant we may find the environment of a dream, or the universe of thought in which we are absorbed, we recognize (at least afterwards) that it was our own creation. Its unpleasantness is due to something unpleasant in us. This is the world of inner, often hidden, desire and of psychic forms. *The Voice of the Silence* calls it the *Hall of Learning* because it is through experience of that state that we learn, first, that we are not the physical body, and secondly, that environment is self-created and is an outer manifestation of our own past acts and thoughts (*karma*). "What is to be learnt from it is that all that happens to us is the inevitable result of what we have thought, and in that plastic world this can be readily seen and grasped. If one's thoughts have been harmonious our Svapna environment, whether in day-time fantasy, at night, or after death, will be a pleasant one (*cf.* the heaven worlds of mythology and spiritualism), which may tempt us to linger enjoying vivid pleasures. How often for example would we not like to prolong those vivid dreams in which, though we have a body, it no longer clogs us with its inert weight and we fly and do all manner of pleasant things with an unheard-of ease?"

Nevertheless "under every flower a serpent is coiled," the serpent of desire. However pleasant it may be, this world is still a world of desire and plurality, and, as the Upanishad says, "As long as there is plurality there is fear."

The disciple must therefore pass on to the third state, the state of Sushupti (dreamless sleep), termed in *The Voice of the Silence,* the Hall of Wisdom. This is the level of buddhi-mahat and is termed the hall of wisdom because in it plurality, the great illusion, has vanished: all is one living Unity of Light. It may be wondered why the dark state of dreamless sleep should be taken to typify this state if it is One of Light. The reason for the darkness of the state as known to most people is that they are centered in the personality (lower manas) and cannot rise to their own true Selves, still less to union with the buddhi above. The result is that when the pluralistic vision of the lower self is transcended nothing is left except a dark blank, retaining of the true Sushupti nothing except its unity.

As Gaudapada puts it in his *Karikas* on the Mandukya Upanishad (iii, 34 and 35):

"The condition of the mind of a wise person in *samadhi* (trance on the Sushupti-level) free from imaginations, is to be distinguished from that of dreamless sleep for it is not the same. In sleep the mind is simply overpowered, but not so in samadhi, for then it is the fearless Brahman blazing with the light of Knowledge." And Shankara comments: "For the condition of the mind immersed, during sleep, in the torpidity of ignorance (*avidya*—i.e. the idea of plurality), and still full of the potential impressions of the cause of experience, is quite distinct from that absolutely independent and perfectly tranquil condition of samadhi, all light."

The above explains why it is that the Upanishads declare that the Soul goes to the Brahman every night in sleep and also why modern readers are apt to feel that, if that is so, going to Brahman can be no very great affair! Again, when the Upanishads declare that the waking feeling "happy I slept" is the memory of the bliss of Brahman (more exactly of the Mahat Atman) they are not referring to a physical feeling of refreshment after sleep but to a phenomenon well known on the Path. In early stages it will happen that, though the personal consciousness of the disciples is not able to unite properly with the buddhi, Sushupti experience is able to be reflected in their personal mind, and they may be aware of it in his waking consciousness either as a memory of a peculiarly vivid dream felt to be charged with spiritual meaning or simply as a feeling of inner bliss felt equally to be of intense significance, though of what it was about he has no knowledge.

The *Turiya* (fourth) state is that of sheer transcendence, the unmanifested Consciousness of the Shanta Atman. It is the Goal and is best left in silence.

It may be added that the Mandukya Upanishad, which deals with these four states, though in a very compressed manner, states that the Mantra Om can be considered as split up into the three elements, A, U, and M. Of these A signifies the Jagrat, U the Svapna, and M the Sushupti, while the Om, taken as a single unity, stands for the "Fourth." The repeated counsel to meditate on the Om has no reference to setting up "vibrations" in the subtle body but to raising the consciousness through the three stages into the Fourth.

Appendix D

Avataras

As chapter four (particularly verses 6 to 8) is the main authority for the doctrine of Avataras or Divine Incarnations it is perhaps desirable to say a word or two on the subject. According to orthodox tradition certain times in the history of the world have been marked by direct Divine "descents." Besides less-known ones, Rama Chandra, Sri Krishna, Buddha, and, by the more liberal-minded, Christ are usually considered as such. There is a well-known list of ten which is generally accepted, though the Bhagavada has a less widely known list of twenty-four. The doctrine is accepted as a relative truth by the Advaita Vedanta school, though in strict accuracy it can find little place in Advaita thought, for which all forms and all births are due to ignorance. In reality the teaching belongs to the Bhagavada (Vaishnava) tradition, though accepted by all others with the exception of one or two "protestant" modern sects.

The Avataras, scholastically defined as descents from beyond the five-fold universe into it (*aprapañchat prapañche avatirna*), are of many sorts. There are manifestations undertaken for a special purpose, such as that of *Nrisingha*, the so-called Man-Lion, and descents in animal forms, probably symbolic, such as the *Matsya* or Fish Avatara, perhaps connected with the Chaldaean Oannes, the Man-Fish who swam up the Persian Gulf to teach wisdom to the Sumerian dwellers in Eridu. Apart from these, there are the "descents" in human form of whom the most famous are Sri Rama Chandra and Sri Krishna. They are classified as partial Descents (*anshavatara*) and full, in the sense that while the former manifest only a particular selection of the Divine Powers, the latter manifest them in their fullness.

It is universally held that Sri Krishna is such a Full Avatara, and indeed, some schools, following the Bhagavada tradition, go further and affirm that He is the actual source or root of all the other Avataras. Be that as it may, tradition represents Him as manifesting in their fullness the Divine Wisdom and Power from the very moment of His birth.

In addition to these types there are many others of which perhaps the only one we need notice is the *Avesha* Avatara, an overshadowing of some highly evolved human soul for a particular purpose. Vyasa, the classifier of the Vedas and revealer of so many other Scriptures, including the Mahabharata itself (and of course the Gita), is sometimes held to be an instance of this type of Avatara in which the Divine Consciousness overshadows and takes possession of a human soul.

Such is the account given by tradition and accepted by Hindus in general. A view has sometimes been put forward that all Avataras are really of this last class, and that, in all cases, the actual *avatarana* is really the answering "descent" called out, as it were, from the Eternal by the aspiration of an "ascending" human soul, and manifesting thereafter through him, so that "he" is no more a man as we understand the term but a vehicle for the manifestation of the Supreme.

Such a view certainly seems to fit the case of the Buddha, who remembered all His past lives of human striving, and, as a matter of fact, it differs only in terminology from the views of some Mahayanist Buddhist schools.

Nevertheless it is certainly not the Hindu view that all Avataras are of this type and, indeed, it would be strenuously denied. In particular, it is definitely held that Sri Krishna is a direct manifestation of the Supreme in a form apparently, but only apparently, human. Sri Madhyacharya as well as Sri Chaitanya Deva, indeed, taught that all *avataric* Forms are actually eternal (*nitya*) and merely manifest on this plane from time to time, a view which, whatever may be its difficulties from the viewpoint of ordinary common sense, has certainly a very important mystical basis.

At any rate, it clearly betrays a very limited conception of the Divine nature to deny *a priori* the possibility of His (or Its) manifesting when, where, and how He pleases in a universe of which the entire structure on all levels constitutes a "descent" of His various powers. Surely the days are past when the "eternal laws of nature" could be held to interpose any obstacle in the way of the Divine Freedom.

Appendix E

Diagram of the Cosmic Levels

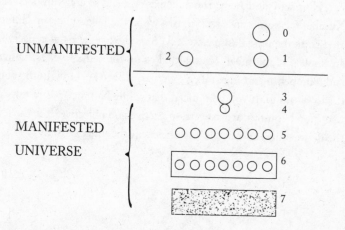

Number 0: Parabrahman Purushottama, beyond all levels.

Number 1: Shanta Atman, Pure Consciousness, Unmanifested Self, Adhyatma, Svabhava.

Number 2: Mula-prakriti, the Matrix, Unmanifested Object, Avyakta.

Number 3: Mahat Atman, Mahat, the One Life, Great Self, adhi-daivata, Cosmic Ideation, Divine Wisdom.

Number 4: Buddhi, knowledge of Number 3, also the faculty by which that knowledge is acquired, jñana atman.

Number 5: Manas, higher Mind, Ahankara, Individual Egos, the "point of view," jiva, Adhiyajña.

Number 6: Lower manas—i.e. united with the desire-nature; personalities; also the *Indriyas* (senses) and their inner objects, Adhibhuta.

Number 7: The outer world, objects of the outer senses, Adhibhuta.

Number 0 and 1 are often taken as one, and so are Numbers 3 and 4. Number 6 is sometimes split in two when the lower manas is differentiated from the pure desire-nature. Where the five levels of consciousness are spoken of, Number 2 is omitted as on the same level as Number 1, and Numbers 6 and 7 are taken together, as both are brought to a focus in the lower mind. It will be noticed that, while Number 7 is purely objective, Number 6 has two aspects, subjective and objective. It is the level of the desire-mind and also of the objects of the inner senses.

Appendix F

The Process of Cosmic Manifestation

The manifestation of a Cosmos depends on the polarization of the One, the Parabrahman, into the transcendental Subject, the Shanta Atman, and the transcendental Object, the Mula-prakriti. While it would be absurd to attempt to explain how that polarization actually occurs, it may be useful to make a few suggestions as to how we may conceive it as occurring.

Let us take as a basis the sublime Creation Hymn of the Rig Veda (x, 129, Griffith's translation):

> *(1) There was not non-existent nor existent;*
> *   there was no realm of air, no sky beyond it.*
> *What covered in, and where? and what gave shelter?*
> *   Was water there, unfathomed depth of water?*

"Existent" (*sat*) must here be taken in the sense of ex-istent; something which "stands forth." Note that while *air* (the moving world of manas and plurality) and *sky* (the calmly shining Cosmic Ideation, Mahat) are negated, that which covered in (the all-enfolding consciousness or Shanta Atman) and the *depth of water* (the Matrix or Mula-prakriti) are not negated but questioned. It cannot be said of them that they are not, though neither can it be said that they are.

> *(2) Death was not there, nor was there aught immortal:*
> *   No sign was there, the day's and night's divider.*
> *That One Thing, breathless, breathed by Its own nature:*
> *   Apart from it was nothing whatsoever.*

The *mortal* personalities and the *immortal* Egos had not come into existence nor was there any division between the dark or lower half of the Cosmos and the *light* upper half. The One, however, was not in a static death-like state, but was characterized by a rhythmic process which will be discussed later.

> (3) *Darkness there was: at first concealed in Darkness*
> *the All was indiscriminated chaos.*
> *All that existed then was void and formless: by the*
> *great power of warmth (*tapas*) was born that Unit.*

So far beyond all thought or imagination is that One that It is only to be conceived as Darkness. In that Darkness was buried the potentiality of all existence. By the power of tapas or self-limitation arose the Unit, the Shanta Atman, or One Consciousness.

> (4) *Thereafter rose Desire (*kama*) in the beginning,*
> *Desire the primal seed and germ of* Manas.
> *Sages who searched with their heart's thought discovered*
> *the existent's kinship in the non-existent.*

With the arising of the unitary Consciousness the other aspect of the One becomes the Object (*Mula-prakriti*) and, attracting the attention of the Consciousness, causes an outpouring of energy which is here termed Desire and which is the root of the individual Self (*manas*). The second half of the verse tells how, by searching within the heart (*manas*), the original undifferentiated Reality is to be found.

> *(5) Transversely was their severing line extended:*
> *What was above it then, and what below it?*
> *There were begetters, there were mighty forces,*
> *free action here and energy up yonder.*

Below these two is a great gulf, the "abyss" of the Kabala, which divides the manifested below from the unmanifested above. Above was the massive energy and "here" (i.e. below) the *begetters*, mighty forces of "desire" spiraling downwards and referred to in Gita (xi, 15) as the Divine Serpents.

> *(6) Who verily knows and who can here declare it,*
> *whence it was born and whence comes this creation?*
> *The Gods are later than this world's production.*
> *Who knows then whence it first came into being?*

The actual first impulse to creation is forever hidden in the Darkness, and that is why the Buddha kept silent on the subject and refused to go beyond Desire. The Gods who are the levels of manifested consciousness came into being later. In other words, Consciousness cannot penetrate to its own root.

> *(7) He, the first origin of this creation,*
> *whether He formed it all or did not form it,*
> *Whose eye controls this world in highest heaven,*
> *He verily knows it, or perhaps He knows not.*

The proximate origin of the creation is *He*, the Shanta Atman, the One Consciousness, whose *eye controls this world in highest heaven*, all the forms being drawn forth and sustained by and in that Consciousness. The ultimate root is, however, even beyond the Atman. Not even for the Shanta Atman can It be an object of knowledge, for to know It is to merge in It and in that merging the separate Knower comes to an end.

One point remains to be noticed. The second verse states that in the One (even during the period of *pralaya*) there is a certain rhythmic process symbolized as breathing. Within the One exist in potentiality the two poles of Subject and Object (which, it will be remembered, were not entirely negated in verse one). We may conceive that "breath" as a rhythmic alternation of polarity between these two. When the pendulum swing has attained a certain amplitude we may conceive something happening comparable to what takes place in ourselves when mental processes that have been going on below the threshold of consciousness rise into the light and emerge as "I am experiencing such-and-such."

Incidentally it may be mentioned that some accounts treat the emergence of the Mula-prakriti as prior to that of the Shanta Atman. The contradiction is not so much real as apparent. It must be remembered that we are in a region beyond time as we know it and the stages are more logical than temporal ones. When the emergence of the Mula-prakriti is taken as prior it is because, from one point of view, consciousness *manifests* only when there is something there to be conscious of, just as light becomes manifest only when there is something to be illuminated. The two (Subject and Object) are two poles of the One Reality and priority in manifestation is largely a matter of viewpoint.

As an illustration of the identity of the inner teaching in the different schools, the following quotation from the *Zohar* may be of interest. The identifications in brackets are somewhat tentative as I have not made an adequate study of the Kabalistic version. The translation is Sperling and Simon's:

"What is within the Thought [the Shanta Atman] none can conceive, much less can one know the *En Soph* [the Brahman], of which no trace can be found and to which thought cannot reach by any means. But from the midst of the impenetrable mystery, from the first descent of the *En Soph*, there glimmers a faint indiscernible light like the point of a needle, the hidden recess of thought [the Shanta Atman], which even yet is not knowable until there extends from it a light in a place where there is some imprint of letters [the Mula-prakriti], and from which they all issue. First of all is *Aleph* [the Mahat Atman], the beginning and end of all grades [the levels], that on which all the grades are imprinted and which yet is always called 'one' to show that though the Godhead contains many forms [the Cosmic Form] it is still one. This is the letter on which depend both the lower and the upper entities" (*Zohar*, i, 21A).

Appendix G

After-Death Paths

Popular Hinduism has sometimes taken the "times" of death mentioned in chapter eight, verses 23-26, literally, and the Mahabharata relates how Bhishma held off death for several months in order that the sunlight might enter on the Northern Path—i.e. till the winter solstice was over. Taken literally, however, contradictions are involved. For instance, what would happen to a person dying in the light fortnight of the month of November—i.e. during the Southern Path? Shankaracharya emphatically affirms that the Path taken after death depends on jñana alone and that the time of death makes no difference whatever. He goes on to say that the various "times" mentioned are symbols for the Gods who are the stages on the Path, a statement which is perfectly comprehensible if we remember that the "Gods" mean the levels of consciousness.

The two Paths are in fact the paths taken, the one by one who identifies with the consciousness, the Light of the Atman, and the other by one who identifies himself with the passing forms that are illumined by that Light.

On the first path the Yogi passes from the consciousness on the desire-level (withdrawn from the objects of desire and symbolized by fire and light—these two are given as one in the Upanishadic version) to the "day" of the higher mind (which persists as a focus throughout the Cosmic Day unless, indeed, destroyed by passing Beyond); thence passing to the bright fortnight, the waxing moon of buddhi, and to the sunlight of eternal summer (in the Mahat Atman).

On the other path travelers are absorbed in the "smoky" contents of the desire-consciousness and so, failing to see the "day" of the higher manas, are lost in the "night." It goes without saying that for them the moon of buddhi wanes (the dark fortnight) and that, though the Light of the Great Atman is within them all the time, they see it not and are left in the darkness of an almost Arctic winter (the six months of the sun's south path) and see only the "moonlight"—here not the Light of "buddhi" but the Light that is entangled in the moon of forms (see Prashna Upanishad, i, 5).

Perhaps it should be added that these two paths are in the nature of "limiting paths," they represent the two extremes. Ordinary people will find themselves somewhere between the two. After death they will find themselves in their desire-body, a subtle body resembling the body in which they now find themselves in dreams, a body which can experience pleasure and pain but which cannot be injured. All in them that is of real worth will then ascend to the higher, though in many cases it will not be conscious of that Ego but will live in it much as a dissociated personality may live within the psyche of someone of the earth. That is called in the symbolism "going to the night" instead of to the "day" of the Ego.

There within the Ego it will experience subjectively the fruits of its good deeds (which the Gita terms enjoying the wide heaven world), culminating in a flash of expanded consciousness as it unites with the Ego. In the ordinary person this flash of union is the immediate precursor of the raying-out of energy that will form the new personality and, inheriting the karma of its predecessor, will be reborn on earth.

It is thus seen that there is a gap between the personalities of two successive incarnations, which explains the lack of memory of the former life. The few cases of memory of a former life that occur sporadically (a well-authenticated case occurred in Delhi a few years ago) are usually ones where, through some strong desire, the ascent to the Ego has not been made and rebirth takes place almost at once, the subtle desire-body remaining unchanged.

In the *Tibetan Book of the Dead*, edited by Dr. Evans-Wentz, it is taught that: "After death thy own consciousness, shining, void, and inseparable from the Great Body of Radiance, hath no birth and death and is the immutable Light—*Buddha Amitabha*." It is stated that the mentality of the dying person momentarily enjoys a condition of balance which is compared to that of a needle balanced laterally on a thread. But it is added that, owing to unfamiliarity with such a state, the consciousness principle of the average human being lacks the power to function in it; "*karmic* propensities becloud the consciousness principle with thoughts of personality . . . and, losing equilibrium, it falls away from the Clear Light" (*Tibetan Book of the Dead*, pp. 96 and 97). It is after this that the visions, pleasant or terrifying, of the after-death state commence.

Students of the Buddhist tradition may find that the above explanation throws light on the well-known difficulty in stating from a Buddhist viewpoint what it is that passes from one life to another. Obviously the personal self cannot transmigrate, since a new one is projected for each life. On the other hand, the higher Self is not really born at all and so cannot be said to transmigrate either. Consciousness cannot be said to transmigrate as it is all-pervading and motionless. All that can be said to pass over from one life to the next is karma, and this, at least by some, has been said to be the Buddhist answer. I am quite aware that most Buddhists would not accept the idea of the existence of the higher Self. This is not the place to go into the reasons for such non-acceptance but it should be pointed out that what the Buddhists object to is a permanent self-entity, while what has in this book been termed the higher Self is not a permanent entity, not, in fact, an entity at all.

The same teaching of the two paths occurs in the Orphic tradition. Speaking of the mystic Y and the path which leads to filth and oblivion the Orphic poem *The Descent into Hades* reads:

"Thou shalt find to the left of the House of Hades a well-spring and by the side thereof a white cypress. To this well approach not near. But thou shalt find another cypress and by this the Lake of Memory, cold water flowing forth. Guardians will be before it. Say unto them: 'I am a child of Earth and Starry Heaven, but my Race is of Heaven alone. This ye know yourselves. Quickly give me the cold water flowing forth from Memory's Lake.' And of themselves will they give thee to drink from the holy well-spring and thereafter shalt thou have lordship together with the rest of the heroes" (from Eisler's *Orpheus the Fisher*).

Appendix H

The Five Elements

It must not be supposed that the Mahabhutas, the so-called five elements, are elements of matter in the sense of the chemist's elements (though even the latter have now vanished as ultimate entities). Indian philosophic thought is concerned with the analysis of experience, not of "matter." The Hindu view has been excellently stated by Pandit J. C. Chatterji (on page 40 of his *India's Outlook on Life*) as follows:

"These are collectively the five *Bhutas* and are produced by the five sensation-generals called *Bhuta-matras* (later *Tanmatras*), inasmuch as they have no other meaning except the inferred, *i.e.* the imagined origins or concomitants, moving or stationary, of the sensations of Odor, Flavor ["taste" would be better here.—K. P.] Color, Temperature and Sound as are actually perceived by means of the senses operating in the physical body, *i.e.* as varieties in these sensations as distinguished from the general ones. And they are produced in the following manner."

The author then goes on to explain in a manner which, whether altogether sound or not, is very interesting, the details of their arising. In the end he sums up as follows:

"Thus from the experience of variation in the five general objects of perception there are produced also the five important factors of the physical, namely Ethereal Space (*Akasha*) and the four others technically and symbolically called Air (*Vayu*), Fire (*Agni*), Water (*Ap*) and Earth (*Prithivi*)—ingredients collectively designated in Sanskrit by the technical name of Bhutas, *i.e.* the ever-passing Have-beens (never the ares) which are but Ghosts (*Bhuta* also means 'ghost') of the Real, the one ever-abiding Being that is the inmost self of them all, as of the universe."

Buddhist tradition is also quite explicit. *The Abhidharma Kosha* (i, 13) explains that the "earth" of common speech merely means a colored shape, while the philosophical earth, water, fire, and air signify forces of firmness (in some accounts repulsion or that which causes extension), cohesion, maturing (energizing?), and flowing-forth or motion. (Note that even the earth of common speech is held quite correctly to be a "colored shape" and not a solid substance.)

Some may detect a slight flavor of artificiality (almost of apologetic) in this account of the five elements. Perhaps they are not entirely wrong. In still older times, older than what we call philosophic thought, the five elements were earth, water, etc., in their natural sense, the sense we still use in such a phrase as "exposed to the elements." But, *at the same time*, they were used in mystical teaching as *symbols* of various levels of being. Later the symbolic reference to the lighter levels was forgotten by teachers who had no knowledge of them and they came to be regarded as just physical-plane realities. The list of five remained, however, sacrosanct and so there was a need for a reinterpretation on philosophical lines. Hence the flavor of artificiality adhering to such interpretations. The Gita, a work which preserves the older mystical symbolisms as well as the newer philosophic thought, uses the elements sometimes in one sense, sometimes in the other. When we read of the earth and fire in chapter fifteen (verses 13 and 14) it is in the symbolic sense that they are used, but in such a verse as Gita, xiii, 5, the sense is "philosophic," and the term should be understood along the general lines set forth above.

In any case, as Chatterji has observed, the five *Mahabhutas* are inferred, not perceived, and the real elements are the elements of sensation (what we should nowadays term sense-data), smell, taste, color-shape, touch, and sound. Even these are elements only in the psychological sense. They represent the elements into which our experience can be analyzed and, even if considered "atomic," the atoms must be regarded as psychological irreducibles and not as "material" atoms.

Glossary

Adityas: A class of Vedic Gods, six, seven, or eight in number, the sons of Aditi, the Infinite. They are golden, many-eyed, unwinking, sleepless, and they support all that moves or is stationary (Macdonnell's *Vedic Mythology*). They represent the levels of consciousness. Later they became twelve in number and were affiliated to the twelve months.

Akasha: Space—rather in the sense of a continuum than of mere emptiness. We read also of *chid-akasha*, the space of consciousness.

Ananda: Bliss as distinguished from mere hedonic pleasure.

Asura: Originally a title of the great Gods, Indra, Agni and Varuna, but later, by a different etymology, it came to mean not-divine, and so a Titanic enemy of the Gods. The Rig-Veda has both meanings, the later Atharva-Veda only the latter. Used in the Gita of the "dark" path of pravritti, q.v.

Atman: Originally (perhaps) meaning breath, the word came to stand for self, or anything that may be considered self, from the body up to the highest Reality. Particularly it signifies the higher Self (*jivatman*), the manifested cosmic Self (*Mahat Atman*), and the Unmanifested transcendent Self (*Shanta Atman*). It is the consciousness, particularly on the higher levels.

Avyakta: The Unmanifested, especially Mula-prakriti, but also (e.g. the Gita, viii, 20) the Parabrahman and the Shanta Atman.

Bhakti: Service motivated by love and worship. Also used for the emotions of love or worship themselves.

Bhishma: A hero in the Mahabharata, the adviser of King Dhritarashtra and a devotee of Krishna though fighting on the other side. In the Gita he stand for blind faith.

Bodhisattva: In Mahayana Buddhism one who treads the Path not for his own salvation alone but for the salvation of all. In the highest sense it is used of one who reaches the Goal, but instead of entering the transcendent Nirvana preserves an apparent individuality in order to help others on the Path.

Brahmacharya: Originally the study of the sacred tradition under a guru. Later, since the period of study, as contrasted with the following period of life as a householder, was characterized by sexual continence, the word came to have this restricted sense of chastity. Whence *Brahmachari*, one who practices sexual restraint. In the Gita the emphasis is an inner one.

Brahman: The name given in the Upanishads for the Supreme Reality. Especially used of the Parabrahman but also of the Shanta Atman and sometimes for the Mula-prakriti (e.g. Gita, xiv, 3). Discussion of the etymology would take us too far afield, but it may be taken as the Greatness (*brih*). It must not be confused with Brahma, the four-headed God, who symbolizes the creative Power of desire, nor with Brahman, a member of the priestly caste, nor Brahmana, a class of scriptures.

Buddhi: An impersonal spiritual faculty giving knowledge of the Cosmic Unity. Also used of the knowledge itself. See Appendix E. It is also the seat of such higher emotions as love. In a lower sense it is used for the purely intellectual aspect of our empirical personalities.

Daivic: Bright, the adjective from *Deva*, a shining power or "God." Used in Gita of the path of nivritti.

Dehi: Literally, the dweller in the body; more exactly, the consciousness focused therein.

Dharma: A difficult word to translate and one having many meanings. Leaving aside meanings which do not occur in the Gita we may take it as the Cosmic Order. Microcosmically it is the law or principle which governs the development of the individual. Secondly, it can be rendered as duty. Dharma and karma were the two aspects into which the Vedic rita (the Cosmic Order) was split up.

Dhritarashtra: The blind king of the Kauravas—see Prolegomena, p. 15;

literally, "he who has seized the kingdom."

Drona: A Brahman who lived as a Kshattriya and was the teacher of the military arts to both Kauravas and Pandavas. In the Gita he stands for the power of ancient tradition, which has to be slain.

Duryodhana: Eldest son of Dhritarashtra: literally, "he who is hard to overcome," the desire-nature.

Ganga: The River Ganges, which traditionally rises from the feet of Narayana and flows through the three worlds purifying all who bathe in its water. From the inner point of view the stream of consciousness flowing through the three states. See Appendix C.

Guna: Literally, quality or "strand"; a technical term for the three moments of the Mula-prakriti—namely, sattva—reflecting power, manifesting as brightness, harmony, purity; rajas—transmitting power, manifesting as desire, energy, mobility; tamas—absorbing power, manifesting as darkness, stagnation, inertia. See chapter 14. The interplay of these three forces makes up all the content of the universe whether physical or mental.

Jagrat: Literally, waking consciousness. See Appendix C.

Jiva: The individual Self. The Light focused in the higher manas; also called jivatman. See under Atman.

Jñana: Knowledge in all senses, from the purely worldly knowledge to gnosis, the intuitional knowledge of the buddhi. In the Gita usually in the latter sense.

Kapila: The original teacher of the Sankhya philosophy. In the Gita (chapter x) he is taken as the archetypal siddha (perfected yogi).

Karma: Literally, action. Especially actions as the elements that manifest the aspect of the Cosmic Order that we know as causal sequence (see also under Dharma). Hence also the law by which actions inevitably bear their fruit.

Karna: In reality a half-brother of the Pandavas, being the son of their mother by the Sun-God. He was abandoned at birth and became the friend and ally of the Kauravas. He was actuated by intense rivalry against Arjuna and the Kauravas placed great reliance on his prowess. In the Gita he signifies the power which genuinely worships ideals but places them in the physical life of the senses, believing there to be no other. In this he may be contrasted with *Jayadrath* (Gita, xi, 34), who is a genuine Kaurava, and who typifies the belief that the sense-life is itself good.

Kauravas: Dhritarashtra and his sons. The Asuric tendencies of pravritti, q.v.

Loka: Literally, "that which is seen" (*lokyate*). This and higher worlds. The levels of consciousness. The lokas are sometimes classified as three (in which case they correspond to Jagrat, Svapna and Sushupti, see Appendix C), sometimes as seven, corresponding to the seven levels (see Appendix E).

Mahat: Same as Mahat Atman but with emphasis on the objective aspect.

Mahatma: One who has identified completely with the One Self (Mahat Atman). Nowadays the term is applied to any holy personage.

Manas: The mind in its two aspects of the true Thinker or individual Self (higher manas) and the empirical thought-system or personality (lower manas). In the higher sense it is symbolized by Arjuna and is that which persists from life to life. The two aspects are symbolized by twin Ashwins in the Vedas.

Manu: An ancient lawgiver and king. In the Gita used in the plural to signify the higher Selves of men as the true lawgivers, rulers and pro-genitors of personalities.

Maruts: A class of Vedic warrior-gods. They are the "heroes," the "sons of heaven" by Vayu, the moving power of air. They are brothers, equal in age, having one birthplace, one mind, and one abode. They have grown on earth, in air, and in heaven (the three worlds). They are self-luminous fires, ride on chariots, and strike downwards with golden spears. See Macdonnell's *Vedic Mythology*. They represent the higher Selves. Their occasional hostile nature is to be understood from Gita, vi, 6.

Mula-prakriti: See Prakriti.

Nara: Literally, man; Arjuna, the higher Self.

Narayana: He who dwells in the Cosmic Waters. The supreme Self. Mythologically the Supreme God who sleeps on the Serpent of Eternity in the Causal Ocean, the Shanta Atman in the Mula-prakriti. From his navel comes forth a lotus on which is born Brahma (*Mahat*) and from the latter the whole universe. Identified with Krishna.

Nirvana: The final Goal; extinction of all selfhood and separateness. Called in the Gita Brahma-Nirvana, indicating that it is not annihilation but extinction of selfhood in the Real (Brahman).

Nivritti: Fulfillment, completion, fruition. Technically the Path of Return, the ascent from "matter" to Spirit, the fulfillment of the Cosmic Play.

Parabrahman: The Supreme Reality. See Brahman, which is also used in the same sense.

Prajña: Wisdom, a synonym of buddhi, especially considered as the Wisdom content of buddhi. Illumination.

Prakriti: The source, original, or material cause of anything. The objective moment of the Parabrahman, the great unmanifested Matrix which is the source of all forms. Often termed Mula (root) Prakriti to distinguish it from its evolutes which, as material causes, are also called prakritis.

Pranava: That which sounds forth. The symbol Om. See Appendix C.

Pravritti: Continued advance, flow, the outward-flowing Cosmic movement, the correlative of Nivritti, q.v.

Purusha: Said to mean "he who dwells in the city" (of the body or the universe). The pure witnessing consciousness. Said in the Gita to be threefold, the perishable purusha or individual Self, the imperishable (the Shanta Atman), and the Purushottama (highest Purusha), the Parabrahman.

Rajas: See Guna.

Sañjaya: The charioteer and adviser of Dhritrashtra. Turning of the thought-system of the lower manas towards the true Thinker (higher manas). Conscience. See Prologomena.

Sankalpa: A bringing-together by the will or imagination. Use of the personal will to formulate some end of oneself.

Sankhya: A system of philosophy said to have been founded by the sage Kapila. Its essence is the discrimination between purusha and prakriti, q.v. The early forms of Sankhya seem to have been monistic and must be distinguished from the alter scholastic form that we have in the Sankhya karikas. See Gita, ii.

Sanskara: An impression or memory-trace. These impressions of past acts and thoughts serve as causative forces for bringing about further developments. A man's knowledge of a foreign language is not always manifested in his mind, but it is always there in a latent form and will issue in actual words under suitable circumstances. Such latent knowledge is a sanskara. There are also sanskaras in the higher Ego and in the Cosmic Mind. The word has other meanings not relevant here.

Sannyasi: One who has renounced the household life to wander about as an ascetic. The sannyasi abandons all the ceremonial observances of the brahmans, including the worship of the sacred fires, hence he is said to be without fire and without rites. The Gita gives an inner meaning to the conception. See Gita, vi, 1.

Sattva: One of the gunas, q.v.

Shastra: An order or command. Usually applied to the scriptural books, also to any science or art. In the Gita it signifies *shasak traya*, the Threefold Inner Ruler (see p. 208).

Tamas: One of the gunas, q.v.

Tapasvi: One who practices tapasya (religious austerities). The word tapas means heat, or glow, and was used of the severe penances performed by Hindu ascetics. In the Gita it stands for self-discipline. It is also said that the Cosmic process was caused by the tapas of the Parabrahman; here tapas means self-limitation.

Tattva: A principle or element of existence, or rather of experience. Any of the "levels" of the Cosmos.

Upadhi: "Limitation, condition (as of time or space)" (Apte's *Dictionary*). A vehicle. That in which the consciousness works, by which its manifestation is limited. The thought-system of the lower manas in the upadhi of the true Thinker or higher manas. The latter is limited and conditioned by the former.

Vedanta: Literally, the conclusion of the Vedas—the Upanishads. Any system of philosophy claiming to be based on the Upanishads, the Gita and the Brahma-Sutras. Especially used of the monistic system formulated by Shankaracharya (8th century AD?), but this system should strictly be called advaita (non-dualist) Vedanta as there are other claimants to the Vedantic title, such as the semi-dualistic and dualistic systems of Ramanuja and Madhva. In the Gita it signifies the final Knowledge, to impart which was the purpose of the Vedas, as of all other traditions.

Virata: A king of the Mahabharata. During the thirteenth year of exile, in which the Pandavas had to remain unrecognized by anyone, they took refuge in various disguised capacities in Virata's service. Arjuna, who had disguised himself as a woman, repaid the debt by acting as charioteer to the young prince and routed, single-handed, an army of the Kauravas who were attempting to drive away Virata's cattle.

Vyasa: A Seer who is credited with having classified the Vedas and with being the author of the Mahabharata and all the Puranas. It was by his blessing that Sañjaya was able to "overhear" the dialogue between Krishna and Arjuna. One of the meanings of the word is diffusion, extension, and we may consider vyasa as symbolizing the power of inspiration, the power which diffuses and extends downwards the higher knowledge.

Yajña: The ritual sacrifices of the Vedas. In the Gita it means sacrifice in the more general sense.

Yoga: Union, joining. The Path on which the self is united to the Self and the Self to the All and the teaching about that Path. Also (as the Sovereign Yoga, Gita, ix, 5) the union of the Shanta Atman with the Mula-prakriti which brings about the Cosmic process.

Yukta: Joined, united; also fit, right, or suitable.

About the Author

Sri Krishna Prem was born in England in 1898 as Ronald Henry Nixon. After service in the Royal Flying Corps, he took his M.A. at Cambridge and in 1920 went to India to pursue his interest in Buddhism and theosophy. There he met his guru, Sri Yashoda Mai, a Bengali woman of profound mystical experience. He followed her to a remote ashram in the Himalayan foothills, took holy orders as a monk of the Hindu Vaishnava sect, and was given the name Sri Krishna Prem. After his guru's death, he was left in charge of the ashram and reluctantly accepted the task of leading the other disciples. Teaching from his own religious insight and retaining only such rituals as he felt to be of universal significance, he became one of the outstanding figures in India's spiritual life. He died in 1965.